my revisio

AQA GCSE (9–1)

HISTORY
SECOND EDITION

Tim Jenner
David Ferriby
Simon Beale
Carmel Bones
Adele Fletcher
Lizzy James

HODDER
EDUCATION
AN HACHETTE UK COMPANY

The Publishers would like to thank the following for permission to reproduce copyright material.

Photo credits: p77 © Pictorial Press Ltd/Alamy Stock Photo; **p83** © TopFoto.co.uk; **p87** © Chronicle/Alamy Stock Photo; **p93** *Daily Mirror*, 12th November 1918 © Mirrorpix; **pp99, 101, 105, 109** Punch Ltd; **p121** SPUTNIK/Alamy Stock Photo; **p127** NASA; **p135** Josef Koudelka/Magnum Photos; **p145** Granger Historical Picture Archive/Alamy Stock Photo; **p151** David Pollack/Corbis via Getty Images; **p153** TopFoto.co.uk; **p159** British Cartoon Archive/Telegraph Media Group Ltd; **p169** De Agostini/A. Dagli Orti/Getty Images; **p173** INTERFOTO/Alamy Stock Photo; **p175** Wellcome Library, London/http://creativecommons.org/licenses/by/4.0/; **p197** Chronicle/Alamy Stock Photo; **p205** Heritage Image Partnership Ltd/Alamy Stock Photo.

Acknowledgements: Barrie & Jenkins: Michael Balfour, *The Kaiser and His Times*, 1964. California State University: Joseph Papp and Elizabeth Kirkland 2003: www.csun.edu/~hflrc001/family.html. Devin-Adair: John T. Flynn, *The Roosevelt Myth*, 1944. Eyre & Spottiswoode: Robert Sherwood, *White House Papers*, 1948. Harper: Eric Foner, *Reconstruction: America's Unfinished Revolution*, 1988. *History Today*: Hugh Lawrence, 1986. John F. Kennedy Presidential Library and Museum: John F. Kennedy, speech from 1963: www.jfklibrary.org/JFK/JFK-in-History/The-Cold-War-in-Berlin.aspx. John Murray: Greg Lacey and Keith Shephard, *Germany 1918–1945*, 1997. Literary Guild: Doris E. Fleischman in *America as Americans See It* edited by F.J. Ringel, 1932. NASA: John F. Kennedy, speech from 1961: www.nasa.gov/vision/space/features/jfk_speech_text.html. Ohio State University: Thomas Jackson, Can today's candidates revive Martin Luther King's "shattered dreams"? writing in 2007. http://origins.osu.edu/history-news/can-today-s-candidates-revive-martin-luther-king-s-shattered-dreams. Oxford University Press: Gordon A. Craig, *Germany 1866–1945*, 1981. Penguin Books: Alan Bullock, *Hitler: A Study in Tyranny*, 1952; John Guy, *Elizabeth: The Forgotten Years*, 2016. Princeton University Press: Eric D. Weltz, *Weimar Germany: Promise and Tragedy*, 2007. Random House: Frances Perkins, *The Roosevelt I Knew*, 1946. University of California Santa Barbara: Lyndon B. Johnson, speech from 1965: www.presidency.ucsb.edu/ws/?pid=26805.

Every effort has been made to trace all copyright holders, but if any have been inadvertently overlooked, the Publishers will be pleased to make the necessary arrangements at the first opportunity.

Although every effort has been made to ensure that website addresses are correct at time of going to press, Hodder Education cannot be held responsible for the content of any website mentioned in this book. It is sometimes possible to find a relocated web page by typing in the address of the home page for a website in the URL window of your browser.

Hachette UK's policy is to use papers that are natural, renewable and recyclable products and made from wood grown in sustainable forests. The logging and manufacturing processes are expected to conform to the environmental regulations of the country of origin.

Orders: please contact Bookpoint Ltd, 130 Milton Park, Abingdon, Oxon OX14 4SE.
Telephone: +44 (0)1235 827827. Fax: +44 (0)1235 400401. Email education@bookpoint.co.uk Lines are open from 9 a.m. to 5 p.m., Monday to Saturday, with a 24-hour message answering service. You can also order through our website: www.hoddereducation.co.uk

ISBN: 978 1 5104 5561 0

© Tim Jenner, David Ferriby, Simon Beale, Carmel Bones, Adele Fletcher, Lizzy James 2018

First published in 2017
Second edition published in 2018 by
Hodder Education,
An Hachette UK Company
Carmelite House
50 Victoria Embankment
London EC4Y 0DZ

www.hoddereducation.co.uk

Impression number   10 9 8 7 6 5 4 3 2 1
Year   2020 2019 2018

Cover photo © Shutterstock/Militarist
Produced and typeset in Bembo by Integra Software Services Pvt. Ltd., Pondicherry, India
Printed in Spain

A catalogue record for this title is available from the British Library.

FSC
www.fsc.org

MIX
Paper from
responsible sources
FSC™ C104740

My Revision Planner

This books covers the most popular options. You will use up to four of the eleven chapters.
- Highlight the chapters you are studying and cross out the ones you are not.
- To track your progress tick each topic as you complete it. One tick when you have learned the content, another tick when you have tackled all the revision tasks.

Section 1A World History Period Studies

CONTENT   TASKS

Section 1B Wider World Depth Studies

CONTENT   TASKS

Section 2A British Thematic Studies

Section 2B British Depth Studies

CONTENT   TASKS

How to use this book

Features

Each topic from the specification is covered in a double-page spread with the following features:

Key term

- Key terms are **highlighted** and defined in the glossary at the end of each chapter.
- These are the terms that you need to understand in order to write clearly about a topic. Precise use of language is very important for top marks.

Revision point

Instead of headings the content is divided into revision points. These are worth learning in their own right. They summarise the three to five key points about each topic. Take the revision points together and you have the course covered.

Bullet points

This is the detailed knowledge you need to back up the revision point. The GCSE course emphasises the use of relevant, precise and detailed knowledge. Think of the revision point as the headline and the bullets the detail you can use in your answer.

- Learn this your own way – make mnemonics, use highlights.
- Mark this up. Use your pen. This should look like your book once you have finished.
- Sometimes we have used tables and charts to make it easier to remember. A good way to revise is turn a table into bullets or turn the bullets into tables. Whenever you change the format of the knowledge your brain has to process it.

Chapter 2 Germany, 1890–1945: Democracy and dictatorship

2.7 Economic changes: employment and rearmament

REVISED

Under Nazi rule **unemployment was reduced** and **industry prospered**, 1933–39

- In 1933, unemployment was over 5 million. By 1939 it was virtually zero. Hitler fulfilled one of his key promises. This was done by:

Public works	Rearmament	Conscription
The **National Labour Service** employed workers to build a network of *autobahns* (motorways), more railways and new houses. These were paid for by the government	Started in secret in 1933 (in defiance of the Treaty of Versailles). Jobs were created manufacturing weapons and army uniforms	**Conscription** was introduced in 1935. Selected Germans were forced to join the armed forces

- These were part of 'The New Plan' devised by Dr Schacht, which ran from 1933–36.
- In 1936 this was replaced by the Four-Year Plan under Hermann Goering. This was intended to make Germany self-sufficient by 1940 so that it did not have to import essential raw materials.

Key point

Many German civilians benefited from the improved economy during the 1930s but they all suffered greatly in the final three years of the war.

Some Germans benefited more than others from the economic changes

- **Industrial workers** mostly gained from Nazi rule in the 1930s. They were glad to have a job and an income. However,

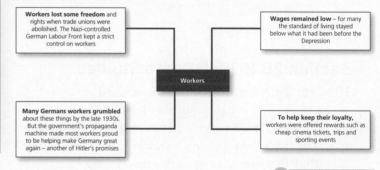

Workers lost some freedom and rights when trade unions were abolished. The Nazi-controlled German Labour Front kept a strict control on workers	**Wages remained low** – for many the standard of living stayed below what it had been before the Depression
Many Germans workers grumbled about these things by the late 1930s. But the government's propaganda machine made most workers proud to be helping make Germany great again – another of Hitler's promises	**To help keep their loyalty,** workers were offered rewards such as cheap cinema tickets, trips and sporting events

Workers

- **Farming communities** were helped with guaranteed food prices and rights to keep their land.
- **Big businesses** were pleased about the Nazis getting rid of the Communist threat and many benefited from government spending.
- **Small businesses** did not benefit from any protection (for example, local shops).
- **Nazi opponents** were excluded from the prosperity. They could not work and could not claim unemployment pay. Jews and other 'undesirables' were victimised and persecuted. Jewish businesses were boycotted or closed down.

Test yourself

1. List five things that most Germans were happy about in the period 1933–39.
2. List three things that most Germans were not so happy about in the period 1933–39.

42   Quick quizzes at **www.hoddereducation.co.uk/myrevisionnotes**

Answers online

At www.hoddereducation.co.uk/myrevisionnotes we have provided model answers for all tasks and exam-style questions. However, just because you write something different from us it does not mean yours is wrong! Often history does not have right and wrong answers. As long as you can explain your point clearly and support your argument with evidence you can say many different things.

Progress tracker

Tick this box to track your progress:
- One tick when you have revised and understood the content.
- Two ticks when you have tackled the Revision Tasks and/or practice questions.

Practice question

- All the main question types are practised either as a part of a revision task or as practice questions.
- Model answers to the practice questions are available online: www.hoddereducation.co.uk/ myrevisionnotes.

From 1942 onwards the war went badly for Germany, which had a huge impact on its people

Shortages	Bombing raids
Rationing started in 1939 on food and clothes, but in the first two years of the war there were no real shortages as imports from defeated countries arrived	From 1942, German cities were bombed first by the British and then also by the Americans
However, from 1942 onwards when Germany started to suffer defeats, the economy was totally directed towards war production	Major bombing of cities such as Berlin and Dresden was intended to break German morale
German civilians began to suffer greatly with increasing shortages of food and other essentials, including fuel	About half a million German citizens died in these raids; 7.5 million became homeless
	By 1945, many became refugees – with millions fleeing the advancing Soviet armies

Part 3: The experiences of Germans under the Nazis

Practice question

Describe two problems faced by German civilians in a city such as Berlin in the final months of the Second World War. **(4 marks)**

Develop the detail

Each of the following statements lacks detail. Add details to show that you understand the statement.

Statement	Detail
Unemployment went down in the period 1933–39	
The Nazis created jobs 1933–39	
Farmers were helped by Nazi policies 1933–39	
Bomb damage was huge during the Second World War	
Food shortages got worse as the war went on	

Revision task

These tasks develop your exam skills. Sometime you write in the book, sometimes you write in your notebook.

Our advice is to work through each chapter twice:
- The first time learning the content.
- The second time using the revision tasks and practice questions.

Answers to revision tasks are provided online.

Essay plan

Look at the essay question below.

Which of the following was the more important reason for most Germans supporting Hitler in the 1930s?

- The Nazis providing jobs.
- Nazi policies encouraging loyalty.

Explain your answer with reference to both reasons. **(12 marks)**

1 List two factors for each of the bullet points to show they are important.
2 Then decide which is more important and explain a reason.

TIP

In your exam you only have about a minute's writing time per mark! So don't waste time on the low-tariff questions. Save time for the 12-marker.

Tip

Throughout the book there are regular tips that explain how you can write better answers and boost your final grade.

Test yourself

- As you revise the content the first time use these to check your knowledge and recall.
- Try answering them without looking at the bullets. See how you get on.
- Usually the answers are obvious but in case they are not there are answers at www.hoddereducation. co.uk/myrevisionnotes.
- Don't worry about these questions second time through. Focus on the revision tasks instead.
- If you want to revise on the move, there are also self-marking knowledge quizzes on each topic here: www.hoddereducation.co.uk/myrevisionnotes. These can to be used on your phone or computer.

Section 1A World History Period Studies

How the Period Study will be examined

Overview of the Period Study

A study of a medium time-span. The focus here is on how events unfold across the period and the narrative of key developments and issues:

In this book we cover:
- America, 1840–1895: Expansion and consolidation
- Germany, 1890–1945: Democracy and dictatorship
- America, 1920–1973: Opportunity and inequality.

Period Studies are about understanding the narrative (story) across a period of important change or developments:

- Each study focuses on **one country** and its **domestic history** (rather than the international situation) over a 50-year period.
- Each focuses on two key related **developments** (for example, Democracy and Dictatorship) and the **impact** these developments had on **people**.
- You investigate these developments from different **perspectives**: political, social and cultural, economic, the role of ideas and of key individuals and groups.
- You will also need to understand and evaluate **interpretations** of the period you have studied.

There are a number of key skills you will need for the Period Study

Comprehending interpretations – you will need to be able to read an interpretation of this period and pick out features which reveal its viewpoint

Clearly describing – you will need to be able to give a short but detailed description of a key event or development

THE PERIOD STUDY

Evaluating interpretations – you will need to be able to look carefully at the content and provenance of two interpretations and explain why they have different viewpoints. You will also need to compare these to your own knowledge to give a judgement about their accuracy

Explaining – you will need to identify but also explain the impact of a development

Coming to overall judgements and supporting them – you will need to make sophisticated judgements based upon the range of evidence used in your answer. You will need to write these in a clear and persuasive manner

There are six main question types in the Period Study

This is Section A of Paper 1. It is worth 40 marks in total. You will be asked the following types of question.

1 How do interpretations differ?   *(4 marks)*

You will be given two interpretations and will need to work out what each is arguing. You will then need to consider how similar or different these arguments are. The focus in question 1 is on the content of the interpretations.

2 Why do interpretations differ?   *(4 marks)*

You will have to explain why the interpretations you have looked at are different. This will involve looking at the provenance of the interpretations and then explaining reasons why they might have different views.

3 How convincing are these interpretations?   *(8 marks)*

You will use your own contextual knowledge of the period to evaluate how accurate (convincing) the content of the interpretations is. You will need to support and challenge the claims made in both interpretations.

Questions 1–3 are closely linked. They deal with the same two interpretations

The rest of the questions test your knowledge and understanding and are not based on the interpretations.

4 Describe ...   *(4 marks)*

You will need to give a brief but precise summary of a key topic, event or development using specific factual knowledge.

5 In what ways ... ?   *(8 marks)*

You will be asked to explain how a key development affected a situation or a group of people. You will need to use specific factual knowledge to show the impacts of this development.

6 Essay question   *(12 marks)*

You will be given two factors, events or individuals and asked to evaluate the extent of their importance or impact, or how extensive the impact of a key development was on them. You will need to structure your answer as an essay, include a range of factual detail and come to a judgement.

How we help you develop your exam skills

■ The **revision tasks** help you build understanding and skills step by step

For example:

Eliminate irrelevance will help you to make your writing more focused on the issues in the question.

Develop the detail will help you improve your ability to explain impacts.

Spot the interpretation will help you to compare interpretations.

Support or challenge will help you to use content to inform your judgement in an essay question.

■ The **practice questions** give you exam style questions.

■ **Exam focus** at the end of each chapter gives you model answers for each question type.

Plus:

■ There are **annotated model answers** for every practice question online at www. hoddereducation.co.uk/ myrevisionnotes or use this QR code to find them instantly.

Chapter 1 America 1840–1895: Expansion and consolidation

1.1 Attitudes to the West

REVISED

The West was a vast area which was difficult to settle

- The area to the west of the Mississippi river was often called 'the West'.
- On the west coast of America was fertile farming land.
- However, the area beyond the Mississippi was a vast grassland called the **Great Plains**.
- The weather on the Plains was extreme, with cold winters and hot summers. There were also frequently very strong winds.
- The Plains was also very dry and there was a lack of wood that could be used for building.

> **Key point**
>
> Attitudes to the West changed from the 1840s, as Americans increasingly saw it as their Manifest Destiny to control the continent from coast to coast.

American attitudes to the Great Plains changed in the 1840s

- Because of these conditions, the Great Plains was dismissed by most Americans as the **Great American Desert**.
- However, some Americans did travel to the West.

California	Texas	Rocky Mountains
There was trade between the United States and California (which was owned by Mexico).	Other Americans settled in Texas which was also a Mexican state.	In the 1820s and 1830s the Plains were crossed by **Mountain Men** who travelled to the Rocky Mountains to catch beavers and sell their fur in the East.

- In 1845 the United States took over Texas, causing the Mexican–American War.
- When the USA won this war in 1848 it gained a huge area of land including California and the land which would become Arizona, Colorado, Wyoming, Nevada, Utah and New Mexico.
- This led to a developing interest in settling the West.

> **TIP**
>
> The key terms in **purple** are defined in the glossary at the end of each chapter.
>
> Make sure that you can spell the key terms, know what they mean and aim to use them in your written work.

The idea of Manifest Destiny became increasingly popular

- The opening of the Oregon Trail (a route across the Plains and Rocky Mountains leading to Oregon) led to more Americans settling in the West.
- Some Americans began to accept the idea that the United States should occupy the whole continent from coast to coast.
- For many, this was also a religious idea. They believed that it was God's will that they spread Christianity and democracy.
- This idea came to be known as **Manifest Destiny**. It was first used by a journalist called John L. Sullivan.
- Some Americans also believed this was right due to the view that the Native Americans who occupied the Plains were savages.
- Many even considered it right for the USA to go to war to control the West. A war with Britain was narrowly avoided and a treaty gave the USA control of Oregon in 1846.

> **Test yourself**
>
> 1 Why was living on the Plains difficult?
>
> 2 Why did attitudes to the West change in the 1840s?
>
> 3 What was Manifest Destiny?

Key events

Complete the flow chart below to show the key events in the changing attitudes to the Plains amongst Americans. The first box has been done for you.

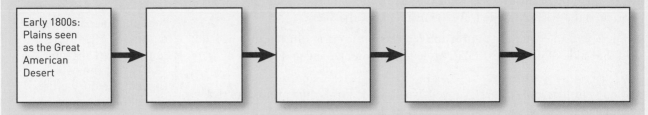

Early 1800s: Plains seen as the Great American Desert → □ → □ → □ → □

 Develop the explanation

Complete the table to explain why each of these reasons led to Americans supporting the idea of Manifest Destiny.

Reasons	Explanations
The Oregon Trail meant more Americans settled in the West.	With more Americans in the West, people began to see it as part of America. The people who had moved there wanted the US government to take control.
Mexico controlled areas in the West. Some Americans viewed Mexicans as lazy and uncultured.	
The USA won a war against Mexico in 1848 and gained control of much of the West.	
The Great Plains was occupied by Plains Indians. Many Americans viewed them as savages.	
Most Americans were Christians.	

 Practice question

Describe two reasons why the belief in Manifest Destiny became popular.   (4 marks)

1.2 Early settlers in the West

Pioneer farmers began to move west in the 1840s

- The opening of the Oregon Trail and the Mountain Men meant that stories reached the East of **fertile** (easy to farm) land in the West.
- There was an economic **depression** (an economic crisis which leads to a fall in the value of goods) in 1837. This led to unemployment and the loss of savings.
- Many families looked to move west across the Plains for the promise of free land and to escape the economic effects of the depression.
- This journey was incredibly tough and covered around 1,000 miles, taking around four months.
- Many died from accidents, starvation when trapped in the mountains, or the spread of disease.

> **Key point**
>
> Religious and economic reasons encouraged a number of settlers to move west in the 1840s, but they still faced huge difficulties in making the journey.

The Mormons faced persecution in the East

- The Mormons were a religious group founded by Joseph Smith. They believed they were God's chosen people.
- Opposition and persecution drove them steadily further west.

Ohio	Missouri	Nauvoo
In Kirtland, Ohio, the Mormons set up important businesses and a successful mill, bank and printing press. However, in the 1837 depression the bank collapsed. Many blamed the Mormons for the loss of their money.	The Mormons were then forced to Missouri. Here they were attacked for their anti-slavery beliefs	In Nauvoo, their leader Joseph Smith announced the Mormon belief in **polygamy** (that Mormon men should have many wives). Many Americans thought this was **blasphemy** (offensive to God). Joseph Smith was shot by a mob. Brigham Young became the new leader of the Mormons.

Joseph Smith led the Mormons to the Great Salt Lake

- In 1846, **Brigham Young** led 16,000 Mormons west to the isolated area around the Great Salt Lake.
- This area was under the control of Mexico until 1848, which meant that American laws did not apply.
- The Mormon journey was well-organised: they set up **Winter Quarters** to allow them to shelter over the winter.
- They also had rest and repair camps along the way and they crossed in wagon trains of 100 wagons.
- To make a success of the dry and barren area around Salt Lake, the Mormons developed an **irrigation** system to water crops.
- They also established a **Perpetual Emigrating Fund** to encourage Mormons to migrate from Europe to Utah.
- By the time Young died, there were 140,000 Mormons in Utah.

> **TIP**
>
> The examiners want you to use relevant and detailed knowledge in your answers. In your revision, you should try to remember a specific piece of information associated with each general idea.

The discovery of gold in California in 1948 encouraged thousands to move west

- News of the discovery was published in a newspaper and spread rapidly. Many local people rushed to the area hoping to get rich by finding gold.
- By 1849, miners were coming from all over the world. By 1852, the population of California had increased from 15,000 to 250,000. This movement was called the **Gold Rush**.
- It soon became clear that there were not enough good **claims** (mining areas) to make everyone rich, leading to serious tensions in the mining towns.
- There were no organised forces of law and order to prevent violence.
- Racial tensions also boiled over, particularly against Chinese miners who were discriminated against by high taxes. There was also serious violence against Mexicans.
- By 1852, the California Gold Rush was over.

Test yourself

1 Why did Pioneer farmers move west?
2 Why did the Mormons move to the Great Salt Lake?
3 What was the Gold Rush?

Develop the detail

Complete the table to explain how each of the following helped the Mormons to travel or settle in the West successfully.

Generalised statement	With developed detail
Winter quarters were built on the eastern edge of the Plains.	Winter was the most dangerous time to travel, so by waiting out the winter the Mormons could make sure their journey across the Plains took place in summer.
Wagon trains of 100 were used to cross the Plains.	
Repair stations were built in advance.	
Irrigation ditches were created to channel mountain water to the Salt Lake area.	
A fund was established to pay for other settlers to move to Salt Lake.	

Eliminate irrelevance

Describe two reasons why the Mormons moved to the Great Salt Lake. (4 marks)

The answer below contains material which is not necessary for a question like this. Cross out any material which you think might be irrelevant to the question.

The Mormons were originally founded by Joseph Smith who claimed to have discovered golden tablets containing religious revelations. The Mormons were initially based in New York, where they gained a number of followers. In Kirtland the Mormons set up a successful bank, but after the economic depression of 1837 (a depression is an economic event where the value of goods falls and this leads to unemployment and lower production) they faced opposition from people who had lost their money and were forced to move. In Nauvoo the Mormon belief in polygamy was announced and this was seen as blasphemous by many white Americans. Joseph Smith was eventually killed by a mob.

1.3 The Plains Indians' way of life

Native American life was **well suited to the Plains**

- Native Americans living on the Plains were also known as **Plains Indians**. Most Plains Indians were **nomadic** (they moved from place to place) and followed buffalo herds.
- Most Native American bands lived in **tipis** (cone-shaped tents made from buffalo skins).
- The shape of tipis deflected the strong winds on the Plains.
- They could also be adjusted to the extreme temperatures of the Plains using ears at the top and by rolling up the bottom or banking it with earth.
- Tipis were made using only 10 wooden poles covered with buffalo skin. This dealt with the lack of resources on the Plains.
- They could be packed up to move in only 10 minutes and loaded on a **travois** for transportation.
- Women owned the tipi and were responsible for it.

> **Key point**
>
> Plains Indians relied on the buffalo and their lifestyle was adapted to help them survive on the Plains.

Plains Indians were divided into **tribes and bands**

- Native Americans were divided into tribes, such as the Arapahoe, Cheyenne, Pawnee and Sioux.
- Small groups, called **bands**, lived and hunted together. Each band had a chief and a council. The council would make most important decisions.
- These bands would usually contain between 10 and 50 families.
- The role of men focused on hunting and protecting the band. All men were part of a warrior society.
- The role of women focused on preparing food, making clothing and having responsibility for the tipi.

Native American survival depended on the **buffalo**

- Perhaps as many as 50 million buffalo lived on the Plains in the early 1800s.
- Native Americans would perform a buffalo dance before the hunt to bring them luck.
- They would use every part of the buffalo:

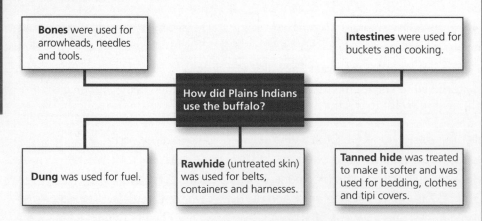

Bones were used for arrowheads, needles and tools.

Intestines were used for buckets and cooking.

How did Plains Indians use the buffalo?

Dung was used for fuel.

Rawhide (untreated skin) was used for belts, containers and harnesses.

Tanned hide was treated to make it softer and was used for bedding, clothes and tipi covers.

- Horses were also vital to Native American life. The wealth of individuals and bands were often measured in the number of horses they owned.

> **TIP**
>
> The highest mark question in your period study exam will be an essay question structured like this Practice Question. The secret of writing a good essay is good planning. Here is a plan:
> - Introduction: Set the context. Why was survival on the Plains a challenge for the Plains Indians
> - Paragraph 1: Explain how they used the buffalo
> - Paragraph 2: Explain how they used the tipi
> - Conclusion: Link the two reasons (if you can), and reach a supported judgement on which is more important.

Indian warfare was often based on raids or non-lethal combat

- The Sioux were widely known as the most warlike tribe. Their traditional enemies were the Crow and Pawnee.
- Warfare was often conducted in small raids.
- After guns arrived on the Plains, Indians often fought by **counting coup** (trying to get close enough to an enemy to touch them).
- There were low casualties. Between 1835 and 1845 the Sioux were at war, but lost on average only four warriors a year.
- Native Americans often took **scalps** (the top of the head, which was cut off and dried) to prevent their enemies from attacking them in the afterlife. These were also displayed to show their bravery.

 Test yourself

1 Why was the tipi well suited to living on the Plains?
2 How did Plains Indians use the buffalo?
3 Why did wars between Indian bands cause few casualties?

Part 1: Expansion – opportunities and challenges

 Topic summary

Complete the following mind map to summarise the features of Native American life on the Plains.

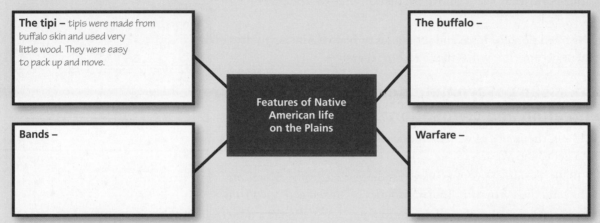

The tipi – tipis were made from buffalo skin and used very little wood. They were easy to pack up and move.

Bands –

Features of Native American life on the Plains

The buffalo –

Warfare –

 Develop the detail

Complete the table to explain how each of the following helped the Native Americans to survive on the Plains.

Generalised statement	With developed detail
Counting coup.	This was a form of non-lethal combat so less Indian men were killed in warfare.
Tipis were made from buffalo skin.	
Tipis could be packed up in 10 minutes.	
Horses.	
Native Americans lived in bands.	

 Practice question

Which of the following was the more important reason why Plains Indians were able to survive on the Plains?

- The buffalo
- The tipi   (12 marks)

1.4 Early American relations with the Plains Indians and the Mormons

Native Americans were **forced west** beyond a **Permanent Indian Frontier**

- At first, the Native Americans were seen as separate nations that the USA would have to negotiate with.
- In 1824, a Bureau of Indian Affairs was set up. This was a government department to manage the relationship with Native Americans.
- Over time, the Native Americans came to be seen as a problem as they blocked the expansion of the USA westwards.
- There was also a conflict of cultures, as many Native American tribes believed that no one could own the land.
- In 1830, the **Indian Removal Act** created a **Permanent Indian Frontier**. All Native Americans had to move beyond this line to make way for American settlers.
- This was often done by force and thousands of Native Americans died. This movement became known as the '**Trail of Tears**'.

> **Key point**
>
> The US government tried to deal with the Plains Indians through a policy of concentration, but the continued movement of settlers west still caused conflict.

The American government developed a policy of **concentration** and **civilisation**

- In the 1840s, thousands of white Americans had started to travel across the Plains to get to the West.
- By the 1850s, even more people were travelling west. Some Americans settled beyond the Permanent Indian Frontier on the edge of the Plains.
- The US government encouraged this movement, but it also felt a duty to protect the Native Americans.
- The **Indian Appropriations Act** in 1851 set up **reservations** (areas of land which were limited to Native Americans and which settlers could not cross, but Native Americans also could not leave).
- Schools were also set up to 'civilise' Native Americans and spread American culture and Christianity.
- The **Fort Laramie Treaty** was also signed in 1851 between the government and the Plains Indian nations.
- Indian nations promised not to attack travelling settlers on the Oregon Trail and allowed some roads and forts to be built on their territory.
- In return they received payments from the government.

Concentration ultimately **failed** to prevent conflict with **Native Americans**

- Some Plains Indian nations (such as the Crow) never accepted the Fort Laramie Treaty.
- Some white Americans, known as **exterminators**, thought it would be getter to get rid of the Plains Indians.
- Despite this, there was very little conflict before 1858.
- In 1854, settlers began to move onto Indian lands in Kansas and Nebraska, breaking the Fort Laramie Treaty.

- In 1858, gold was discovered in Colorado and around 100,000 settlers moved onto Indian lands to try to get rich in the **Colorado Gold Rush**.
- The government did nothing to stop these movements or enforce the treaty.

The US government also **increasingly took** control of the Mormon territory of **Utah**

- Opposition to the Mormons continued to grow as many settlers complained of them charging high prices for goods.
- Others were afraid that the Mormons and Indians were planning to join forces to attack white Americans. People criticised Utah for being a **theocracy** (a state which followed religious rules, rather than the laws of the USA).
- In 1857, a new non-Mormon governor was sent to Utah with troops. Brigham Young mobilised troops to stop their advance.
- During this **Mormon War** a group of over 100 settlers were murdered by Mormons following a dispute. This event was called the **Mountain Meadow Massacre**.
- The Mormons were pardoned (not punished) but had to accept a non-Mormon governor.
- Eventually in 1896, the Mormons banned polygamy and Utah became a US state.

 Test yourself

1 Why had attitudes to Plains Indians changed by the 1850s?
2 What was the policy of concentration?
3 Why did concentration fail to prevent conflict?

 Match up the definitions

Match up the policies in column 1 with the impacts in column 2.

Policies	Impact
Indian Removal Act	Set up reservations
Trail of Tears	Set up a 'Permanent Indian Frontier'
Indian Appropriations Act	Gave government grants and allowed forts to be built
Fort Laramie Treaty	The violent movement of Indians west

 Key events

Complete the flow chart to summarise the main events in the early relationship between the US government and the Native Americans.

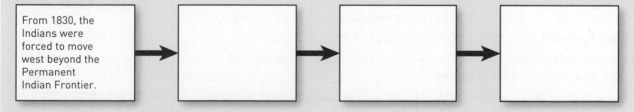

From 1830, the Indians were forced to move west beyond the Permanent Indian Frontier.

 Practice question

In what ways were the lives of Native Americans affected by the movement of Americans westwards? (8 marks)

TIP

The Practice Question is the kind you will meet as Question 5 in your exam. Don't think of it as an essay. There is no need for an introduction or a conclusion. The question asks 'In what ways ...' and you should focus on explaining the different ways clearly.

1.5 The Indian Wars

The **Cheyenne War** broke out in 1863

- Due to the Colorado Gold Rush, from 1859, the number of miners, settlers and railway surveyors passing through Indian lands increased. Conflict developed with the Plains Indians.
- In 1861, the Cheyenne and Arapahoe began to attack settlers passing through their lands.
- By 1863 the Cheyenne were at war with white American **militia** (unofficial armed forces drawn from local men). Militia were used because regular soldiers were fighting in the Civil War which was going on at this time.
- Indians attacked ranches and small settlements on the Southern Plains.
- In 1864, some Cheyenne signed a treaty to end the fighting and moved onto a new reservation.
- However, fighting continued and in 1865 the fort at Julesburg was attacked by over 1,000 warriors from the Sioux, Cheyenne and Arapahoe.
- The war ended in 1867, but many Cheyenne continued to fight and joined in Red Cloud's war.

The **Sand Creek Massacre** was an attack on a band of peaceful Indians

- The Colorado militia was one of the many militia which had been formed to fight against the Cheyenne.
- In 1864, a band of Cheyenne led by Black Kettle had agreed to peace talks and moved onto a reservation at Sand Creek.
- Black Kettle flew a US flag over his tipi as a symbol of peace.
- Colonel Chivington led 700 soldiers in an attack on the camp. Around 150 Indians were killed. Initially this was seen as a great victory for the militia.
- In a Congressional enquiry, it was revealed that most of the dead were women, children and the elderly. The soldiers also scalped the Indians.
- Although Chivington was never punished, the event became known as the Sand Creek Massacre.

War with the Sioux (Red Cloud's War) broke out in 1865

- In 1862, gold was discovered in the Rocky Mountains. A new trail, the **Bozeman trail**, was created to allow miners to access the area.
- This trail passed through Sioux lands and new mining towns were built. This again broke the Fort Laramie Treaty.
- The government encouraged miners to move to the area, as the country was short of money after four years of Civil War.
- In 1865, the Sioux began to attack travellers along the trail. The Sioux warrior **Red Cloud** led a force of many Sioux bands and even some allies from the Cheyenne and Arapahoe.
- The government tried to open peace talks, but continued to build forts along the trail. Red Cloud broke off negotiations and attacked the army.
- Although the Indians could not capture the US forts, they were able to lay siege to them (trap the soldiers inside) and attack parties that left the forts.
- The Indian forces also managed to prevent travellers from using the trail and even continued fighting throughout the winter.

Key point

The discovery of gold led to war between the Indians and US government. Neither side could fully defeat the other, leading to further negotiation over land.

 Key events

Complete the flow chart to summarise the key events of the Cheyenne War and Red Cloud's War.

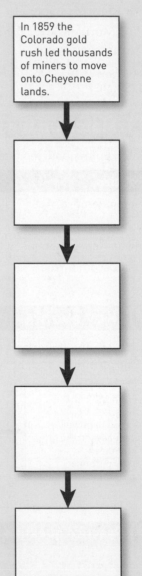

In 1859 the Colorado gold rush led thousands of miners to move onto Cheyenne lands.

80 US soldiers were trapped and killed in the Fetterman Massacre

- Fort Phil Kearney was surrounded by Indian forces. The commander Colonel Carrington ordered his soldiers not to stray too far from the fort to avoid an ambush.

- In December 1866, a group of 80 men led by Captain William Fetterman rode out from the fort to protect a wood train.

- They were ordered not to ride past Lodge Trail Ridge, but Fetterman saw an opportunity to inflict a defeat on the Indians.

- His men were lured into a trap and ambushed. All of the men were killed and their bodies mutilated.

- Some historians blame Fetterman for falling into the Indian trap.

The war was ended by a Second Fort Laramie Treaty

- The government was not able to defeat the Indians led by Red Cloud and they were forced to negotiate.

- In 1868 the Second Fort Laramie Treaty was agreed.

- The US forces withdrew from the forts and the Great Sioux Reservation was created. No non-Indians were ever to be allowed to enter this area.

- The Sioux burned the forts and many moved onto the reservation.

- Red Cloud agreed to the Treaty, but some Sioux continued fighting under the leadership of Crazy Horse and Sitting Bull.

Test yourself

1 What were the causes of the Cheyenne War and the Sioux War?

2 What was the Sand Creek Massacre?

3 What was the Fetterman Massacre?

4 What was the Second Fort Laramie Treaty?

TIP

In your exam you have about 1 minute writing time per mark! So in these interpretation questions don't waste time on the first two lower-tariff questions. Save time for the 8-mark question.

Practice question

Study Interpretations A and B.

1 How do these two interpretations differ? (4 marks)

2 Why might these two interpretations differ? (4 marks)

3 Which of these interpretations do you find most convincing about the events at Sand Creek? (8 marks)

INTERPRETATION A *An editorial (leading article) from the* Rocky Mountain News, *a newspaper published in Colorado.*

The Indian camp was well supplied with defensive works. For half a mile along the creek there was an almost continuous chain of rifle-pits, and another similar line of works crowned the adjacent bluff. Pits had been dug at all the salient points for miles. After the battle twenty-three dead Indians were taken from one of these pits and twenty-seven from another.

Whether viewed as a march or as a battle, the exploit has few, if any, parallels. A march of 260 miles in but a fraction more than five days, with deep snow, scanty forage, and no road, is a remarkable feat, whilst the utter surprise of a large Indian village is unprecedented. In no single battle in North America, we believe, have so many Indians been slain.

INTERPRETATION B *From* A Misplaced Massacre *by historian Ari Kelman, who uses the testimony of George Bent (an eyewitness to the Sand Creek Massacre)*

Bent related that when the soldiers arrived at Sand Creek just before dawn, he had heard shouts warning of their approach. Startled, he dashed from his lodge and "saw that Black Kettle had a flag up on a long pole to show to the troops that the camp was friendly." Chivington's men ignored the signal and "opened fire from all sides." Bent then discovered "[hiding Indians] who had dug pits under the high banks of the creek." These makeshift holes in the sand were the trenches that Chivington later insisted proved that the Cheyennes and Arapahoes had prepared in advance for combat.

1.6 The American Civil War

Differences between the North and South were a long-term factor in the Civil War

Key point

The issue of slavery and westward expansion led to a devastating war between North and South.

- The climate in the South was well suited to crops such as cotton and tobacco. The South made a lot of money selling cotton to Britain and Europe.
- Much of this was grown on plantations worked by slaves. Around a quarter of the population of the South depended on slavery for their income.
- The Northern states were more industrialised. Slavery had disappeared in the North by 1804. Northerners were worried about competing with slave labour and there was a growing **abolition** movement to abolish slavery.
- The Anti-Slavery Society was set up in 1832 and called for an end to slavery and equal rights for freed slaves.
- There was also disagreement about trade, with the South favouring open trade and the North wanting their industries protected from competition.
- However, because there were equal numbers of Northern **free states** (states where slavery was banned) and Southern **slave states**, both sides had to compromise.

Westward expansion increased conflict between North and South

- As territories in the West were settled, they could eventually apply to become US states.
- The states joining the Union were balanced between slave and free states, but in 1819 Missouri was due to join as a slave state.
- The Missouri Compromise allowed Missouri to join, but Maine was also created as a free state to maintain the balance. No new slaves states were allowed in the North.
- With the increased expansion after 1848 the balance was upset. This led to the Compromise of 1850, which allowed California to join as a free state.
- It gave power to the states in the south-west to decide on whether to become free or slave states.
- When two new states (Kansas and Nebraska) were created in 1854 it was decided that these states could also vote on whether to become slave states.
- This led to the formation of the **Republican Party** which was a Northern party opposing slavery.
- It also led to chaos in Kansas where pro-slavery supporters poured in to vote for Kansas to become a slave state. Violence broke out between the two sides in a period referred to as **Bleeding Kansas**.

Fears of abolition led **Southern states** to leave the Union

- In 1859 a famous abolitionist called **John Brown** attacked a weapons store at **Harpers Ferry**.
- He was captured and hanged, but rumours spread that Brown had been planning to lead an armed slave rebellion.
- Many Southerners became afraid that the North intended to attack the South and end slavery.

- Then in 1860, **Abraham Lincoln** was elected as the first Republican President. He was a strong opponent of slavery.
- Although Lincoln claimed he had no intention of ending slavery in the South, a number of Southern states seceded (left the Union) in fear. These states formed the **Confederacy**.
- This lead to the four year civil war between the Union and the Confederacy.

The American Civil War had a **devastating impact** on both North and South

- **Conscription** (forced recruitment into the army) was introduced in both the North and South. This caused a lot of anger because there were **exemptions** (ways to avoid conscription) for the rich.
- In 1863, the **Emancipation Proclamation** ended slavery in the United States. Many African-Americans joined the Union forces.
- By the end of the war in 1865, a number of industries in the North had been badly affected.
- There was also **inflation** (rising prices) at the same time as wages fell.
- However, the economic effects in the South were even worse.
- The railroad system was destroyed and the crucial cotton industry was badly disrupted.
- Inflation in the South became so bad it was classed as **hyperinflation**.

 Test yourself

1. Why did Westward expansion cause conflict between North and South?
2. Why did Southern states leave the Union in 1860?
3. What were the effects of the war on the South?

 Develop the explanation

Copy and complete the table below to explain how each of the following factors led to conflict between North and South

Factor	Developed explanation
Economic differences between North and South.	The North wanted to protect its industries, but the South wanted free trade for cotton exports.
The creation of new states.	
Kansas and Nebraska joining the Union.	
The founding of the Republican Party.	
John Brown's attack on Harpers Ferry.	
The election of Abraham Lincoln.	

 Improve the paragraph

Which of the following was the most important reason for conflict between North and South?

- Slavery
- Westward expansion   (12 marks)

The paragraph below is missing a key feature of a successful answer. Work out what is missing and rewrite the answer to improve it.

Slavery was an important reason for the development of conflict. The North did not want slavery and the South did. Some states that joined the union had slavery and some did not. This was fine as long as they were balanced, but when they weren't balanced this led to violence. People in the South got more and more worried and so eventually they left.

1.7 The aftermath of the American Civil War

The **status of former slaves** and the **Confederate states** were the main issues after the war

- The period after the war is known as the **Reconstruction**. Before the war ended, Lincoln developed a plan to readmit the Southern states into the Union.
- Lincoln was assassinated in 1865 and replaced by President Andrew Johnson.
- Johnson wanted to allow all of the Southern states to rejoin the Union. Southerners had to swear an oath of allegiance to the Union and they would then have their property returned.
- The state governments in the South also had to agree to the new **Thirteenth Amendment** which formally ended slavery in the USA.
- They also had to agree to scrap loans made to the North during the war, which a number of states refused to do.
- The Southern states also passed **black codes**, which restricted the rights of freed slaves.

> **Key point**
>
> The Reconstruction period saw the Southern states readmitted to the Union, but failed to fully guarantee the rights of African-Americans.

Congress attempted to force a **Radical Reconstruction** on the South

- In 1866, the Republicans gained control of Congress.
- They attempted to use the law to force the Southern states to guarantee African-American rights in a period known as Radical Reconstruction.
- Johnson attempted to **veto** (block) the Civil Rights Act to make freed slaves citizens.
- However, Congress overrode this and passed the law as the **Fourteenth Amendment**.
- This was a crucial change as the federal (national) government was interfering with state control over civil rights.
- Congress then divided the South into five districts controlled by a military governor. They would force the Southern states to write new constitutions and approve the Amendment.
- Johnson opposed this and Congress tried but failed to **impeach** him (force him out of office).
- In 1869, the **Fifteenth Amendment** was passed which gave freed slaves the right to vote in elections.
- By 1870 all of the Southern states had rejoined the Union.

Reconstruction failed in some key areas

Successes	Failures
• Education was now available to over 600,000 black pupils in the South.	• Many freed slaves were forced into share cropping where they were prevented from being free because of debt.
• Much of the infrastructure of the South had been repaired or rebuilt.	• Literacy tests and property requirements were used to prevent African
• A number of freed slaves moved north, or to farms in the south-west where they could earn higher wages. Thousands also moved to Kansas.	• Americans from voting in the South. • The Ku Klux Klan was formed in 1866 and used violence and intimidation to attempt to prevent African-Americans from voting.

- By 1877, Reconstruction had come to an end and the federal government was focused on other issues such as conflict with Plains Indians and the expansion westwards.
- There was hatred in the South of **carpetbaggers** (Northerners who came to the South during Reconstruction) and **scallywags** (poor Southern farmers who had supported the Union in the war).

Support or challenge?

In your exams you will often have to reach a judgement and support it with evidence. This task helps you practice. Read this statement:

Reconstruction successfully guaranteed the rights of African-Americans.

Below is evidence from this period. For each one, decide whether it supports or challenges the overall statement above.

Statement	Support	Challenge
The 15th Amendment guaranteed African-Americans the right to vote.		
Literacy tests were used to disqualify black voters.		
Thousands of African-Americans were able to attend schools.		
Black codes were introduced in Southern states.		
Many African-Americans became share croppers.		

TIP

When examining an interpretation always read the caption. It will include important information about who wrote it and when.

Practice question

Study Interpretations C and D.

1 How do these interpretations differ? (4 marks)
2 Why might these interpretations differ? (4 marks)
3 Which interpretation do you find most convincing about the impact of Reconstruction? (12 marks)

INTERPRETATION C *An extract from historian Albert B. Moore who in his 1972 article '100 years of Reconstruction' argues that Radical Reconstruction was too forcefully imposed on the South.*

The political enfranchisement of four million Negroes . . . is the most startling fact about [Radical] Reconstruction. . . . There is nothing in the history of democracy comparable to it. To give the Negroes the ballot and office—ranging from constable to governor—and the right to sit in state legislatures and in Congress, while depriving their former masters of their political fights and the South of its trained leadership, is one of the most outstanding facts in the history of Reconstruction. . . . It was a stroke of fanatical vengeance and design.

INTERPRETATION D *An extract from historian Eric Foner in his book* Reconstruction: America's Unfinished Revolution *(1988).*

In some areas, violence against blacks reached staggering proportions in the immediate aftermath of the war. In Louisiana, reported a visitor from North Carolina in 1865, "they govern . . . by the pistol and the rifle." "I saw white men whipping colored men just the same as they did before the war," testified ex-slave Henry Adams, who claimed that "over two thousand colored people" were murdered in 1865 in the area around Shreveport, Louisiana. In Texas, where the army and Freedmen's Bureau proved entirely unable to establish order, blacks, according to a Bureau official, "are frequently beaten unmercifully, and shot down like wild beasts, without any provocation."

1.8 The continued settlement of the West

After the Civil War, thousands of homesteaders went west

- The homesteaders moved onto the Plains to set up small farms.
- There were a number of reasons why so many homesteaders moved west after the Civil War:

> **Key point**
>
> The promise of free land encouraged thousands of homesteaders to move west. They faced significant difficulties but many of these were eventually overcome.

Land	The Civil War	The railroad
• The government encouraged settlers onto the Plains with the offer of free land. • The **Homestead Act** (1862) gave families 160 acres of free land on the Plains to farm. • Extra land was available for homesteaders who planted trees or cultivated desert land. • Millions of acres of land were made available, most of it land which had once been settled by Plains Indians.	• Many Americans had been uprooted by the war and sought a new start in the West. • Many **demobilised** soldiers (soldiers who had left the army) were now unemployed and so set up as farmers on the Plains. • Many freed slaves moved west to escape continuing racism in the South.	• The earliest homesteaders travelled by wagon, but in 1869 travel was made far easier by the opening of the **transcontinental railroad** across the Plains. • This also helped homesteaders obtain equipment and supplies to support their farms. • The railroad companies also sold off cheap land either side of the railroad.

Homesteaders faced a number of problems living and farming on the Plains

- The extremes of weather and the lack of building materials made shelter a serious problem for homesteaders.
- There was also a lack of water and the **sod houses** (houses made of mud bricks) could be dirty and disease-ridden.
- Farming on the Plains was also difficult. Many homesteaders could not afford the most fertile land, which was bought up by companies.
- The land was difficult to plough and traditional crops did not grow well in the dry soil.
- Crops could also be destroyed by extreme weather, wind, trampling by buffalo or by huge clouds of grasshoppers.

The homesteaders found some solutions to these problems

- Many homesteads failed, especially during the severe droughts of the 1870s.
- However, some homesteaders managed to build successful farms.
- One successful technique was **dry farming** where the land was ploughed after rain to trap moisture in the soil.
- The introduction of **hard winter wheat** by Russian immigrants also helped as it was more suited to the soil on the Plains.
- Some homesteaders used a machine called a **sod-buster** to break through tough roots and ease farming on the Plains.
- The opening of the railroad made it easier to transport machinery to the Plains and in 1874 the **wind pump** was invented which allowed water to be drawn from the ground.
- The invention of barbed wire in the same year also allowed land to be fenced off cheaply.

 Test yourself

1 Why did homesteaders move west?

2 What problems did the homesteaders face?

3 How were these problems solved?

Match the problems and solutions

Match up the problems in the left column with the solutions in the right column.

Problems
The ground was too dry to support crops.
Crops could be trampled.
There was a lack of wood.
There was a lack of rainfall.
The land on the Plains was tough to plough.

Solutions
Sod-buster
Barbed wire
Dry farming
Sod houses
Wind pump

 Summary pyramid

Complete the pyramid below to summarise the key details of the topic.

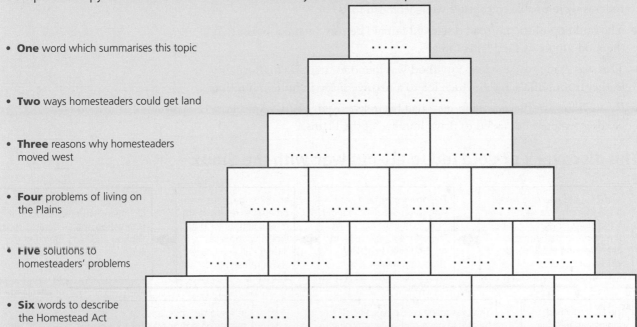

- **One** word which summarises this topic
- **Two** ways homesteaders could get land
- **Three** reasons why homesteaders moved west
- **Four** problems of living on the Plains
- **Five** solutions to homesteaders' problems
- **Six** words to describe the Homestead Act

 Practice question

Which of the following was the most important reason why the homesteaders went west?

- The end of the Civil War
- The opening of the transcontinental railroad

(12 marks)

TIP

The highest marks in the mark scheme are reserved for candidates who show 'complex thinking'. What this means varies according to the type of question. Complex thinking for this question would be showing that you can explain the different **nature** of the impact – how many people were affected by each development, and over what time scale.

1.9 The resolution of the 'Indian Problem'

The end of the Civil War led to **increased conflict with the Plains Indians**

- The movement of thousands of homesteaders onto the Plains caused conflict with the Native Americans on the Plains.
- The US Army also had a number of well-trained troops available because of the end of the Civil War.
- Officers in the army began to develop new strategies such as **total war**. This involved fighting against the whole Indian population by destroying their food and shelter. This forced many Indians onto the reservations.
- The army also began to fight **winter campaigns** when it was much more difficult for Indian bands to move or retreat.
- The network of forts on the Plains also helped the army to resupply and the Indians were unable to capture well-defended forts.
- The building of the railroad disrupted buffalo herds which put pressure on the food supply of the Plains Indians.
- This was made worse when a method was found for making high-quality leather from buffalo hide, which led to a massive surge in buffalo hunting.
- By 1875 the Southern buffalo herd had been destroyed. Native American bands attempted but failed to drive hunters off the Plains.

> **Key point**
>
> Following the end of the Civil War, the US Army waged total war against the Native Americans and forced them onto reservations which destroyed their culture and lifestyle.

The discovery of gold led to all-out **war with the Sioux**

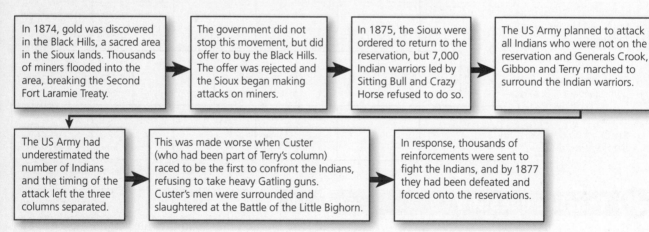

In 1874, gold was discovered in the Black Hills, a sacred area in the Sioux lands. Thousands of miners flooded into the area, breaking the Second Fort Laramie Treaty. → The government did not stop this movement, but did offer to buy the Black Hills. The offer was rejected and the Sioux began making attacks on miners. → In 1875, the Sioux were ordered to return to the reservation, but 7,000 Indian warriors led by Sitting Bull and Crazy Horse refused to do so. → The US Army planned to attack all Indians who were not on the reservation and Generals Crook, Gibbon and Terry marched to surround the Indian warriors.

The US Army had underestimated the number of Indians and the timing of the attack left the three columns separated. → This was made worse when Custer (who had been part of Terry's column) raced to be the first to confront the Indians, refusing to take heavy Gatling guns. Custer's men were surrounded and slaughtered at the Battle of the Little Bighorn. → In response, thousands of reinforcements were sent to fight the Indians, and by 1877 they had been defeated and forced onto the reservations.

Reservations attempted to break Native American culture and fighting spirit

- The destruction of the buffalo continued and by 1883 the Northern herd had been destroyed.
- Reservations were split up into smaller areas of land, which prevented the Indians from following a nomadic lifestyle.
- Rations were soon distributed to families rather than chiefs to reduce their power over bands.
- In 1887, the **Dawes Act** broke up the reservations further into small individual plots of land. Indians were encouraged to become farmers.
- Native Americans were also banned from leaving the reservations to hunt or fight.
- Native American religious ceremonies were also banned and boarding schools attempted to eradicate Native American culture among children.

 Test yourself

1 Why was there increased conflict following the end of the Civil War?

2 How did the reservations destroy Native American culture?

3 What was the Battle of Little Bighorn?

4 What was the Ghost Dance movement?

The **Battle of Wounded Knee** finally ended the resistance of Native Americans

- A new religious movement called the **Ghost Dance Movement** spread through the reservations from 1889.
- Many Indians believed that the dead would come back to life, the buffalo would be restored and the white Americans would disappear.
- The US government was threatened by this and the army was ordered to force all Indians back on to the reservations.
- In 1890 a band of Indians were moved to Wounded Knee where they were shot. 146 Indians were killed in the **Wounded Knee Massacre**.
- The removal of the final Indian bands from the Plains opened up millions of acres of land for Americans to settle.

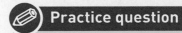
Practice question

Describe two reasons why the US Army was able to force Native Americans onto the reservations.

(4 marks)

Topic summary

Complete the mind map to summarise the reasons why the US Army was able to defeat the Native Americans.

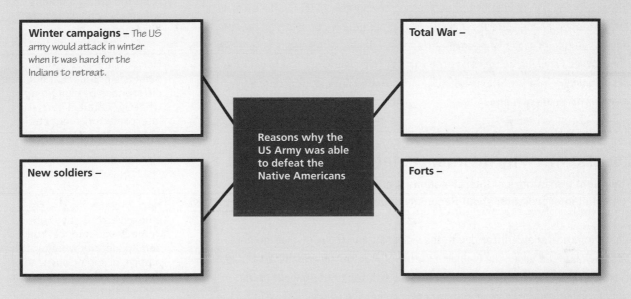

Winter campaigns – The US army would attack in winter when it was hard for the Indians to retreat.

Total War –

New soldiers –

Forts –

Reasons why the US Army was able to defeat the Native Americans

Develop the explanation

Explain how each of the following helped to destroy Native American culture and lifestyle.

Feature or action	Explanation
Boarding schools	Tried to eradicate Indian culture and raise Indian children to be Christian and follow American values.
The Dawes Act	
Destruction of the buffalo	
Ban on religious ceremonies	
Rations distributed to families	

Model answers

Here are model answers for each of the question types on the America Period Study. The annotations highlight what makes it a good answer.

These questions are based on Interpretations A and B on page 21.

Question 1: How do interpretations differ?

How does Interpretation A differ from Interpretation B about the impact of Reconstruction in the South? **(4 marks)**

These interpretations differ in their view of the impact of Reconstruction in the South. Interpretation A suggests that the Reconstruction transformed the rights of African-Americans in the South by giving them political power, even stating that 'there is nothing in the history of democracy comparable to it'. On the other hand, Interpretation B suggests the impact of Reconstruction was much more limited, due to the rise of violence against African-Americans. It describes violence in some areas reaching 'staggering proportions'. This clearly contrasts with the sense given in Interpretation A of fully emancipated African-Americans who enjoyed full political rights.

> The answer opens by clearly addressing the question. It gives a way in which the interpretations are different.

> The answer then uses details from the interpretations which show how they are different.

> Here the answer explains what is significant about these differences by explaining what the detail in each interpretation suggests.

Question 2: Why do interpretations differ?

Why might the authors of Interpretations A and B have a different interpretation about Reconstruction? **(4 marks)**

These interpretations differ due to the viewpoint and focus of their authors. Although both consider the changing status of African-Americans after the Civil War, the author of Interpretation A also focuses on the impact on the rights of the former slaveowners, suggesting that they were 'deprived of their former rights'. The author of Interpretation A also takes a broad view of Reconstruction, focusing on the 'enfranchisement of four million', whereas the author of Interpretation B instead highlights individual accounts of violence carried out against African-Americans which makes the Reconstruction seem far less positive. The title of Foner's book calls Reconstruction an 'unfinished revolution' which suggests that his view is that Reconstruction failed to fully transform the rights of ex-slaves, and this argument is clearly reflected in this extract.

> Here the answer clearly addresses the question in the first sentence. You should identify whether the nature, origin or purpose of the interpretations helps to explain the differences.

> Here the answer identifies information about the provenance of the interpretation which helps to explain its view.

> Here the answer explains in detail why the provenance of the interpretation would affect its view.

Question 3: How convincing are these interpretations?

Which interpretation do you find more convincing about Reconstruction? **(8 marks)**

Interpretation A is convincing as it suggests that the Reconstruction marked a radical break with the former rights of African-Americans. The author suggests that four million African-Americans were 'enfranchised', which was the result of the Fifteenth Amendment which gave all Americans the right to vote regardless of race. This followed the ending of slavery in the Thirteenth Amendment and the granting of citizenship in the Fourteenth Amendment. Despite the hyperbole of the statement, there is even some truth in the claim that former slaveowners were 'deprived of their political rights', as during the Radical Reconstruction phase the South was placed under the control of military governors to ensure compliance with the amendments. However, despite this guarantee of the right to vote, the reality was very different for many African-Americans who were prevented from voting by black codes, literacy tests and property qualifications.

> The answer opens by directly addressing the question and dealing with one of the interpretations given.

> Here the answer identifies a detail in the interpretation and explains what it suggests.

Interpretation B rightly identifies violence as a problem for many African-Americans in the South following the Civil War, quoting one witness as suggesting that African-Americans were 'frequently beaten unmercifully'. The KKK was formed in the immediate aftermath of the Civil War and used violence and intimidation to prevent African-Americans from exercising their political rights. This was the reason why many African-Americans, such as the exodusters, left the South in the decades following the Civil War. However, the interpretation does ignore some of the genuine achievements of Reconstruction, such as the growth of public education for African-Americans in the South.

Overall, Interpretation B is slightly more convincing in its view of what life was like for African-Americans who remained in the South, particularly the Deep South. Interpretation A addresses many of the changes made at federal level, but fails to appreciate the limited impact of these changes for many African-Americans.

> Specific own knowledge is used to evaluate the information in the interpretation.

> The answer closes with an overall judgement about which interpretation is most convincing and explains this decision.

Question 4: Describe two ways

Describe two reasons why the belief in Manifest Destiny became popular. **(4 marks)**

One reason the belief in Manifest Destiny became popular was due to the movement of Americans West. The opening of the Oregon Trail led to more Americans settling in Oregon and California and so these were increasingly seen as areas which the US had a right to claim. Another reason was the Mexican-American War, which led the US gaining control of much of the land in the West, leading to a desire to control the entire continent.

> The answer starts by directly addressing the question and giving one relevant detail.

> Here the answer adds a little explanation to show the relevance of the point given.

> The answer also gives a second relevant detail.

Question 5: In what ways ... ?

In what ways were the lives of Native Americans affected by the development of reservations? **(8 marks)**

One effect of reservation policy on Native Americans was to develop a dependency on the government. After the Great Sioux War, the amount of land given over to reservations was limited, which made the reservations unsuitable as hunting grounds for buffalo herds which moved throughout the year. Native Americans were banned from leaving the reservations to hunt. As a result, they depended on rations distributed by the government in order to survive. To break other ties of loyalty, the rations were soon distributed to individual families rather than the chief, so that each family owed its loyalty to the government and its Indian Agents.

Another effect was to destroy Native American culture. Native American children on the reservation were often taken away to attend white boarding schools, with the aim of making them Christians and removing their culture. Important religious practices like the Sun Dance were also banned, and the Dawes Act broke up the reservations into small family plots of land, which forced the Native Americans to farm and damaged the cohesion of the bands. This destroyed their nomadic lifestyle, and the importance of the band in their culture, which undermined many of the other practices which Native Americans had followed for centuries.

> Each paragraph opens with one clear point which addresses the question.

> Specific own knowledge is used to develop this point.

> The answer explains the relevance of this knowledge by linking back to the question at the end of the paragraph.

Question 6: Which reason?

Which of the following was the most important reason for conflict between North and South?

- Slavery
- Westward expansion

Explain your answer with reference to both reasons. **(12 marks)**

Slavery was one important reason for the conflict between North and South. These arguments led to violence in 'Bleeding Kansas' as thousands of settlers moved into the territory in order to influence the vote over whether Kansas should be a slave or free state. This led to violent attacks like the one at Lawrence, which escalated to a conflict in which hundreds were killed. John Brown's attack at Harpers Ferry also convinced many in the South that Northern abolitionists wished to encourage a slave rebellion, and this, combined with the election of Lincoln in 1860, eventually sparked the Civil War. Even though Lincoln insisted he would not end slavery in the South, Southerners had become convinced that this was the aim of the Republican Party, and therefore a number of Southern states seceded.

However, many of these conflicts had their roots in westward expansion. The conflict over Kansas had actually been triggered by the proposed route of a new railroad to support the further expansion West, and which created the new territories of Kansas and Nebraska. The issue of new territories had been problematic since the accession of Missouri in 1820, and continued to cause problems. This came to a head in 1850 when the balance of free and slave states was broken, and although a temporary compromise was reached, it was not long until this led to conflict in Kansas.

Although slavery was the immediate trigger for the Civil War, it would never have become a national issue if it had not been for the westward expansion. By continually reigniting the debate between pro-slavery and free-soil groups, westward expansion was the reason why disputes over slavery erupted into violence and conflict.

> Each paragraph addresses one of the reasons given in the question. It opens with a sentence showing which reason is being considered.

> The answer uses specific own knowledge to show the role of this reason.

> The answer then links back to the question and explains the importance of this reason.

> The answer gives a judgement about which reason was most important. This judgement is supported. You can show how one reason had more of an impact than the other, or look at how the reasons might be linked.

Glossary: America, 1840–1895: Expansion and consolidation

Abolition Opposition to slavery.

Bands Small groups of Plains Indians who lived and hunted together.

Blasphemy Speaking about God or religious matters in a rude or disrespectful manner.

Bozeman Trail A new trail which was opened across Indian lands, causing conflict with white settlers.

Conscription Forced recruitment into the army.

Concentration The US policy of moving Native Americans onto reservations and limiting their travel.

Counting coup A non-lethal form of Indian warfare where fighters tried to touch each other with sticks.

Dawes Act A law which broke up the reservations into smaller areas of land.

Dry farming A farming method where the ground is ploughed just after rain to hold moisture.

Exterminators White Americans who believed that Native Americans should be removed from their land or killed.

Fifteenth Amendment A law which gave all Americans the right to vote, including ex-slaves.

Fort Laramie Treaty A treaty in 1851 which agreed Indian lands and gave government support if they agreed not to attack white settlers.

Fourteenth Amendment A law which gave ex-slaves citizenship.

Free state A state where slavery was banned.

Ghost Dance Movement A movement which promised that the buffalo would return and white Americans would disappear from Indian lands. **Depression** An economic crisis which tends to lead to unemployment.

Gold Rush A rapid movement of people to any area where gold has been discovered, as in California in 1849.

Great American Desert A way Americans referred to the Great Plains in the 1820s.

Great Plains Region in central USA between the Rocky Mountains and the Mississippi river.

Hyperinflation When prices rise so quickly that money becomes effectively worthless.

Impeach To force a President out of office.

Indian Appropriations Act A law in 1851 which set up reservations.

Indian Removal Act A law passed in 1830 which set up a permanent frontier which Native Americans had to live beyond.

Irrigation Man-made water channels to water crops.

Manifest Destiny The idea that the US had a God-given right to take control of the whole continent of America.

Militia An unofficial group of soldiers drawn from local men.

Mountain Meadow Massacre An attack on white settlers by a group of Mormons which led to criticism of the Mormons.

Permanent Indian Frontier A boundary which marked out Indian land, created in 1830.

Perpetual Emigrating Fund A fund set up by the Mormons to pay for the travel of European migrants to join the settlement at Salt Lake.

Polygamy Having more than one husband or wife at the same time.

Reconstruction The efforts to bring the Southern states back into the Union after the Civil War.

Republican Party A US political party created in the 1850s. It was mostly anti-slavery.

Reservations Areas of land where Native Americans were forced to live. White settlers were not supposed to cross these areas.

Scalping Taking the skin from the top of the head of an enemy after defeating them in battle.

Share cropping A system of work where workers were kept in debt and forced to work without payment.

Sod house A mud-brick house built by homesteaders on the Plains.

Theocracy A state which follows religious rules.

Thirteenth Amendment A law which banned slavery in America.

Tipi A cone-shaped tent-like structure which many Plains Indians lived in.

Total War The US Army strategy to attack Native American homes and livestock, as well as fighting their warriors.

Travois A sled used for transporting the tipi.

Winder campaigns The US Army strategy of continuing to fight Plains Indians in the winter, when they were unable to move.

Chapter 2 Germany, 1890–1945: Democracy and dictatorship

2.1 Kaiser Wilhelm and the difficulties of ruling Germany, 1890–1914

Kaiser Wilhelm II controlled the government and had extensive powers

- The **Kaiser** appointed the **Chancellor** (head of the government) and other officials. No decision could be made without his agreement.
- However, Wilhelm II did not govern consistently because he was moody and unstable and had violent rages.
- **Parliamentary government** developed. There were several major political parties. None had a majority so governments were coalitions.
- **Right-wing** parties were strong and keen to expand the German Empire.
- **Left-wing** parties were gaining support from the increasing number of industrial workers.
- One of the 25 states, Prussia, was more powerful than the others. It had two-thirds of the population and half the territory. Some other states felt powerless to influence German policy.

> **Key point**
>
> Under Kaiser Wilhelm II the new country of Germany was becoming a leading industrial power. The Kaiser wanted to expand its power and influence even more.

Germany was becoming more industrialised and richer

- By 1914, Germany led the world in chemical and steel industries. For example, it produced twice as much steel as Britain. It produced one-third of the world's electrical goods.
- The population was growing rapidly (from 40 million in 1871 to 68 million in 1914). This provided manpower for the growing industries.
- Farmers could not supply all the food needed by the growing population so food imports were increasing.

> **TIP**
>
> The key terms in **purple** are defined in the glossary at the end of each chapter.
>
> Make sure that you can spell the key terms, know what they mean and aim to use them in your written work.

Tensions in society led to demands for social reforms

- German society was traditional, both in the rural areas and in the cities.
- Many people were very conservative in their political views. For example, they expected the upper classes to rule.
- At the same time, the **socialist** movement was growing, supported by industrial workers who wanted reform.
- Governments tried to meet workers' demands by introducing pensions and sickness insurance schemes.
- Support for the left-wing Social Democrat Party increased. It had about 30 per cent of seats in the **Reichstag** in 1912.

The army and navy had high status. There was much support for German expansion

- The army in Prussia swore obedience to the Kaiser.
- Wilhelm II wanted to expand the German navy to match that of Britain's.
- The Navy Laws allowed the building of many more battleships.
- The Kaiser wanted Germany to have an overseas empire as France and Britain both had. This led to international crises in the years leading up to 1914 and was one cause of the First World War.

 Test yourself

1 What were the Naval Laws?

2 List two strengths and two weaknesses in German society in the years before 1914.

Compare interpretations

Questions 1–3 of your exam will ask you to compare the content of interpretations. You need to read carefully, understand what is said, compare with your own knowledge and make inferences. This task practises question 1.

Study Interpretations A and B. How do they differ in their views on Kaiser Wilhelm II? (4 marks)

> **INTERPRETATION A** *First impressions of Wilhelm II as Kaiser. From G. Craig,* Germany 1866–1945 *(1981).*
>
> Most people were impressed by the new ruler's vitality, his openness to new ideas, the diversity of his interests, and his personal charm. A Court official later wrote that William was 'a dazzling personality who fascinated everyone who appeared before him. He was well aware of his ability to do this and developed this talent with much effort and refinement to an extra-ordinary perfection'.

> **INTERPRETATION B** *Concerns about Wilhelm II. From Michael Balfour,* The Kaiser and His Times *(1964).*
>
> The main cause of alarm was William's [Wilhelm's] lack of tact. ... The chief danger is that he is absolutely unconscious of the effect which his speeches and actions have upon princes, public men and the masses. For example, he astonished the British Ambassador by the way he talked about the diminutive [small] King of Italy whom he referred to as 'the Dwarf' while calling the Queen 'a peasant girl' and 'the daughter of a cattle thief'.

Summarise in a sentence the overall difference in their view of the Kaiser and choose two extracts from each interpretation to support this.

 You're the examiner!

Question 5 of your exam focuses on how a key development affected a situation or a group of people. For example:

In what ways did the style of German government under Wilhelm II affect how the country developed? (8 marks)

For a top-level answer, an examiner is looking for an explanation that:
- includes accurate and detailed knowledge
- uses the knowledge to answer the question.

Question 5 is not an essay. There is no need for an introduction and a conclusion.

Connect the comments to the highlighted elements to show the good features of the answer below.

Wilhelm II was powerful and made sure that the Reichstag leaders were kept under control. This meant that he could decide policies – such as the expansion of the navy, which the Reichstag agreed to by passing the Navy Laws. The Reichstag had representatives from many political parties, with an increasing number of socialist members – about 30 per cent by 1914. This meant that, with coalition governments, the left wing had influence to get policies implemented that they favoured. For example, Germans gained old-age pensions and sickness and unemployment insurance before the end of the nineteenth century. Lastly, the ruling conservative elite kept much power, which meant that traditional attitudes remained strong.

Key words showing how the answer is organised.

Relevant, detailed knowledge to support the main point.

Key phrase to ensure you explain not just describe.

2.2 The impact of the First World War on Germany

By 1918 the **German people** were suffering **war-weariness**

- Living standards were low, especially in many cities. There were food and fuel shortages and a major flu epidemic swept the country.
- There were 600,000 widows and 2 million children without fathers.
- The country was virtually bankrupt and industrial production was only two-thirds of what it had been in 1913. Much of that was geared towards fighting the war.
- Divisions in society had deepened during the war, with huge differences in living standards between rich and poor.
- War shortages, suffering and inequality boosted support for left-wing parties who wanted to overthrow the Kaiser's government.

When **Germany surrendered** in November 1918, the Kaiser fled

- When the Allies counter-attacked in August 1918, it was clear that Germany was losing the war.
- There were riots by German sailors at Kiel and among German workers.
- The Socialists (left-wingers who hated the Kaiser's rule) led uprisings in ports and cities. A socialist republic was declared in Bavaria.
- On 9 November, the Kaiser fled to the Netherlands and **abdicated** (gave up his throne).
- On 11 November, representatives of the Social Democrat Party led by Friedrich Ebert signed the **Armistice** (agreement to stop fighting).

A new **constitution** made Germany very **democratic**

- Ebert became leader of the new German **Republic** because he was leader of the largest political party in the Reichstag.
- A new **constitution** was drawn up quickly which made Germany much more democratic than under the Kaiser.

President (the head of state)	Chancellor (the prime minister)	Reichstag (the parliament)	The people (the electorate)
Elected by the people every seven years	**Chosen** from the Reichstag by the President but must have (and keep) Reichstag support	**Elected** by the people by **proportional representation** (each party gets the same proportion of seats as they get votes)	All Germans over the age of twenty could **vote** for the President and the members of the Reichstag

- One exception to these democratic principles was **Article 48**. This said that, in a crisis, the **President** could rule the country directly using emergency powers. This proved to be a very important power in later years.

The new government faced **political chaos** and was further damaged by the **Treaty of Versailles**

- With a new system of government, dissatisfied soldiers returning home and new political parties emerging, it is not surprising that there was political unrest. Each group wanted to seize the opportunity to gain control.
- Ebert's government crushed a right-wing revolt on 6 December 1918 and a left-wing Communist revolt on 5 January 1919 (see page 34).

Key point

After the First World War, Germany was weaker than it had been before – politically and economically. The war led to a complete change of government which got off to a very shaky start, with political and economic chaos. The very unpopular Treaty of Versailles made things worse.

- Amid this chaos there were free elections on 19 January 1919 and Ebert became President on 11 February.
- The new government met in Weimar because Berlin was too unstable. The government became known as the Weimar Republic.
- A further crisis came when Ebert's government had to sign the Treaty of Versailles in June 1919. It weakened his government because its opponents always blamed it for the problems caused by the treaty.
- The war defeat had damaged German pride. The Treaty of Versailles made it even worse because it blamed Germany for the war. The German people resented that.

Germany faced major economic problems from 1919 to 1923 including hyperinflation

- Because of the war, many of Germany's traditional industries were weak.
- Germany's pre-war international trade had also disappeared. It was difficult to re-establish trading links at a time when industry was weak and Germany was being blamed for the war.
- To make matters worse, under the Treaty of Versailles, Germany was forced to agree to pay **reparations** (compensation for war damage) of £6600 million (£6.6 billion) to the victorious countries.
- The first instalment was paid in 1921, but nothing was paid in 1922 and so in January 1923 French and Belgian troops entered the **Ruhr** (an industrial area of Germany), to seize raw materials and goods as an alternative to the unpaid reparations.
- German workers went on strike in protest. Factory production collapsed.
- The government was running out of money so it printed more. **Hyperinflation** followed. Prices rose so quickly that bank notes and savings became worthless. Those on fixed incomes suffered badly.
- Hyperinflation damaged the reputation of the Weimar Republic – particularly among the middle classes whose wealth was wiped out.

Test yourself

1 List two reasons why support for left-wing parties increased in 1918.
2 What is hyperinflation?

TIP

One common error is to confuse hyperinflation (which happened in 1923) and the Depression which happened after 1929. They were very different events with very different causes. Don't make that mistake.

Key events

Copy and complete the flowchart to outline how German government changed from late 1918 to early 1919.

Autumn 1918	9 Nov 1918	11 Nov 1918	6 Dec 1918	5 Jan 1919	19 Jan 1919	February 1919
German armies in retreat. German people not informed of desperate situation						The newly elected democratic government met at Weimar

Challenge: create a second flowchart to show how post-war economic problems led to hyperinflation.

Topic summary

Complete a diagram like the one opposite to classify the different problems faced by Germany in 1919. This will make it easier to write analytical answers. Try to be as specific as possible as the mark schemes ask you to use specific and detailed knowledge. The first one has been started for you.

Political
Left-wing opposition from Spartacists

Economic

International

Problems faced by new Weimar government in 1919

Social

2.3 The new Weimar government: initial problems and recovery under Stresemann

In the **early 1920s** the Weimar government faced **political unrest** and **rebellions**

- The three most important rebellions were:

Date	Rebellion	Aims and outcome
January 1919	The **Spartacist** rebellion	The Spartacists were Communists who wanted to copy what Communists had achieved in Russia in 1917. They tried to seize control, helped by some soldiers, sailors and factory workers. Their leaders, Karl Liebknecht and Rosa Luxemburg, were killed
March 1920	Kapp Putsch	Dr Wolfgang Kapp led a march in Berlin of 5000 *Freikorps* (ex-soldiers). They wanted to make Germany powerful again with something like the old dictatorial style of government. The **putsch** (an attempt to seize power) was defeated by the workers who declared a general strike
November 1923	Munich Putsch	Hitler, leader of the small Nazi Party, had some support in Bavaria. At a meeting in a beer hall, Hitler announced that he and his supporters were going to seize power and marched towards the government building. The putsch was quickly defeated. Hitler was arrested, put on trial and sentenced to five years in prison. While in prison he decided that in the future the Nazis should seek power by election and not by putsch

- The government survived these rebellions. **However**, the rebellions showed how dissatisfied some people were with Weimar democracy.

Under Stresemann Germany **appeared to recover** and Weimar **culture flourished**

- In 1923, Germany was in a chaotic situation: it faced political weakness, hyperinflation and the French occupation of the industrial area of the Ruhr.
- Gustav Stresemann rescued Germany. He was the most powerful politician in Germany from late 1923 to 1929, as Chancellor, then as Foreign Minister.

Date	Measure	Significance
1923	New currency introduced	The Rentenmark replaced the old worthless marks. This stabilised prices and the economy
1924	The Dawes Plan	Germany was loaned 800 million marks by the USA, and reparations payments were spread over a longer period of time
1929	The Young Plan	Reparations payments were reduced to £2.2 billion and Germany was given longer to pay

- By early 1929, Germany appeared to be regaining its prosperity. For example, Germany was second (behind the USA) in industrial output.

However,

- unemployment was rising (it was six per cent by 1928) and the economic benefits were not equally shared. Farmers got poorer in the 1920s.

International agreements restored Germany's international reputation and pride

- As Foreign Minister, Stresemann signed agreements with Germany's former enemies, France and Britain, promising not to invade each other.
- In 1926, Germany was allowed to join the League of Nations, which restored its 'great power' status and boosted German pride.

Key point

The new Weimar Republic faced huge problems in the early 1920s. In the later 1920s, under Stresemann, successes seemed to outweigh failures. Germany appeared to be on the road to recovery.

TIP

The examiners want you to use relevant and detailed knowledge in your answers. In your revision you should try to remember a specific piece of information associated with each general idea.

However,

- Stresemann had to accept the Treaty of Versailles, and some Germans, particularly right wingers, thought Stresemann was weak and had given in to Germany's enemies.

There was a **cultural revival**

- Under the Kaiser there had been strict censorship.
- When censorship was removed under the Weimar government, painters, writers, musicians and architects revelled in the new freedom – particularly in cities such as Berlin.
- Clubs and cinemas thrived. German art and architecture became internationally famous.

However,

- A lot of Germans were not happy about this. Many (particularly in the countryside) thought Weimar culture showed moral decline.

Test yourself

1 Who were the Spartacists and what happened to them?

2 What was the Dawes Plan and why was it significant?

Develop the detail

Each of the following statements is vague and lacks detail. Using the past four pages and your own knowledge, on a separate piece of paper, add details to show that you understand the general point made. One example has been done for you.

Generalised statement	With developed detail
The President could act like a dictator	Article 48 of the Constitution allowed the President, if there was an emergency, to pass laws without the approval of the Reichstag
It was difficult for any party to get a majority	
The Spartacists were Communists	
Stresemann ended hyperinflation	
Germany was becoming more prosperous	
Germany's progress depended on the USA	

Support or challenge?

In your exams you will often have to reach a judgement and support it with evidence. This task helps you to practise. Read this statement:

In the 1920s the Weimar Republic seemed like a new strong government for Germany.

Below is a list of events and situations. For each one, decide whether it supports or challenges the overall statement above.

A The *Freikorps* wanted the return to strong government as under the Kaiser.

B All Germans over the age of 20 could vote.

C Attempts to overthrow the Weimar Republic were defeated.

D Hyperinflation was ended and a new currency introduced by Stresemann.

E Germany was allowed to join the League of Nations in 1926.

F German prosperity depended largely on US loans.

G Unemployment was rising by the end of the 1920s.

2.4 The impact of the Depression on Germany

The **Great Depression** had a huge **impact** on Germany

- The Wall Street Crash in the USA in 1929 led to a global **Depression**.
- The Depression had a huge impact on Germans because Germany depended on loans from the USA and because it still owed reparations to the **Allies**.
- American loans were recalled. German businesses could not pay, so many businesses went bankrupt.
- Millions of German workers lost their jobs. There were 6 million unemployed by late 1932.
- The mood of optimism in Germany disappeared.

> **Key point**
>
> The Great Depression severely damaged the German economy and undermined Weimar democracy. This gave the Nazis an opportunity to win support for their extreme policies, which they exploited very effectively.

As Weimar government struggled, **extremist parties** including the Nazis gained **support**

- The Weimar government failed to end the crisis. The shortcomings of the Weimar system became more obvious. No party was strong enough to take decisive action.
- Extremist parties exploited this situation.

←	→
Many workers turned to the Communist Party with its promises to the working classes of a workers' revolution	Others, particularly rich and middle classes, were attracted by right-wing parties promising strong rule and to restore Germany's status

- The Nazis were also fiercely anti-Communist which made them even more popular with the bosses who feared a Communist revolution.

Nazi slogans appealed to many Germans

Promises	Culprits (to blame for German problems)
<ul><li>To make Germany great again</li><li>To abolish the Treaty of Versailles and rearm Germany</li><li>To end the economic crisis by providing jobs for workers</li></ul>	<ul><li>The 'November Criminals' who surrendered when the war could have been won</li><li>France and Britain, who created the Treaty of Versailles in order to cripple Germany</li><li>Communists who wanted to make revolution in Germany</li><li>Jews who had too much influence in Germany (although the Jews were not much emphasised in the early years)</li></ul>

- Nazi policies lacked detail. They were more like slogans. It was therefore hard to criticise them.
- The slogans were backed up with effective **propaganda** (rallies, marches, posters and pamphlets) organised by Josef Goebbels.
- Hitler was a brilliant speaker. He travelled around Germany (by plane) to speak to as many people as possible. This was an innovation.

At **election** time there were **violent clashes** between right- and left-wing groups

- The **SA** members with their smart uniforms gave an impression of law and order. The SA often fought Communist gangs in the streets.
- The SA often had the support of the police and army when it disrupted meetings of its political opponents.

Test yourself

1 What was the SA?
2 List three reasons for increased support for the Nazis.
3 Which do you think was the most important and why?

Quick quizzes at **www.hoddereducation.co.uk/myrevisionnotes**

Compare interpretations

An essential exam skill is comparing two interpretations. You need to read carefully, understand what is said, compare with your own knowledge and make inferences. Use these questions to guide you.

1 List reasons why the speaker in Interpretation C supported the Nazis.
2 How can you infer that she was not wholeheartedly in support?
3 Why might that be?
4 Did the speaker in Interpretation D support the Nazis for the same reasons?
5 Why did he think of the Jews as a 'problem'?

INTERPRETATION C *From an interview in the 1960s with a housewife who had lived in a town in northern Germany in the 1930s.*

The ranks of the Nazi Party were filled with young people. Those serious people who joined did so because they were for social justice, or against unemployment. There was a feeling of restless energy about the Nazis. You saw the swastika painted on the sidewalks or found them littered with pamphlets put out by the Nazis. I was drawn by the feeling of strength about the party, even though there was much in it that was highly questionable.

INTERPRETATION D *From an interview in the 1960s with a man who had been the head of a secondary school in the same town in Germany in the 1930s.*

I saw the Communist danger; their gangs breaking up middle-class meetings, the Nazis being the only party that broke terror by anti-terror. I saw the complete failure of the other parties to deal with the economic crisis. Only National Socialism offered any hope.

Nazis mostly did not hate Jews individually, but they were concerned about the Jewish problem. Most Jews persisted in being loyal to their Jewish fellows, so that more and more Jews got positions in trade, banking, the newspapers, etc. Many people saw the danger of that problem. Nobody knew of any way to deal with it, but they hoped that the Nazis would know.

 Develop the explanation

The first column in the table below lists reasons why Hitler became popular by 1933. For each reason, add details to explain how this made him popular.

Reasons	Explanation
Hitler's skills as a speaker	Hitler was a powerful speaker who gave the impression he knew what was wrong with Germany and how to solve the problems. This made him the Nazis' main attraction. Hitler travelled around Germany by plane at election time so as many people as possible could hear him speak
The Nazis' private army – the SA	
Nazi propaganda	
The Depression	

 Practice question

Describe two ways in which Germany suffered economically after the Wall Street Crash. (4 marks)

2.5 The failure of Weimar democracy: Hitler becomes Chancellor, January 1933

REVISED

The **democratic system** of Weimar government **did not cope well** with the crisis

- Proportional representation was a good idea in theory. It was supposed to ensure that all groups in Germany were well represented in the Reichstag.
- However, in practice it meant that there too many small political parties in the Reichstag who disagreed with each other, which made it difficult to take action.
- Chancellor Brüning (Chancellor from 1930 to 1932) dealt with this problem by getting President Hindenburg to use Article 48. This allowed the President to pass emergency laws without the approval of the Reichstag.
- Using this power in 1930, Brüning cut government spending and welfare benefits. This actually made the economic problems worse for many Germans.

A series of **elections** allowed the Nazis to **exploit people's disillusion** with Weimar government

- Hindenburg and Brüning decided to call an election in 1930.
- Hitler and the Nazis ran a powerful campaign criticising the Weimar government.
- The Nazis won 107 seats. They were not yet the largest party but it was a massive increase on the twelve seats they had won in 1928.
- The largest party was still the **Social Democratic Party** (the left-wing party supported by most workers).
- The Weimar government was still unstable so there were two further elections in 1932. The Nazis gained 230 in July and then 196 seats in November. They became the largest party, but still not with a majority.
- Also in 1932, Hitler stood against the respected President Hindenburg in the presidential election.
- Hitler lost, but he gained 13 million votes (Hindenburg gained 19 million). This boosted his profile and made him seem an important national figure in German politics.

Hindenburg reluctantly made **Hitler Chancellor** because only he had enough **Reichstag support** to govern

- Through 1932 Hindenburg avoided making Hitler Chancellor, even though he led the largest party in the Reichstag. Instead, von Papen was made Chancellor in 1932.
- Von Papen did not have a majority to support him in the Reichstag, so he resigned in December 1932 and von Schleicher took over. He ran into the same problems.
- In January 1933, Hindenburg and von Papen met with other leading right-wing politicians and army leaders to discuss the political crisis.
- Von Papen persuaded Hindenburg to appoint Hitler as Chancellor with himself (von Papen) as Vice-Chancellor and with a majority of non-Nazis in the government. They thought that in this way Hitler would be controlled.

> **Key point**
>
> After the elections in 1932, the Nazis were the largest party. President Hindenburg did not want Hitler as Chancellor but in the end he had little choice because Hitler was the only person who had enough support in the Reichstag to lead a government.

> **TIP**
>
> In your answers use words like 'because', 'therefore', 'which meant that' or 'so' to remind you to explain rather than describe.

When **Hitler** became Chancellor in January 1933 many thought he would **not last long** in the job

- Hitler became Chancellor on 30 January 1933.
- Many Germans believed that Hitler's new government would not last long when he faced the problems of actually ruling the country.

Test yourself

1 What was Article 48?
2 How did Chancellor Brüning try to solve the problems caused by the Depression?
3 Why did Hindenburg make Hitler Chancellor in January 1933?

TIP

Candidates find it hard to give time to planning in an actual exam, which is why it is so important to practise it **before** the exam so that it becomes instinctive.

Essay plan

The highest mark question in your Period Study exam will be an essay question structured like this.

Which of the following was the more important reason why Hitler was appointed Chancellor of Germany in 1933?

- **The effects of the Wall Street Crash.**
- **The role of Nazi propaganda.**

Explain your answer with reference to both reasons.   **(12 marks)**

The secret of writing a good essay is good planning. Here is a plan.

Plan	Purpose/points to include
Introduction	You show that you know why Hitler becoming Chancellor was such an important event
Paragraph 1	You explain how the Wall Street Crash helped to lead to this outcome. For example: American loans were withdrawn so businesses went bankrupt
Paragraph 2	You explain how Nazi propaganda led to this outcome
A conclusion	You link the two reasons (if you can) Reach a judgement on which is more important and support that judgement

- Step 1: note down evidence or points you will include in paragraphs 1 and 2.
- Step 2: make a decision on which reason to argue for. There is no right or wrong answer but you need have good historical reasons to justify your choice. Practise writing your conclusion.

2.6 The establishment of Hitler's dictatorship in the years 1933–34

REVISED

The **Reichstag Fire** gave Hitler an excuse to **crush the Communists**

- Once he was Chancellor, Hitler immediately called an election for early March 1933.
- A week before the election, on 27 February, the Reichstag building was set on fire.
- The Nazis may have started the fire but they blamed the Communists.
- The Nazis used the fire as an excuse to pass an emergency decree to give the police extra powers to arrest people without trial and to ban meetings.
- Police arrested 4000 Communists and anti-Communist propaganda was increased.
- In the election on 5 March, the Nazis got their best ever result – 288 seats.
- With the support of the Nationalist Party, the Nazis had a majority.

> **Key point**
>
> Hitler acted quickly to establish a dictatorship. He crushed opposition before it got organised. He was able to do this because of the Enabling Act.

The **Enabling Act** allowed Hitler to **create a dictatorship**

What?	The **Enabling Act** in March 1933 gave Hitler power to pass laws for four years without consulting the Reichstag
How?	The Reichstag approved the Act by a huge majority after Hitler intimidated its members, using the SA and the **SS**
Results	Only the Nazi Party was allowed. The Nazis rounded up political opponents and imprisoned them in **concentration camps**
	The Nazis took control of the media such as newspapers and radio stations
	Trade unions were banned. Workers had to join the new Nazi-controlled **German Labour Front**

The **threat of the SA** was removed on the **Night of the Long Knives**

- The SA had been the basis of Nazi success since the 1920s, particularly by intimidating opponents. It had grown massively to 2.5 million members.
- It was now seen as an unruly mob and a threat to Hitler's control. It was also a rival to the army, which had only 100,000 soldiers.
- In the **Night of the Long Knives** (June 1934), SA leaders including Ernst Röhm were killed.
- The SA continued to exist but was much less important. Many members moved to the army or the SS.
- The SS came under the direct control of Hitler as his private army.

Hitler became **Führer** in August 1934

- President Hindenburg died in August 1934, aged 84. Hitler declared himself President in addition to being Chancellor.
- The army swore an oath of personal loyalty to Hitler.
- Hitler was now Supreme Leader (**Führer**).

 Test yourself

1 How many seats did the Nazis win in the March 1933 elections?

2 What was the Enabling Act?

3 How many people were in the SA in 1933–34?

4 Who was Ernst Röhm?

Explain significance

1 Link up the heads and tails in the table below to show why each feature was significant in establishing the Nazi dictatorship.

2 Put the features in chronological order by numbering them 1–5.

Feature	Significance
The Enabling Act	... removed the SA as a potential threat to his authority
Proportional representation	... led to a severe depression in Germany with high unemployment
The Reichstag Fire	... gave Hitler power to pass laws without the Reichstag for four years
The Night of the Long Knives	... meant that no party ever gained a majority in the Reichstag, which made it hard to agree solutions to the economic crisis
The Wall Street Crash	... gave the Nazis an excuse to clamp down on the Communists

Evaluate the interpretations

Read the two interpretations below about the Reichstag Fire. Then answer the exam-style questions.

INTERPRETATION E *From an account written in 1950 by Rudolf Diels, a Nazi and head of police in Berlin in 1933.*

I think van der Lubbe started the Reichstag Fire on his own. When I arrived at the burning building, some police officers were already questioning him. His voluntary confession made me think that he was such an expert arsonist that he did not need any helpers. Why could not one person set fire to the old furnishings, the heavy curtains and the bone-dry wood panelling? He had lit several dozen fires using firelighters and his burning shirt, which he was holding in his right hand like a torch when he was overpowered by Reichstag officials.

INTERPRETATION F *From* Hitler – A Study in Tyranny *by the British historian Alan Bullock (1952).*

Goering had been looking for an excuse to smash the Communist Party. He at once declared that van der Lubbe was only part of a larger Communist plot to start a campaign of terror. The burning of the Reichstag was to be the signal for Communist revolt.

In fact, I believe that the burning of the Reichstag was planned and carried out by the Nazis themselves. Van der Lubbe was picked up by the SA and allowed to climb into the Reichstag and start a fire on his own in one part of the building while Nazis started the main fires.

Question 1 asks you to compare the interpretations. Identify the overall message and support that with detail from the interpretation.

1 How does Interpretation E differ from Interpretation F about the Reichstag Fire? (4 marks)

Question 2 asks you to compare the provenance (purpose and authorship) to explain why they might differ.

2 Why might the authors of Interpretations E and F have a different interpretation about the Reichstag Fire? (4 marks)

Question 3 is worth more marks. Use your knowledge to explain which you think is more accurate (convincing).

3 Which interpretation do you find more convincing about the Reichstag Fire? (8 marks)

TIP

When examining an interpretation always read the caption. It will include important information about who wrote it and when.

2.7 Economic changes: employment and rearmament

Under Nazi rule unemployment was reduced and industry prospered, 1933–39

- In 1933, unemployment was over 5 million. By 1939 it was virtually zero. Hitler fulfilled one of his key promises. This was done by:

Public works	Rearmament	Conscription
The **National Labour Service** employed workers to build a network of *autobahns* (motorways), more railways and new houses. These were paid for by the government	Started in secret in 1933 (in defiance of the Treaty of Versailles). Jobs were created manufacturing weapons and army uniforms	**Conscription** was introduced in 1935. Selected Germans were forced to join the armed forces

> **Key point**
>
> Many German civilians benefited from the improved economy during the 1930s but they all suffered greatly in the final three years of the war.

- These were part of 'The New Plan' devised by Dr Schacht, which ran from 1933–36.
- In 1936 this was replaced by the Four-Year Plan under Hermann Goering. This was intended to make Germany self-sufficient by 1940 so that it did not have to import essential raw materials.

Some Germans benefited more than others from the economic changes

- **Industrial workers** mostly gained from Nazi rule in the 1930s. They were glad to have a job and an income. However,

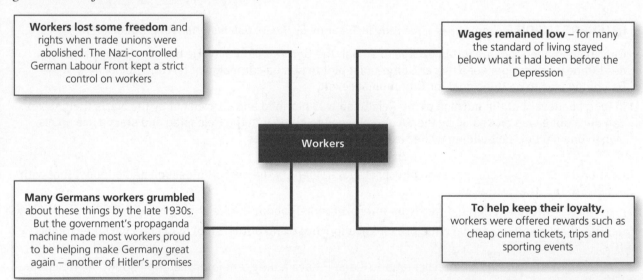

Workers lost some freedom and rights when trade unions were abolished. The Nazi-controlled German Labour Front kept a strict control on workers

Wages remained low – for many the standard of living stayed below what it had been before the Depression

Workers

Many Germans workers grumbled about these things by the late 1930s. But the government's propaganda machine made most workers proud to be helping make Germany great again – another of Hitler's promises

To help keep their loyalty, workers were offered rewards such as cheap cinema tickets, trips and sporting events

- **Farming communities** were helped with guaranteed food prices and rights to keep their land.
- **Big businesses** were pleased about the Nazis getting rid of the Communist threat and many benefited from government spending.
- **Small businesses** did not benefit from any protection (for example, local shops).
- **Nazi opponents** were excluded from the prosperity. They could not work and could not claim unemployment pay. Jews and other 'undesirables' were victimised and persecuted. Jewish businesses were boycotted or closed down.

 Test yourself

1 List five things that most Germans were happy about in the period 1933–39.

2 List three things that most Germans were not so happy about in the period 1933–39.

From 1942 onwards the **war went badly** for Germany, which had a **huge impact** on its people

Shortages	Bombing raids
Rationing started in 1939 on food and clothes, but in the first two years of the war there were no real shortages as imports from defeated countries arrived	From 1942, German cities were bombed first by the British and then also by the Americans
However, from 1942 onwards when Germany started to suffer defeats, the economy was totally directed towards war production	Major bombing of cities such as Berlin and Dresden was intended to break German morale
German civilians began to suffer greatly with increasing shortages of food and other essentials, including fuel	About half a million German citizens died in these raids; 7.5 million became homeless
	By 1945, many became refugees – with millions fleeing the advancing Soviet armies

Practice question

Describe two problems faced by German civilians in a city such as Berlin in the final months of the Second World War.

(4 marks)

Develop the detail

Each of the following statements lacks detail. Add details to show that you understand the statement.

Statement	Detail
Unemployment went down in the period 1933–39	
The Nazis created jobs 1933–39	
Farmers were helped by Nazi policies 1933–39	
Bomb damage was huge during the Second World War	
Food shortages got worse as the war went on	

Essay plan

Look at the essay question below.

Which of the following was the more important reason for most Germans supporting Hitler in the 1930s?

- **The Nazis providing jobs.**
- **Nazi policies encouraging loyalty.**

Explain your answer with reference to both reasons. (12 marks)

1 List two factors for each of the bullet points to show they are important.
2 Then decide which is more important and explain a reason.

TIP

In your exam you only have about a minute's writing time per mark! So don't waste time on the low-tariff questions. Save time for the 12-marker.

2.8 The impact of Nazi social policies

Women, children and young people had a key role to play in Nazi society

- Hitler wanted all Germans to think of themselves as part of the German state.
- Hitler wanted a woman's role to be a wife or a mother.
- Married couples were encouraged to have more children – and were given rewards for doing so.
- Married women were restricted in what work they could do – until there was a shortage of workers in the late 1930s.
- Children were taught to be good Nazis:
  - ○ at school where subjects such as History were angled to teach Nazi ideas
  - ○ outside school through the **Hitler Youth** (for boys) or the **League of German Maidens** (for girls).
- Physical fitness was seen as very important for both girls (for child-bearing) and boys (future German soldiers). Youth camps took children off to explore the countryside.

Nazi attempts to control the German Churches had mixed results

- Hitler signed a **Concordat** (an agreement) with the Catholic Church in 1933, promising not to interfere so long as the Church did not interfere in politics.
- Hitler set up the **Reich Church** (an official state Protestant Church), which many Germans supported to start with – before they became aware of the evil of some Nazi policies.
- Some Protestant Church leaders such as Martin Niemöller stood up to Hitler by setting up their own independent churches.

Nazi racist ideas led to increasing persecution of Jewish people through the 1930s

- The Nazis believed in the superiority of the **Aryan** race (the white-skinned race of northern Europe). Other racial groups were persecuted, including gypsies and Jews.
- Laws were passed restricting what Jews could do. For example, in 1935 the Nuremberg Laws stated that Jews were not German citizens and could not marry Germans.
- In November 1938, discrimination turned into persecution in a Nazi-organised purge known as *Kristallnacht* (Night of Broken Glass):
  - ○ Jewish properties including synagogues were attacked
  - ○ many Jews were killed or injured
  - ○ 20,000 Jews were taken to concentration camps
  - ○ other Jews left the country
  - ○ hundreds of synagogues were destroyed.

Hitler's actions against the Jews got worse, ending in the genocide of the Holocaust

- Once the war began and the Germans invaded other countries, Hitler's campaigns against the Jews spread from Germany to newly conquered territories such as Poland.

Key point

Hitler intended to transform German society to reflect Nazi ideals and beliefs. There was no room for alternative views. This affected all sections of society – and especially the Jews.

 Test yourself

1 What was the role of women in Nazi Germany?
2 What was the Concordat?
3 What was *Kristallnacht*?

TIP

The highest marks in the mark scheme are reserved for candidates who show 'complex thinking'. What this means varies according to the type of question. Complex thinking for the 'Support or challenge' question on page 45 would be showing that you really understand how **variable** people's experiences were under the Nazis depending on who you were or when you lived.

Quick quizzes at **www.hoddereducation.co.uk/myrevisionnotes**

- They escalated in stages into a programme of extermination.

Ghettos	*Einsatzgruppen*	The Final Solution
In 1939, the Jewish population was rounded up and forced to live in overcrowded **ghettos** (areas of a city with little sanitation or food). Many people died of disease or starvation	From 1941, after the invasion of Russia, half a million Jews in German-occupied areas were rounded up and shot by SS squads called *Einsatzgruppen*	In 1942, the Nazis started what they called the Final Solution. This was the deliberate policy to wipe out the Jewish population by taking Jews to **death camps** such as Auschwitz or Treblinka in Poland. They were worked to death or murdered with poison gas

- Other groups who the Nazis wanted to get rid of, such as Jehovah's Witnesses, homosexuals and Soviet prisoners of war, were also murdered in these death camps.
- There is no agreement among historians about how much Hitler was personally responsible, but there is no doubt that he knew what was happening.
- Other countries gradually found out about what the Nazis were doing but they found it hard to believe the full extent of it and little specific action was taken.

 Develop the detail

Add details to the blank boxes in the right-hand column to summarise the stages by which Hitler's hatred of the Jews became the actions of the Holocaust.

Before 1933	Hitler developed racial theories that justified Aryan superiority
1933–35 List Nazi actions against the Jews	Once in power …
1936	There was reduced persecution of the Jews – Olympic Games held in Berlin
1938 List further actions against the Jews	
1939 onwards Explain how the war changed things	There were many Jews living in countries occupied by the Nazis …
1942–45: The Holocaust Summarise key developments and their impact	

 Support or challenge?

For each piece of evidence below, decide whether it supports or challenges this overall statement.

'German people benefited from Nazi rule in the years 1933–39.'

A   German children were taught that they were members of a master-race.

B   Married couples were given financial rewards if they had four or more children.

C   Children were taught by teachers who supported the Nazis.

D   Women were restricted in what careers they could have.

E   The Jews were no longer German citizens after the Nuremberg Laws were passed in 1935.

F   Most German boys were keen to join the Hitler Youth movement.

Challenge: now list as many other points as you can on each side of the argument, using the information on these two pages and your own knowledge.

2.9 The Nazi dictatorship

Ideas were controlled by **propaganda** and **censorship**

- Propaganda stressed the importance of the Nazi state and the superiority of the German people.

- Every year the Nazis put on a spectacular and colourful **Nuremberg Rally** with vast meetings and marches. These rallies showed how Nazis brought discipline and order out of chaos.

- Goebbels controlled what was broadcast on the radio and in newspapers. Books that did not reflect Nazi values were burned.

- Goebbels restricted what artists, writers and musicians were allowed to show or perform. All films had to have a pro-Nazi message.

- However, German people were not simply brainwashed. Many Germans in the 1930s genuinely valued the Nazis' economic achievements, Hitler's foreign policy and the restoration of stable government.

> **Key point**
>
> Nazi Germany was a police state. German people could not think or speak openly. They were controlled through a combination of terror, propaganda and censorship. The result was that the Nazi leadership faced only limited opposition.

Nazi Germany was a **police state**

- The SS and **Gestapo** intimidated people into accepting Nazi rule.

Organisation	Leader	Role
SS	Himmler	Responsible for destroying opposition to the Nazis and carrying out Nazi racial policies
Gestapo (state secret police)	Heydrich	Could arrest on suspicion and send people to concentration camps without trial

- So-called concentration camps were set up from the first months of Hitler's regime to detain and terrorise political prisoners and Nazi critics.

Resistance was punished harshly as **an example** to others

- There was not much resistance to the Nazis. People were afraid to speak out. Many felt that the benefits of Nazi rule outweighed their bad points.

- Even in the early years of the Second World War, actual opposition groups and resistance were slow to develop.

- Young people opposed the regime in different ways and some were punished harshly for it.

> **TIP**
>
> Don't confuse concentration camps with 'death camps', where the mass murder of Jews started in 1942.

White Rose Group	Swing Youth	Edelweiss Pirates
A group of students at Munich University who used leaflets, posters and graffiti to criticise the Nazis. The leaders were arrested, tortured and killed	Middle-class teenagers who rebelled against Nazi values, for example by playing American jazz music that the Nazis had banned. The Nazis disapproved but did not take this seriously enough to impose severe punishments	Disaffected, mainly working-class, teenagers who made fun of the Nazis and their policies. Again mostly ignored until in wartime when some were hanged after committing acts of espionage

- Various plots were hatched to kill Hitler. Only one came close to success – the Stauffenberg bomb plot in July 1944, organised by army officers. Their bomb went off but Hitler was only slightly injured.

- The Nazi response to the **July Bomb Plot** was typically violent. The plotters were all executed. The SS rounded up another 5000 opponents and killed them by shooting, hanging or torture.

Eliminate irrelevance

In what ways did the lives of children change in the 1930s under Nazi rule? (8 marks)

Cross out the elements in the sample answer below that are not relevant to the question.

Children's lives changed a lot in the 1930s because at school they were taught how to be good Nazis. They were taught why the Nazis were the ruling race at this time in history.

The Nazis believed that they were destined to rule the earth, and therefore they wanted to conquer as many other territories as possible. Women were also involved with working for Hitler by being good mothers at home. Children were strongly encouraged to join the Hitler Youth movement and learn military drill as well as keeping fit by strenuous exercise.

 Essay plan

Which was the more important reason for the Nazis achieving a high degree of control over the German people, 1933–39?

- **Nazi propaganda and censorship.**
- **The work of the SS and Gestapo.**

Explain your answer with reference to both reasons. (12 marks)

1 Write a list of points you would use for each bullet point.
2 Decide which bullet point you think was more important.
3 Write your essay conclusion.

 Test yourself

1 What were the Nuremberg rallies?
2 List three reasons why there was little opposition to Hitler in the 1930s.
3 List three groups who resisted Hitler during the Second World War and say what happened to them.

 Practice question

INTERPRETATION G *From the memoirs of Henry Metelmann, who grew up in Germany. His father was a Communist sympathiser. Published in 1990.*

Even though my father hated everything connected with the Nazis, I loved being in the Hitler Youth. I liked the comradeship, the marching, the sport and the war games. We were brought up to love our Führer who to me was like a second god. There was no law to join the Hitler Youth. Even so, only one of my classmates managed to stay out of it.

INTERPRETATION H *From an interview with Karma Rauhut about her experiences growing up in Nazi Germany. Published in 1993.*

My friend and I went to every American film going, no matter how bad it was. And there were shops where you could go and buy jazz records in the back room. What you did NOT do was live up to the Nazi ideal of beauty and culture. A woman's life under Hitler was completely dreadful.

1 How does Interpretation H differ from Interpretation G about the attitudes of young people towards Nazi rule in Germany in the 1930s? Explain your answer using Interpretations G and H. (4 marks)
2 Why might the authors of Interpretations G and H have different views about life for young people in Nazi Germany in the 1930s? Explain your answer using the interpretations and your contextual knowledge. (4 marks)
3 Which interpretation do you find more convincing about the attitudes of young people towards Nazi rule in the 1930s? Explain your answer using the interpretations and your contextual knowledge. (8 marks)

Model answers

Here are model answers for each of the question types on the Germany Period Study. The annotations highlight what makes it a good answer.

These questions are based on Interpretations E and F on page 41.

Question 1: How do interpretations differ?

How does Interpretation E differ from Interpretation F about the Reichstag Fire?   **(4 marks)**

The two interpretations have different beliefs about how the fire started. Interpretation A says that the fire was started by van der Lubbe on his own without any help. He was caught red-handed at the scene. Interpretation B says that the fire was planned and started by the Nazis who wanted an opportunity to act against the rival Communist Party.

> Opening sentence clearly addresses the question

> Shows clear understanding of the interpretations and how they are different

> Includes relevant detail from the interpretation. Note that this is only 4 marks so you have about 5 minutes to answer this question, including reading the interpretations. You won't have time to write much!

Question 2: Why do interpretations differ?

Why might the authors of Interpretations E and F have a different interpretation about the Reichstag Fire?   **(4 marks)**

The authors have different motives. Rudolf Diels is trying to protect his reputation from when he was in charge of the Berlin police force at the time. He is writing after the Nazis have been defeated and he is keen to justify his actions at the time. The British historian has no sympathy whatsoever with Hitler's actions – as seen in the title of the book. It was written soon after the war when anti-German feelings were running high in Britain and elsewhere. Bullock is aware of how strange a character van der Lubbe was, and argues that he was incapable of carrying out the fire on his own.

> Clear summary of the purpose of the interpretation using information about the provenance

> Develops the explanation of how this purpose might affect the author's interpretation

> Clearly addresses the question in the first sentence. You could focus on other reasons (for example, nature or origin of the interpretation) but you only have a short time so it is best to focus on one reason only and explain it fully

Question 3: How convincing are these interpretations?

Which interpretation do you find more convincing about the
Reichstag Fire?   (8 marks)

Interpretation E is less convincing. I know that van der Lubbe was a strange
character, and was easily influenced. He was not even a strong Communist
Party member, and could be made to confess with little difficulty. The fire started
simultaneously in quite a few places, and so one person, however expert, would
have had difficulty in achieving such a raging fire so quickly. Although the author
of F is obviously biased, he has knowledge to support his argument. Goering and
Hitler were very quick to condemn the fire as a Communist outrage – too quick to
have had time for any investigations. The Nazi headquarters was next door to the
Reichstag and there was a passage which led from one to the other. It would have
been easy for Nazis to have started the fire and then escaped from the scene.
Most historians now assume that van der Lubbe was the unfortunate victim in
Hitler's desire to outwit the Communists.

> Starts by directly addressing
> the question and giving an
> overall judgement

> Specific own knowledge
> is used to evaluate the
> information in both
> interpretations

Question 4: Describe two ways

Describe two ways in which Germany suffered economically after
the Wall Street Crash.   (4 marks)

Germany suffered economically from the USA withdrawing its loans. These had
been needed for helping the growth of German industry and trade. Many industries
could not survive; many Germans became unemployed; and this affected living
standards. Six million were unemployed by early 1933.

> Directly addresses the
> question and gives one
> relevant detail

> Adds a little explanation
> or extra detail to show the
> relevance of the point given

Question 5: In what ways ... ?

In what ways did the style of German government under Wilhelm II
affect how the country developed?   (8 marks)

Wilhelm II was powerful and made sure that the Reichstag leaders were kept under
control. This meant that he could decide policies – such as the expansion of the
navy, which the Reichstag agreed to by passing the Navy Laws.

The Reichstag had representatives from many political parties, but increasingly
there were more socialist members – about 30 per cent by 1914. This meant that,
with coalition governments, the left wing had influence to get policies implemented
that they favoured. For example, Germany gained old-age pensions and sickness
and unemployment insurance before the end of the nineteenth century.

Lastly, the ruling conservative elite retained much power, and this meant that
traditional attitudes towards society remained strong.

> Each paragraph opens
> with one clear point which
> addresses the question

> Specific own knowledge is
> used to develop this point and
> clearly linked to it

Question 6: Which reason?

Which of the following was the more important reason why Hitler was appointed Chancellor of Germany in 1933?

- The effects of the Wall Street Crash.
- The role of Nazi propaganda.

Explain your answer with reference to both reasons.   (12 marks)

One important reason why Hitler was able to gain the position of Chancellor in January 1933 was the effects of the Wall Street Crash. Germany had been very dependent on loans from the USA, and Germany still owed reparations to the Allies. Even though the amounts had been reduced in the Dawes and Young Plans of 1924 and 1929, the payments still represented a huge burden to the German economy that had only been buoyant because of American money.

> Each section clearly addresses one of the reasons given in the question. It opens with a sentence showing which reason is being considered

Many businesses went bankrupt, leading to high unemployment, which reached 6 million in early 1933. The optimism of the 1920s quickly disappeared as many families suffered a drastic decline in their living standards and many relied on soup kitchens to provide basic food. Many Germans had come to accept their new system of government in the Weimar Republic but the Crash reopened criticisms about its structure and its underlying weaknesses again became paramount. Thus, the Wall Street Crash provided opportunities for Hitler and the Nazis to gain support at the expense of traditional political parties.

> The answer uses specific own knowledge to show the role of this reason

> The answer then links back to the question and explains the importance of this reason

On the other hand, the role of Nazi propaganda was important. The Nazis seized on the weaknesses of the Weimar government and promised a return to strong rule – as before the First World War under the Kaiser. The Nazis promised to restore Germany's position in the world and overturn the hated Treaty of Versailles. Lost territory would be regained and the restrictions on Germany's armed forces would be ended. Germans would be able to hold their heads high again among European nations. Nazi propaganda also promised jobs and employment.

Nazi propaganda was effective and therefore important because of its methods. It was often visual and colourful – with posters and banners. Parades along city streets by smartly dressed Nazi Stormtroopers conveyed to onlookers the spirit of determination to address Germany's problems that the leaders of the Weimar government appeared to lack. Nazi propaganda seized the opportunities that a weak government allowed.

However, I believe that the Wall Street Crash was more important as it created the circumstances that allowed the Nazis to build up support with their propaganda and promises. Before the Crash, in 1928, the Nazis only had twelve members in the Reichstag. The Nazis were the eighth largest party. This emphasises the importance of the sudden change in economic circumstances prompted by the Wall Street Crash.

> The answer gives a judgement about which reason was more important. This judgement is supported. You can show how one reason had more of an impact than the other, or look at how the reasons might be linked

Glossary: Germany, 1890–1945: Democracy and dictatorship

Abdicate Give up a throne

Allies The countries that fought Germany and the other Central Powers during the First World War

Armistice A ceasefire – an agreement to end fighting

Article 48 The part of the Weimar constitution that allowed the President to take emergency powers without consulting the Reichstag

Aryan In the Nazi sense, a master race of white northern Europeans

Autobahn German word for motorway

Chancellor Leader of the German government

Concentration camp A camp used by Nazis to hold political opponents in Germany

Concordat An agreement between the papacy and a state

Conscription A means of raising an army; eligible people are forced to join the armed forces of a country

Constitution Rules that regulate how a country is governed

Death camp A place for the mass murder of Jews and others by the Nazis

Depression Long period of financial problems, leading to lower living standards. The Great Depression of the 1930s affected many countries around the world

Einsatzgruppen A death squad consisting of SS, police and local people

Enabling Act Allowed Hitler power to pass laws for four years without consulting the Reichstag

Freikorps Ex-soldiers in Germany after the First World War who supported right-wing political parties

Führer The German word for leader; in this sense the absolute dictator of Germany

German Labour Front The Nazi-controlled trade union

Gestapo Secret police in Nazi Germany who had a network of informers

Ghetto Part of a city, especially a slum area, occupied by a minority or persecuted group, usually in crowded and insanitary conditions

Hitler Youth An organisation for boys where they were taught militaristic skills

Hyperinflation Where prices increase very rapidly and out of control

July Bomb Plot A failed attempt by German army officers to assassinate Hitler

Kaiser Title of ruler of Germany from 1871 to 1918. Equivalent of Emperor

Kristallnacht The Night of Broken Glass; the shattered glass fragments looked like crystals

League of German Maidens An organisation for girls where they were taught home-making skills

Left wing Socialist or progressive attitudes favouring state control of industry

National Labour Service Unemployed workers were forced to work for the Nazi state

Night of the Long Knives The night (actually a weekend) in June 1934 when Hitler used the SS to kill leaders of the SA and others who had recently angered him

November Criminals An abusive term for those German politicians who had signed the armistice to end the First World War

Nuremberg Rally The annual mass meeting of the Nazi Party, which was held in Nuremberg

Parliamentary government Elected representatives having responsibility for policies and law-making

President Elected head of state. In Germany, the President was elected for seven years

Propaganda Intensive use of mass media to spread political ideas

Proportional representation (PR) An electoral system where political parties get seats in proportion to how many votes they get

Putsch A revolt designed to overthrow an existing government and seize power

Reich Church A Nazi-controlled Protestant Church

Reichstag German Parliament

Reparations Compensation to be paid by Germany to France, Belgium, Britain and other states as a result of the First World War

Republic A country with no hereditary ruler; the head of state is elected

Right wing Conservative or traditional attitudes favouring authoritarian government

Ruhr An industrial region in western Germany

SA Brownshirts or stormtroopers; the private army of the Nazi Party

Social Democratic Party A left-wing political party; the popular party in Germany in the 1920s

Socialist Left-wing political party or views, defending the rights and welfare of ordinary people, particularly working-class people, and wanting controls on business

Spartacists Communists in Germany in 1919 who wanted a revolution in Germany similar to the 1917 revolution in Russia

SS Organisation within the Nazi Party which began as Hitler's bodyguard but expanded to become a state within a state

Chapter 3 America, 1920–1973: Opportunity and inequality

3.1 The economic boom

REVISED

Republican policies helped to make America wealthier during the 1920s

- During the First World War, America had exported weapons and food to Europe which made American companies very rich by 1918.

- After the war, there was a depression as businesses contracted and turned to peacetime production. However, by 1923 the economy was booming again boosted by the policies of Republican Presidents:

Laissez faire	Tariffs	Low taxes
The Republicans believed in a *laissez-faire* approach to the economy. This meant they left businesses alone as much as possible to make as much profit as possible	The Republicans introduced **tariffs** (a type of tax) on imports. This meant that goods built and made in the USA were cheaper. This encouraged people to buy American, boosting American industries hugely	Wages increased but taxes stayed low so workers had more money to spend on American products, which increased sales and boosted profits even more

- The people who benefited most in the short term were businessmen. Company profits increased. But this improved the wages of workers too.

People's confidence in the economy improved and so they bought more goods

- During the early 1920s the economy grew because of increased sales of **consumer items** such as radios, vacuum cleaners and washing machines.

- This was driven by four main factors:

Mass production	Tariffs	Advertising	Credit
Goods were made on a large scale in purpose-built factories using machines rather than skilled workers. This meant consumer goods could be made much cheaper	Tariffs made overseas versions of these products expensive, so people bought American goods	New advertising techniques encouraged people to spend. Newspapers ran adverts persuading people they needed the latest products	Wages increased but not much. The real secrets of the boom were **hire purchase** (paying in instalments) and **credit** (like a loan). People didn't need to have the money at the time they wanted to purchase a car or a radio

- The increased confidence also encouraged some people to invest in the **stock market** (by buying shares in a company).

- Some people took out loans to buy shares hoping that they would increase in value and bring profit when sold.

Ford's car factory is an excellent case study for the boom

- In 1913, Ford created the first **production line**. Each worker had one or two jobs as each car went past them. This was a form of **mass production**.

- In 1927, one car was produced every ten seconds. Costs fell so a lot more people could afford a car. Ford's most popular car was the **Model T**.

- By the late 1920s, the car industry was the biggest employer in the USA. Thousands worked in the car factories themselves but tens of thousands more worked in associated industries: steel, leather and road building.

Key point

The First World War, improved technology and government policy all helped the US economy boom in the 1920s. Wages and confidence increased. However, this did not benefit all parts of society.

TIP

All the key terms in **purple** are defined in the glossary at the end of each chapter.

Make sure that you can spell the key terms, know what they mean and aim to use them in your written work.

- The Model T shows the sense of entitlement people had throughout the 1920s. Most Americans felt that they deserved wealth and the newest things, like the car, and were prepared to borrow to buy them.

Not everyone shared in the increased wealth

- Farmers struggled in the 1920s as demand for food fell dramatically after the First World War.
- Workers in old industries lost their jobs. New technology and new materials replaced workers in the coal and textiles industries.
- African-Americans, Hispanics and immigrant groups were most likely to be unemployed in the 1920s.
- The *laissez-faire* approach of the Republicans meant they did very little to help the poor, believing that the situation would sort itself out.

 Test yourself

1 Name two Republican policies which fuelled the economic boom.

2 Why didn't farmers benefit from the boom?

 Practice question

Describe how two Republican policies affected the economic boom in the 1920s.

(4 marks)

 Topic summary

In your exam answers you are expected to use precise, relevant and detailed knowledge. The diagram below shows features of the economic boom. For each one, on a separate piece of paper, add supporting detail from these two pages or your own knowledge. One example has been done for you.

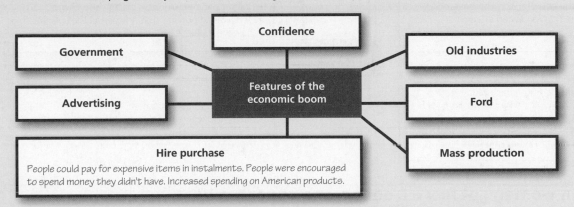

Confidence

Government

Advertising

Features of the economic boom

Old industries

Ford

Mass production

Hire purchase
People could pay for expensive items in instalments. People were encouraged to spend money they didn't have. Increased spending on American products.

 Develop the explanation

Each of the following statements is vague and lacks explanation. On a separate piece of paper, add further details and explanations to show that you understand the general point made. One example has been done for you.

'Some people didn't benefit from the economic boom …'
because their industries were not in demand during the 1920s. Food was no longer required abroad so farmers could not charge as much and were overproducing food. In other industries like textiles and coal, new materials and technology were replacing workers and reducing demand. This meant these groups did not have increased wages or additional income

'Hire purchase was important in the boom because it encouraged people to spend more money …'

'The role of government was crucial in causing the boom as its policies encouraged spending …'

TIP

In your answers use words like 'because', 'therefore', 'this meant that' or 'so' to remind you to explain rather than describe.

3.2 Social and cultural developments in the 1920s

The 1920s were called the 'the Roaring Twenties' because of the massive social and cultural changes

- There were great changes in technology, music, dance and fashion. Many young people in cities rejected traditional values. As the name suggests a wind of change was roaring through society!

- People had more time and money to spend on leisure activities. Average wages rose by 11.1 per cent and average working hours fell by five hours a week.

- These changes were particularly experienced by people in cities. In the rural areas traditional values still ruled.

- Mass production made cars more affordable. Car ownership gave people a greater sense of freedom in both cities and rural areas.

> **Key point**
>
> The 1920s saw big changes in society. Better wages meant people could access entertainment, and many women started to enjoy greater opportunity.

New forms of entertainment became widely available

Radio
- In 1921 there had been one registered radio station
- By the end of 1922, there were 508
- Most homes owned a radio

Jazz
- African-American performers brought jazz to the cities
- It was particularly popular among the young
- Jazz inspired new dances such as the **Charleston**
- Jazz was so popular that this period is also sometimes called the 'Jazz Age'

Entertainment

Cinema
- The film industry boomed. Hollywood produced 800 films a year
- 100 million cinema tickets were sold every week
- Film actors such as Charlie Chaplin and Mary Pickford became stars

Sport
- Professional sport boomed
- Baseball became hugely popular attracting huge crowds

Urban women got more freedom and opportunity

	Before the 1920s	Greater freedom in the 1920s
Dress and behaviour	Women wore restrictive clothing. They did not wear make-up. They had to behave politely They didn't attend sporting fixtures. They were not expected to smoke in public If they were unmarried and wanted to spend time with a man, a **chaperone** came with them (to make sure they behaved appropriately)	**Flappers** were young urban women who cut their hair short and wore daring clothes and smoked in public Hollywood films, newspapers and magazines presented a range of glamorous female role models Women could go out with men unaccompanied. There was greater sexual freedom
Work	There were few paid jobs for middle-class women Unmarried women could work as teachers or secretaries. Married women were expected to stay at home	The First World War challenged these views. Women worked in munitions factories and earned great respect Labour-saving devices, for example vacuum cleaners and washing machines, gave women more free time By 1929, there were 10 million women in paid work (24 per cent more than in 1920)
Rights	Women could not vote	In 1920 women won the right to vote
Society	These traditional views were strong in rural areas and were influenced by the Church	These modern views were particularly common in the cities

Many women still faced **inequalities and limitations**

- Traditional views of women's role continued, especially in rural areas.
- While more women had paid work they were still paid less than men.
- Women had gained the vote, but there were few female politicians.

Test yourself

1 List three new forms of entertainment available in the 1920s.

2 List three limitations on the lives of women in the 1920s.

Structure the detail

Question 5 of your exam focuses on how a key development affected a situation or a group of people. For example:

In what ways were the lives of Americans affected by changes in entertainment in the 1920s? (8 marks)

Here are some facts about entertainment in the 1920s. Turn these into a paragraph answering the question.

A African-Americans started to move towards cities.

B The Charleston became popular.

C There were 508 radio stations at the end of 1922.

D 100 million cinema tickets were sold every week.

E Wages rose by 11 per cent

F More people owned cars.

Spot the interpretation

Look at Interpretation A. Next to it are some inferences that you can draw from it.

1 Link each inference to a specific detail in the interpretation.

2 For each inference, add a specific piece of your own knowledge that supports or challenges this inference.

INTERPRETATION A *From Doris E. Fleischman writing about the 1920s in America as Americans See It (1932). Fleischman was a famous journalist and campaigner for women's rights.*

It is wholly confusing to read the advertisements in the magazines that feature the enticing qualities of vacuum cleaners, refrigerators and hundreds of other devices which should lighten the chores of women in the home.

On the whole the middle classes do their own housework with few of the mechanical aids.

Women on farms – the largest group in the United States – do a great deal of work besides caring for their children, washing the clothes, caring for the home and cooking. Thousands still labour in the fields ... help milk the cows.

[There was little hope for] the vast army of unskilled, semi-skilled and skilled workers. The wages of these men are on the whole so small [that] wives must do double duty – caring for the children and the home and toil on the outside as wage earners.

A Women in the countryside had a harder time than women in the city.

B Richer women did have access to labour-saving devices.

C Working-class women did not benefit from these freedoms.

D Child-rearing and housework were regarded as women's work.

Practice question

In what ways did changes in society affect the role of women in the 1920s? (8 marks)

TIP

Don't think of question 5 as an essay. There is no need for an introduction or a conclusion. The question asks 'In what ways ...' and you should focus on explaining the different ways clearly.

3.3 A divided society

REVISED

Prohibition **banned** the production and sale of alcohol in the USA

- Many groups in the USA feared that alcohol was damaging America.
- The **Temperance Movement** (a Christian group campaigning for prohibition) argued that the health of children was at risk and that alcohol was destroying family life.
- This was all part of a divide in American society between urban values and the traditional country values. Lawlessness in cities was blamed on alcohol.
- The prohibition movement had powerful support. A national ban was introduced by the **Volstead Act** of 1920.
- Prohibition reduced alcohol consumption – but only by 30 per cent.
- In some states, the law was widely ignored, particularly in the cities. The government appointed **enforcement officers**. They had little success.

Prohibition led to an **increase** in organised **crime**

- Despite the ban, it was easy to find **speakeasies** (secret illegal bars) in cities.
- These were supplied by **bootleggers** who smuggled alcohol into the USA (often from Canada).
- Rival gangs ran this illegal but profitable trade. Gang warfare was common. In Chicago, there were 130 murders and no arrests in 1926–27.
- Few people were sent to prison for these crimes because of **corruption**. Police officers and judges were bribed to 'look the other way'.
- The most famous gangster was Al Capone. In 1929 he organised the St Valentine's Day massacre. Members from a rival gang were killed.
- It seemed to many that what they called the 'noble experiment' of prohibition had created more problems than it had solved.
- The St Valentine's Day massacre was a symbol of this and helped to bring about the end of prohibition which was **repealed** in 1933.

Racial tensions **continued to be a problem** in the 1920s

- The USA had a history of racism, particularly in the South where African-Americans had worse education and housing than whites and could not vote in elections.
- African-Americans also faced violence and intimidation from the **Ku Klux Klan** (KKK) who believed that white people were better than black people.
- Between 1919 and 1925, 300 African-Americans were **lynched** (killed by a mob without trial).
- Membership of the KKK surged through the early 1920s. It peaked in 1925 at 4.5 million. However, by the end of the 1920s membership was falling.
- Many African-Americans moved from the South to the more industrial North to find work and greater freedom. However, many still faced poverty and discrimination in the North.

The 1920s also saw increased **political discrimination** against **immigrants** and **suspected Communists**

- After the Russian Revolution in 1917, there was an increased fear of Communism in the USA.

Key point

America in the 1920s was not a unified society. If you were not white or Protestant or a supporter of capitalism you might face prejudice, discrimination and violence.

 ### Spot the mistakes

This paragraph attempts to answer the following question:

In what ways was American society affected by prohibition? (8 marks)

However, there are four factual mistakes in the paragraph. Find them and correct them.

> After the Volstead Act of 1922, one effect on the US was the increase in organised crime. New gangs started to appear as they smuggled alcohol across the border in an act known as 'booze legging'. The gang rivalries soon started to spill into violence, for example in the Christmas Day massacre. There was a lot of money to be made as a gangster but the majority of people only saw the corruption of law officials. This meant there was an increased division between the urban areas that supported prohibition and those who did not.

Quick quizzes at **www.hoddereducation.co.uk/myrevisionnotes**

- When post-war economic problems in the USA led to strikes and riots, this turned into a **Red Scare** (the colour red was associated with Communism).
- Trade unionists who campaigned for better pay and conditions were accused of wanting a Communist uprising.
- Americans were particularly suspicious of immigrants from Europe (where Communist ideas were more popular). Some were accused of being Communists or **anarchists** and of planning bombings. Some were deported.
- In 1927, two Italian immigrants, Sacco and Vanzetti, were tried, found guilty and executed for a burglary and murder. The judge was prejudiced. Many argue that they were executed simply because they were Italian immigrants and because they held anarchist political beliefs.

America **reduced immigration** in the 1920s

- Fear of immigrants and their political impact meant that **quotas** were introduced. The quotas prioritised immigrants from north-west Europe.
- The first restrictions were created in 1921. Quotas were further reduced in 1924. By 1924 the USA was accepting 150,000 per year as opposed to 500,000 before 1914.
- Those who arrived had poor housing and poorly paid jobs.
- Immigrants often lived in the same areas as each other meaning there was little integration.

 Test yourself

1 Which gang-related incident helped to bring prohibition to an end?

2 Which two new political ideas were US governments most afraid of?

TIP

In your exam you have about a minute writing time per mark! So don't waste time on the low-tariff questions. Save time for the 12-mark questions.

 Support or challenge?

In your exams you will often have to reach a judgement and support it with evidence. This task helps you practice. Read this statement:

America was an appealing place for immigrants.

Below is evidence from this period. For each one, decide whether it supports or challenges the overall statement above.

Evidence	Support	Challenge
Immigrants often found themselves in worse living conditions		
The KKK membership increased in the 1920s		
There were more job opportunities in the North		
Immigrant groups often stayed close to each other in new cities		
There was a desire to have more immigrants from the north-west of Europe		
Sacco and Vanzetti were Italian immigrants		
There were immigration quotas put in place in the early 1920s		

Practice question

Which of the following reasons was the more important for the ending of prohibition in 1933?

- The failure of law enforcement against illegal speakeasies.
- The violence of gangsters controlling the illegal trade in alcohol.

Explain your answer with reference to both reasons.   (12 marks)

Part 1: American people and the 'Boom'

3.4 American society in the Depression

The **Wall Street Crash** led to an economic **depression** with **bankruptcies** and high **unemployment**

- In the 1928 election Hoover stressed how prosperous (wealthy) America was, and how fortunate people were to have luxury items.
- Most Americans agreed. Hoover easily won the election.
- Investment in the stock market was at an all-time high. People believed the economy would keep growing, so share prices would keep rising.
- **Speculators** borrowed money from banks to buy shares they could not afford in the hope of a quick profit. This depended on confidence.
- This all changed in autumn 1929 when the stock market crashed.
- It started with worries that the economy was not as strong as people hoped. Share prices started to go down. Investors panicked and tried to sell their shares. Prices plunged. Speculators could not repay money they had borrowed to buy shares. This is called the **Wall Street Crash**.
- The crash had disastrous consequences for the American economy. It was a downward spiral into Depression.

> **Key point**
>
> The Wall Street Crash in 1929 led to the Great Depression. There was high unemployment, low wages and homelessness. For most Americans life became much harder.

Banks recalled loans (from USA and abroad) → Businesses who could not repay went bankrupt → Bankrupt companies laid off workers so unemployment soared → Unemployed people bought less, **so** companies sold less, **so** made less profit, **so** further reduced wages or laid off more workers → Production dropped 40 per cent between 1929 and 1933. Unemployment soared to 14 million. Average wages fell by 60 per cent

- **Hoovervilles** (shanty towns for homeless people) appeared in cities.
- People relied on charities such as soup kitchens.
- In 1931, 238 people were admitted to New York hospitals suffering from severe malnutrition.

Farmers suffered badly from the **Depression** and **Dust Bowl**

- Farmers had struggled in the 1920s. The Depression made it harder still.
- Demand for food went down at home and abroad. American exports fell from $10 billion in 1929 to $3 billion in 1932.
- Demand for meat dropped so much that it cost more to take animals to market than you could sell them for.
- Many farmers went bankrupt. They lost their jobs but also their homes.
- Some southern states had the added problem of the **Dust Bowl**. Over-farming put the soil in a bad condition. Drought and wind caused erosion and dust storms which destroyed farms and made land unusable.
- More than 2.5 million farmers **migrated** to the west coast to look for work, but there was very little there for them.

Hoover's weak response to the Depression led to a rejection of Republican 'do nothing' policies

- As a Republican, Hoover believed people should help themselves not rely on the government.
- He did introduce tax cuts and encouraged businesses to keep wages as high as possible. He also put tariffs (taxes) on overseas goods but this just reduced international trade.

> **TIP**
>
> The examiners want you to use relevant and detailed knowledge in your answers. In your revision, you should try to remember a specific piece of information associated with each general idea.

- However, many saw Hoover as the 'do nothing' President.
- In 1932, some ex-soldiers facing poverty marched to Washington to ask for their war pension to be paid early.
- Hoover refused to meet with these so-called **bonus marchers**.
- The protest continued for many days. Eventually troops were sent for and tear gas was used. This damaged Hoover's reputation still further.

Roosevelt was elected President in 1932 on the promise of improving the American economy

- Roosevelt was a Democrat.
- In his campaign he promised a **New Deal** for the American people.
- He promised active government. He would spend money to create jobs and use experts to advise how to boost the economy.
- He was confident he would win as Hoover was so unpopular. However, he also travelled 20,800 km around the USA giving over 76 speeches.
- He won by a massive majority of 7 million. Democrats also won a majority in the Senate so it was easier for him to pass laws.
- It was the Republicans' worst defeat ever.

 Test yourself

1 What were Hoovervilles?
2 List two things that damaged Hoover's reputation.
3 List two promises made by Roosevelt.

 Practice question

In what ways was American society affected by the Depression?
(8 marks)

 Topic summary

Copy and complete this topic summary pyramid to records key facts about the Wall Street Crash and Depression.

- **One** word that summarises this topic
- **Two** consequences of the Wall Street Crash for businesses
- **Three** consequences of the Depression for farmers
- **Four** words to describe Hoover's response to the Depression
- **Five** examples of how life was difficult in the Depression
- **Six** words to summarise Roosevelt's 1932 election promises

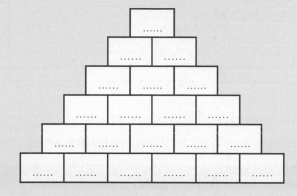

 Spot the interpretation

Look at Interpretation A below. Next to it are some inferences. Match each statement to a phrase or sentence that seems to support this inference.

INTERPRETATION A *From* White House Papers *(1948) by Robert Sherwood, one of Roosevelt's speechwriters.*

Hoover failed lamentably. He first coldly assured the people that the Depression was an illusion which it was their patriotic duty to ignore; then, when economic collapse occurred in Europe, he angrily denounced the Depression as something un-American from which we should isolate and insulate ourselves; and finally scolded the people for blaming the Depression on his own Republican Party which had taken full credit for the preceding boom.

A Hoover would not take responsibility for the Depression.

B Hoover wanted people to focus on the positives.

C Hoover didn't really appreciate the impact of the Depression.

D The Republicans were inconsistent.

E Hoover was not a good communicator.

3.5 The New Deal

Roosevelt's Hundred Days aimed to restore confidence, reduce poverty and create jobs

- As soon as Roosevelt took office he took action. He passed new laws and created the **Alphabet Agencies** to tackle the most urgent problems.

- This three-month period is known as the **hundred days**.

> **Key point**
>
> The measures introduced by Roosevelt under the New Deal started to help America recover from the Depression of the early 1930s. They had many successes but faced some significant opposition.

Restoring confidence
- He closed all banks then gradually reopened the healthy ones
- He broadcast **fireside chats** (friendly radio broadcasts explaining what the government was doing)

Tackling poverty
- Federal Emergency Relief Administration: provided soup kitchens, nursery care and blankets for the poorest
- Home Owners Loan Corporation: rescued around 20 per cent of American mortgages

The Hundred Days

Tackling unemployment
- National Recovery Administration: controlled industry and boosted wages
- Public Works Administration: built schools, dams, bridges and airports, creating millions of jobs
- Civilian Conservation Corps: gave unemployed young men low paid work in conservation (for example, planting trees to stop erosion). Helped around 2.5 million under 25s

Helping farmers and the environment
- Agricultural Adjustment Administration: set quotas for farm production (to steady food prices) and gave machinery to farmers (to help with production)
- Tennessee Valley Authority: built dams and irrigation channels on the Tennessee River which created jobs, prevented erosion and made land more fertile for farmers

The New Deal divided opinion. That is not surprising because it had both achievements and shortcomings

Achievements	Criticisms
Restored confidence	Some (for example Huey Long) said that the New Deal did not go far enough. Businesses still had too much power
Helped trade unions	
Created millions of jobs	
Improved banking system	Others (for example business leaders) felt that Roosevelt was interfering too much.
Fewer businesses failed	Some measures were declared unconstitutional by the Supreme Court
Standards of living rose for many	
African-Americans benefited from some of the Alphabet Agencies	Took power away from local government
Native Americans got money to improve their living conditions	USA recovered more slowly than some countries in Europe. Unemployment problem only ended when the USA entered the Second World War
Roosevelt was very popular. Got re-elected three times	
	Failed to challenge discrimination against African-Americans, women and Native Americans

The 1930s saw **changes** in **popular culture** for most Americans

- The most popular forms of entertainment were radio and film.
- 28 million homes owned radios. Big companies increasingly used advertising on the radio.
- The development of talkies (films with sound) in the late 1920s made the 1930s boom years for Hollywood.
- Studio profits soared. The 1930s is called the Golden Age of Hollywood.
- Musicals, gangster and horror films were particularly popular.
- Films took people's minds off the Depression and helped to restore confidence in America.

 Practice question

Describe two ways that the New Deal helped the American economy.
(4 marks)

 Compare interpretations

1 Look at the interpretation below. Next to it are some inferences that could be drawn from it. Match each statement to a phrase or sentence that seems to support this inference.

INTERPRETATION C *Frances Perkins was Secretary for Labor in Franklin D. Roosevelt's first cabinet. She wrote about this period in her book,* The Roosevelt I Knew *(1946).*

In one of my conversations with the President in March 1933, he brought up the idea that became the Civilian Conservation Corps. Roosevelt loved trees and hated to see them cut and not replaced. It was natural for him to wish to put large numbers of the unemployed to repairing such devastation. His enthusiasm for this project, which was really all his own, led him to some exaggeration of what could be accomplished. He saw it big. He thought any man or boy would rejoice to leave the city and work in the woods.

A The CCC was important to Roosevelt.

B Roosevelt passionately believed in the New Deal.

C Roosevelt understood that re-employment was an important part of recovery.

D Roosevelt had bigger plans than could be accomplished.

E Roosevelt assumed that people would support the New Deal measures.

2 Now read Interpretation D and write some similar inferences around it.

INTERPRETATION D *From* The Roosevelt Myth *(1944) by John T. Flynn, a journalist who helped found the 'America First' movement. He supported Roosevelt's election but became an opponent particularly when Roosevelt took the USA into the Second World War.*

Roosevelt did not restore our economic system. He did not construct a new one. He substituted an old one which lives upon permanent crises and an armament economy. And he did this not by a process of orderly architecture and building, but by a succession of blunders, moving one step at a time, in flight from one problem to another, until we are now arrived at that kind of state supported economic system that will continue to devour a little at a time the private system until it disappears altogether.

3 Write an answer to this exam style question. Focus on the provenance (authorship).

Why might the authors of Interpretations C and D have a different interpretation about the New Deal?
Explain your answer using Interpretations C and D and your contextual knowledge. (4 marks)

TIP

When examining an interpretation always read the caption carefully. It will include important information about who wrote it and when.

Part 2: Bust – Americans' experiences of the Depression and New Deal

3.6 The impact of the Second World War

The war **boosted** American **industry**

- In 1942, Roosevelt established the War Production Board to organise production and recruitment of workers to meet the increased demand for war goods.
- Business leaders who had criticised the New Deal now helped their President.
- Main contracts went to 100 big companies but the benefits multiplied. 500,000 new businesses were established during the war.
- **Lend Lease** was set up to send weapons to America's allies immediately, receiving payment later. This stimulated production. $10 billion of goods were sent to Europe.
- By 1944, the USA was making half of all of the world's weapons.
- Civilians were encouraged to invest in **War Bonds**. They gave the government money and were promised a return in later years.
- Farmers also got huge boost as food exports increased.

> **Key point**
>
> The war had a positive impact on the American economy. It solved some problems that the New Deal hadn't solved. For minority groups there was some limited change.

The war **ended** the problem of **unemployment**

- 14 million Americans worked in factories producing war goods.
- General Motors (which had been the biggest vehicle maker in the USA before the war) took on 750,000 new workers making shells, bombers, tanks, machine guns and engines.
- Many unemployed people moved to cities and states where workers were needed.
- Others were drafted into the army.
- With unemployment ended and with workers in demand, wages increased. Workers now had more money to spend.

There was **some change** for **African-Americans** as a result of the war

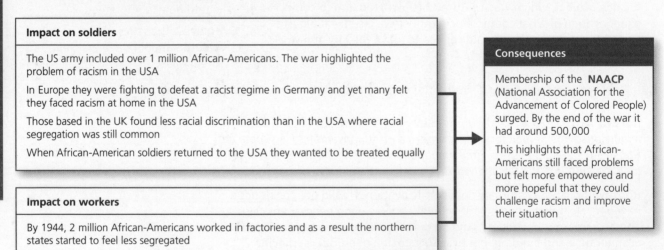

Impact on soldiers
The US army included over 1 million African-Americans. The war highlighted the problem of racism in the USA
In Europe they were fighting to defeat a racist regime in Germany and yet many felt they faced racism at home in the USA
Those based in the UK found less racial discrimination than in the USA where racial segregation was still common
When African-American soldiers returned to the USA they wanted to be treated equally

Impact on workers
By 1944, 2 million African-Americans worked in factories and as a result the northern states started to feel less segregated

Consequences

Membership of the **NAACP** (National Association for the Advancement of Colored People) surged. By the end of the war it had around 500,000

This highlights that African-Americans still faced problems but felt more empowered and more hopeful that they could challenge racism and improve their situation

Women also saw some change due to the Second World War

- The percentage of women in paid employment increased from 35 per cent in 1941 to 50 per cent in 1944.
- Women often replaced male workers who had gone to fight.
- For many of these women it was the first time that they had been in the workplace.

- Women worked in many industries and often did jobs that were fiddly and required small hands such as electronics. One-third of workers in plane construction were women.
- Women's wages increased as they proved how important they were in the war effort. Sixty per cent of managers said that their best workers were women.
- Despite these changes there were still stereotypical views of the role of women. They were expected to return to looking after the household once the war was over.

1 List two impacts of the Second World War on American industry.

2 What was the purpose of the War Production Board?

TIP

Candidates find it hard to give time to planning in an actual exam which is why it is so important to practise it before the exam so that it becomes instinctive.

Practice question

In what ways were the lives of African-Americans affected by the Second World War?
(8 marks)

Improve the paragraph

The paragraph below has been written to answer the following question:

Describe two ways in which the Second World War improved the American economy. (4 marks)

However, the paragraph is not very good, and needs improving. Identify what the areas of weakness are and suggest some improvements this candidate could make.

> The first way the economy improved was that it got better. Lots of new businesses were set up. Wages increased. America made about 75 per cent of all the world's weapons. This meant that America became very rich. There was more money for people to spend on other American businesses.

Essay plan

The highest mark question in your period study exam will be an essay question structured like this.

Which of the following was the more important reason why the USA recovered from the Depression:

- **The work of the New Deal?**
- **The opportunities created by the Second World War?**

Explain your answer with reference to both reasons. (12 marks)

The secret of writing a good essay is good planning. Here is a plan:

Plan	Purpose/points to include
Introduction	Set the context. Was it the New Deal or the Second World War that was more important?
Paragraph 1	Explain how New Deal measures tried to solve the problem of Depression. Describe some successes and some limitations
Paragraph 2	Explain how the Second World War boosted American industry where the New Deal had failed
Conclusion	Link the two reasons (if you can). More important: reach a judgement on which is more important and support that judgement

Step 1: Note down evidence or points you will include in paragraphs 1 and 2.

Step 2: Decide which reason to argue for. There is not a right or wrong answer. You simply need to give good historical reasons to justify your choice. Practise writing your conclusion.

3.7 Post-war society

In post-war America **consumer spending** increased as people pursued the **American Dream**

- After the lean years of the Depression and the challenge of wartime, the 1950s were a time of great prosperity.

- Unlike the 1920s, more people shared the wealth. An average American earned three times the average wage or salary in the UK.

- There was a consumer boom. The USA produced half of the world's goods. They consumed a lot of them too!

- Part of the **American Dream** was to own your own home filled with the latest goods such as a well-stocked fridge.

- Many middle-class people moved out of cities into newly created suburbs where there was more space and a better quality of life.

- Goods could be bought on hire purchase or with the first credit card.

Key point

After the war, most Americans found their quality of life improved. However, the Cold War made Americans fearful of Communism or anything that challenged this way of life.

Television ownership **increased** dramatically and affected people's **attitudes** and spending

- In 1948 less than one per cent of people in the USA owned a TV. By 1958, 83 per cent of households did.

- The most popular shows were children's shows, soap operas and sport.

- Families watched programmes together.

- Programmes were interrupted with regular adverts promoting the latest consumer goods. Soap operas showed houses overflowing with the most up-to-date gadgets and furnishings.

- TV also exposed people to a wider range of role models, news and ideas.

A distinct **youth culture** emerged in the 1950s particularly based around **rock and roll** music

- In the 1950s the **teenager** emerged as a distinct social group. Teenagers were old enough to be independent, had money to spend but had no work or family responsibilities.

- Teenagers identified themselves from their parents through different clothes and different leisure activities and different music.

- Rock and Roll music became popular particularly with young people. The most famous singer, Elvis Presley, had over 170 hit records.

- Some teenagers were seen as rebels and were disapproved of.

- James Dean summed up this image in his film *Rebel Without a Cause* which was about misunderstanding between older and younger generations.

Fear of Communism increased which led to another **Red Scare** and **McCarthyism**

- The Second World War was followed by the **Cold War** (a period of tension between the capitalist USA and the Communist USSR).

- It also caused a nuclear arms race between the USA and USSR which made ordinary people anxious and made the government worried about spies stealing their nuclear secrets.

- Against this background there was another Red Scare as in the 1920s. There were two main strands as summarised in the table on page 65.

Test yourself

1 List three reasons why TV was important in the USA in the 1950s and 1960s.

2 Why were teenagers seen as rebels?

3 What was the HUAC?

House Un-American Activities Committee (HUAC)	McCarthyism
People had to show complete patriotism. Anyone who criticised America was seen as a potential Communist	**McCarthyism** was named after Senator Joseph McCarthy. It means extreme anti-Communism
HUAC had been set up before in 1938 to investigate suspected Communists	McCarthy was a Senator so never a member of HUAC
After the war, HUAC gained fame by investigating film stars	He gained notoriety when he claimed to have a list of Communists working in government
Some stars were **blacklisted** (barred) from working in Hollywood (which was very anti-Communist) because of the committee's investigation	The Senate set up its own committee to investigate (separate from HUAC). Its hearings were shown live on TV
	McCarthy fell out of favour when he started accusing people in the army. He was accused of being a bully
	This damaged the reputation of the USA

 Practice question

Which of the following was more important in explaining why Senator McCarthy was so successful in encouraging the fear of Communism?

- The international situation around 1950.
- The situation in America around 1950.

Explain your answer with reference to both reasons. (12 marks)

 Topic summary

Copy and complete this topic summary pyramid to record key facts about post-war America.

- **One** word to summarise post-war America
- **Two** words to explain the American economy
- **Three** features of teenage culture
- **Four** key words to summarise the new entertainments
- **Five** key points on McCarthyism and the Red Scare

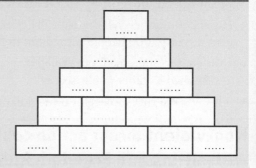

 Develop the detail

In what ways were American attitudes affected by television in the 1950s and 1960s? Explain your answer. (8 marks)

Each of the following statements is true but is vague and lacks detail. Add details to show that you understand the general point made and can link it back to the question above. One example has been done for you.

Statement	Development
More people watched television	83.2 per cent of houses had a television by 1958 which made it the most important shared experience for Americans in the 1950s
TV encouraged people to buy more	
People watched a lot of soap operas	
Anti-Communist hearings were shown on TV	

TIP

For a top-level answer an examiner is looking for an organised answer that:
- includes relevant, accurate, and detailed knowledge
- shows understanding of that knowledge
- uses the knowledge to answer the question.

Include at least two ways in your answer, a paragraph on each. Make sure they cover different angles, for example positive or negative effects.

3.8 Civil Rights campaigns

Legal challenges were the first step to ending segregation in the USA

- In 1954, the NAACP helped mount a legal challenge to school segregation. It brought the case of Linda Brown, an African–American girl who had to walk past white schools to get to her own.
- This case is known as Brown vs Board of Education.
- Linda Brown won her case. The judge declared that school segregation was **unconstitutional** and therefore the laws had to change.
- Some states refused to comply. In 1957, Arkansas said it could not integrate as it was not able to keep students safe.
- In Little Rock, President Eisenhower sent troops to enforce integration.

Martin Luther King got involved in the Civil Rights movement with the Montgomery Bus Boycott

- In 1955, Rosa Parks started a protest against segregation on buses in Montgomery, Alabama. She refused to give up her seat to a white passenger although the law said she should. She was arrested.
- The **MIA** (Montgomery Improvement Association) was formed to help organise a bus **boycott**. Its first leader was Martin Luther King.
- Passenger numbers fell dramatically. The bus company's profits fell by 65 per cent. Over 10,000 people turned out to hear Martin Luther King speak.
- In 1956, the Supreme Court ruled that segregation on buses was illegal. This also applied to other public spaces.
- This was the first success for **non–violent direct action**.

Non-violent direct action continued into the 1960s with sit-ins and Freedom Rides

- **Sit-ins** began with a segregated café in Greensboro, North Carolina in 1960. Black students used 'white' seats. The companies changed their policy and 126 cities desegregated by the end of 1960.
- **Freedom Rides** began in May 1961. Mixed groups of black and white students travelled by interstate bus into areas such as Birmingham, Alabama that were ignoring the order to desegregate.
- Freedom Riders were attacked by white mobs and arrested by police. President Kennedy had to step in to stop the violence and arrests.

Some Civil Rights activists advocated violent tactics

- Some **black nationalist** groups rejected non–violent direct action.
- The **Nation of Islam** was led by Malcolm X. He wanted African–Americans to form their own state. Malcolm X was assassinated in 1965.
- The **Black Panther** movement thought that black people should arm themselves and force white people to give them equality.
- 1965–67 saw race riots, for example in the Watts area of Los Angeles. The cause was poor relations between the police and African–Americans.
- These radical Black Power groups gained national press attention. However, their actions alarmed many and they were blamed for causing the race riots. Some argue violence slowed the pace of change.

Key point

There was racial discrimination, tension and violence in 1950s America. The Civil Rights movement successfully challenged this, through non-violent direct action and more radical methods. As the campaign gathered pace, various groups worked together: Martin Luther King set up the **SCLC** (Southern Christian Leadership Conference), black and white students formed the **SNCC** (Student Non-violent Coordinating Committee) and James Farmer established CORE (Congress of Racial Equality).

Under the leadership of Martin Luther King the campaign achieved the passing of the Civil Rights Acts

- **August 1963**: 200,000 African-Americans and 50,000 white Americans marched to Washington where King gave his 'I have a dream' speech.
- **1964 Civil Rights Act**: made it illegal to discriminate against people in housing and employment.
- **1965 Voting rights marches**: only 2.4 per cent of African-Americans in Selma, Alabama were registered to vote. This campaign aimed to persuade people to register and to challenge the intimidation tactics used to stop them doing so. The marching faced violence organised by the sheriff.
- **1965 Voting Rights Act**: allowed states to ensure that voting took place properly. It also removed reading tests as a qualification to vote.
- **1968 Civil Rights Act**: stopped discrimination in housing based on race, religion, nation of origin or gender.
- **1968 Martin Luther King was assassinated**. There had been huge improvements by 1968. However, major inequalities still remained.

 Test yourself

1 What was the outcome of Brown vs Board of Education?

2 Name two radical protest groups in Civil Rights campaigns.

3 What was made illegal in the 1964 Civil Rights Act?

Part 3: Post-war America

 ## Develop the explanation

Draw your own flow chart to summarise the main developments in the Civil Rights movement. Complete each box to explain how that development helped the cause of African-Americans. Add arrows to link between events.

In 1954 the NAACP helped by …

In 1955 Rosa Parks …

Martin Luther King continued this type of protest by setting up …

Greenboro saw the start of …

Freedom Rides were …

In August 1963 …

Non-violent direct action helped the Civil Rights movement because …

Some significant laws of the 1960s that show progress are …

 ## Practice question

Which of the following was the more important reason why the Civil Rights movement made progress in the 1960s?

- The policies and activities of Martin Luther King.
- The policies and activities of the Black Power movement.

Explain your answer with reference to both reasons.   (12 marks)

 ## Spot the interpretation

1 Look at Interpretation E. Below it are inferences that could be drawn from it. Match each statement to a phrase or sentence that seems to support this inference.

INTERPRETATION E *US historian Thomas Jackson, writing in 2007.*

Martin Luther King Jr. was no mere dreamer. As the civil rights revolution's most famous strategist and self-proclaimed 'symbol', King stood at the forefront of a mass political movement with many leaders and agendas. African-Americans and their white allies organized, protested, and voted, forcing politicians to make hard choices and progressive commitments.

A King was the most significant member of the Civil Rights movement.

B King helped unite African-Americans and some white Americans.

C King was self-important.

D King placed significant political pressure on politicians.

2 For each inference, choose a piece of evidence that either supports or challenges the interpretation.

 TIP

The highest marks in the mark scheme are reserved for candidates who show 'complex thinking'. What this means varies according to the type of question. Complex thinking for this question would be to show you really understand how different causes worked together.

3.9 The Great Society

President Kennedy introduced important social reforms as part of his 'New Frontier'

- In his first speech as President in January 1961, John F. Kennedy (JFK) appealed to American idealism and invited Americans, particularly young ones, 'to ask not what your country can do for you but what you can do for your country'.

- One part of JFK's so-called 'New Frontier' was tackling poverty in the USA. He got reforms through Congress such as increasing the minimum wage, and improving inner-city housing.

- JFK was assassinated in November 1963. It was left to Vice-President Lyndon Johnson (LBJ) to continue this work.

> **Key point**
>
> Through the 1960s, Presidents Kennedy and Johnson introduced measures to tackle poverty with mixed success. Women campaigned for equal opportunities through the 1960s but faced on-going opposition.

President Johnson continued Kennedy's policies to create a 'Great Society'

- Johnson (LBJ) was more of a reformer than Kennedy. He declared 'war on poverty'. He said he wanted to create a 'Great Society'.

- Under Johnson Congress approved:

1964: the Economic Opportunities Act	1964: the Development Act	1965: Medicare and Medicaid
Improved education and training for disadvantaged young people so they could find work	Provided money to remove slum housing	**Medicare and Medicaid** provided medical insurance for the over 65s and hospital care for the poor

- The Republicans criticised these measures. They believed that poor people should help themselves and the state should not interfere.

- It was quite an achievement to pass this legislation at all. It shows LBJ's political skill that he did. But Johnson's reputation has been defined by another battle – the Vietnam War.

- Johnson is therefore seen as the President responsible for the disastrous war in Vietnam rather than the reforming 'Great Society' President.

- This has also obscured the fact that LBJ was the President who passed the Civil Rights Acts. However, his 'Great Society' reforms were criticised for not doing enough for African-Americans.

Women made progress in the fight for equal rights

- In the 1950s, some American women felt trapped in stereotypical roles.

- In the early 1960s, a strong feminist movement emerged to challenge these limitations. Feminists wanted to help women break free so the movement was sometimes called 'women's liberation'.

- In 1966, the **National Organization of Women** (NOW) was formed. In 1968, its members adopted a bill of rights calling on the government to ban sex discrimination at work; guarantee maternity leave; offer tax breaks for child care; provide equal education and training; and allow access to abortion and contraception.

- The campaign for women's equality ran side by side with the battle for African-American Civil Rights. For women the breakthrough year was 1972 as summarised in the timeline on page 69.

 Test yourself

1 Name two reasons for resistance to feminism.

2 How did Roe vs Wade help women?

Quick quizzes at **www.hoddereducation.co.uk/myrevisionnotes**

1963	1972		1973
Equal Pay Act set the principle of equal pay for men and women but there many exceptions	Equal Rights Amendment Act tried to close some of the loopholes. Women still only earned 70 per cent of what men earned for doing the same job	A Supreme Court decision ensured that contraception was legally available to unmarried women just as it was available to married couples	**Roe vs Wade**: the Supreme Court decision made abortion in the first three months legal. It also ensured that the law was consistent across state lines. Access to abortion gave women more independence and control over their reproductive lives

Opposition to the equal rights campaign came from many different groups and progress was slow

Changing a law did not mean changing people's ideas

The campaign did not have the support of all women

Many middle-class women were comfortable and did not see the need for feminism

Reasons for slow progress towards women's equality

Religious influences affected some people's views, especially on abortion and contraception

A lot of women only cared about the changes that would affect them, like equal pay

Protests against sexist institutions (such as the Miss World contest or men only clubs) were largely ignored or were ridiculed

Spot the interpretation

Look at the source below. Next to it are some inferences you can draw from it. Match these to specific parts of the interpretation.

SOURCE A *President Johnson outlines his Great Society aims, in a speech in 1965.*

I want to be the President who educated young children to the wonders of their world … who helped to feed the hungry and to prepare them to be taxpayers instead of tax-eaters … who helped the poor to find their own way and who protected the right of every citizen to vote in every election … who helped to end hatred among his fellow men and who promoted love among the people of all races and all regions and all parties … who helped to end war among the brothers of the earth.

A Johnson's aims were political.

B Johnson wanted to help all parts of society.

C Johnson may have been concerned about his own reputation.

D Even when the policies are about the USA, there is one eye on other countries.

E Johnson also references the Civil Rights movement that was happening at the same time.

F Johnson may have been looking towards the next election and winning votes.

Support or challenge?

Below is a statement. Use these two pages and your own knowledge to provide evidence that supports the statement, and evidence that challenges the statement. Copy and complete the table by writing the evidence you find into it.

Kennedy and Johnson successfully built a 'Great Society'.

Supports	Challenges

Practice question

Describe two improvements towards female equality in the 1970s. (4 marks)

> **Model answers**
>
> Here are model answers for each of the question types on the USA Period study. The annotations highlight what makes each one a good answer.

These questions are based on Interpretations C and D on page 61.

Question 1: How do interpretations disagree?

How does Interpretation C differ from Interpretation D about President Roosevelt's New Deal?   (4 marks)

Interpretation C explores how Roosevelt was passionate about helping the American economy. It stresses that he 'saw it big' implying he had confidence, and that he had great 'enthusiasm'. This suggests he was central to any improvements.

Uses details from the interpretations to show how they are different

In contrast, Interpretation D focuses more on failures, both of the New Deal and Roosevelt as a leader. It suggests that the New Deal was 'a series of blunders' by Roosevelt and that it 'did not restore' the economy. It is critical of the New Deal and Roosevelt.

Therefore C suggests success and that Roosevelt was important to this, whereas D implies failure and that this was due to Roosevelt's mistakes.

Includes relevant detail from the interpretation

Question 2: Why might interpretations disagree?

Why might the authors of Interpretations C and D have a different interpretation about President Roosevelt's New Deal?   (4 marks)

Interpretation C was by the Secretary of Labor who worked for Roosevelt's government at a high level. Therefore, she has a knowledge of the events that took place in the White House. She would have seen the passion of the President as she helped him to put the measures of the New Deal in place. The date it was written in is also significant. It is unlikely that an ally of his would release an overly critical books so soon after his death.

Develops the explanation of how this purpose might affect the author's interpretation

In contrast, Interpretation D was written whilst Roosevelt was still President. Flynn might have felt more comfortable in criticising the leadership. In addition, the title of the book suggests that Flynn had a particular motive with his writing. The fact it is called 'The Roosevelt Myth' strongly suggests that he is looking to contrast the admiration so many had for the President.

Clear summary of the purpose of the interpretation using information about the provenance

Question 3: Which is more convincing?

Which interpretation do you find more convincing about President Roosevelt's New Deal? Explain your answer using Interpretations C and D and your contextual knowledge.

(8 marks)

I find Interpretation C to be more convincing as it provides more specific examples to show the impact, successes and failures of Roosevelt's New Deal.

Interpretation C is accurate. It mentions the 'Civilian Conservation Corp' and Roosevelt's 'enthusiasm' for the endeavour. This was indeed a measure introduced early in Roosevelt's presidency and we know it worked for 2.5 million people. Therefore, Perkins is right to show the positive impact Roosevelt had. This view also shows Roosevelt's leadership. By stressing how 'he saw it big' there are connections to the fireside chats where Roosevelt would reassure the American public. Therefore, Interpretation C is convincing as it uses examples and references that match what we know about the period.

Interpretation D is less convincing due to its generalised claims. There is some credibility in the fact that Flynn mentions 'blunders' that took place. Indeed there were criticisms that the New Deal was poorly organised and there were also constitutional concerns raised by the Supreme Court.

However, there is no specific reference to the TVA which did co-ordinate efforts across many states and Flynn ignores the Second New Deal which resolved some of the concerns of the Supreme Court. Instead, he seems to suggest it was only the Second World War that solved the problems of the economy. This is less convincing as it lacks examples and ignores too many of the positive decisions made by Roosevelt before 1942.

> The answer opens by directly addressing the question and dealing with one of the interpretations given

> The answer identifies a detail in the interpretation and explains what it suggests

> The answer links back to the question evaluating how convincing the view is

Question 4: Describe two ways

Describe two ways in which the Civil Rights Acts of the 1960s helped to end racial discrimination.

(4 marks)

The 1964 Civil Rights Act aimed to end social discrimination. It made it illegal for local governments to racially discriminate in either housing or employment meaning everyone had equal opportunities.

In addition, the 1965 Voting Rights Act aimed to end racial discrimination in the access to democracy. It allowed the federal government to ensure that all voting was taking place according to the law and removed literacy tests giving greater access to all.

> Directly addresses the question and giving one relevant detail

> Adds a little explanation to show the relevance of the point given

> Gives a second relevant detail

Question 5: In what ways?

In what ways did changes in society affect the role of women in the 1920s?   (8 marks)

The first change was that women were no longer expected to dress in certain ways. In the 1910s, women had to dress conservatively and could not wear makeup. However, the influence of Jazz and Hollywood allowed women more freedom. 'Flapper girls' had shorter dresses, and changed their hair styles. This was an important social change. However, it did not affect everyone and in the countryside the role of women hardly changed at all.

> Each paragraph opens with one clear point which addresses the question

> Specific own knowledge is used to develop this point

The second change was more economic. It became more acceptable for women to work. There was a 24 per cent increase in the number of working women by the end of the 1920s. This allowed some women to have more freedom and opportunities. Luxury household items gave women more time out of the house to access the new forms of entertainment.

> The answer explains the relevance of this knowledge by linking back to the question at the end of the paragraph

However, society's view did not change completely and for many women life remained the same. Christian views remained strong in the countryside, and, even if women did work, they were paid less than men. Therefore, change was more limited than it might have been in the 1920s.

Question 6: Which reason?

Which of the following reasons was the more important reason for the failure of prohibition?

- **The failure to enforce the law.**
- **The violence of gangsters.**

Explain your answer with reference to both reasons.   (12 marks)

The violence of gangsters was significant in ending prohibition as it changed public opinion. The most famous gangster, Al Capone, shows how violence became an issue. Initially he was admired due to his wealth. However, after the St Valentine's Day massacre in 1929, there was a growing sense that the violence was getting out of hand, and that maybe prohibition needed to end. The violence of gangsters was very important in ending prohibition. It dramatically altered people's opinion on gangsters and meant there was a push to end prohibition. People were fearful that if prohibition continued it may start affecting more people.

> Each paragraph addresses one of the reasons given in the question

> The answer uses specific own knowledge to show the role of this reason

In addition, the violence of gangsters showed how incompetent the law enforcement was. The agencies responsible for enforcing prohibition were understaffed and underfunded so officers had to control too large an area. Officers were often bribed meaning that when there was illegal activity or violence, it was ignored and no arrests were made. This was important as people were fearful of how corruption and violence would get worse making people more openly critical of the law. One reason Roosevelt won his election in 1932 was because of his promise to end prohibition.

> The answer then links back to the question and explains the importance of this reason

In conclusion, the violence of the gangsters was the more important factor in the end of prohibition because it triggered feelings of fear that put pressure on the government to repeal the law. The failures of law enforcement officers to control the violence was important, but only because it allowed the violence to escalate to the point where the government had no choice but to change the law.

> The answer gives a judgement about which reason was more important. This judgement is supported

Quick quizzes at **www.hoddereducation.co.uk/myrevisionnotes**

Glossary: America, 1920–1973: Opportunity and inequality

Alphabet Agencies Organisations established under the New Deal

American Dream The belief that everyone has the right to be successful

Anarchist A political person who doesn't believe in any type of government

Black nationalists African-Americans who were prepared to establish a separate African-American state

Black Panthers A black nationalist group set up in the 1960s

Blacklisted Barred

Bonus marcher Former soldier who demanded his war pension sooner than it was due

Bootlegger A smuggler of alcohol during prohibition

Boycott A form of protest where you refuse to buy something or use a service

Charleston A popular dance from the 1920s with very fast hand and body movements

Cold War A period of tension between the capitalist USA and the Communist USSR

Consumer items Goods that are sold direct to ordinary people for their home, for example TVs (as opposed to goods sold to other businesses)

CORE Congress of Racial Equality. Set up in 1942 by James Farmer. Led the Freedom Rides

Corruption Dishonest conduct by those in power

Credit A kind of loan

Dust Bowl An environmental disaster of the 1930s. Over-farming and drought made land infertile

Enforcement officers Government agents who had to stop the transport and sale of alcohol under prohibition

Fireside chats Roosevelt's radio broadcasts to the nation. His way of reassuring the American public

Flapper A young middle-class woman who drank, smoked and cut her hair short

Freedom Rides Civil Rights campaigners took long bus rides to show that public transport was still segregated in the early 1960s

Hire purchase Paying in instalments

Hooverville A shanty town for the homeless in US cities during the Great Depression

Hundred days The first 100 days of Roosevelt's presidency when the New Deal was put in place

Ku Klux Klan A white supremacist organisation that was popular in the southern states of the USA

Laissez-faire To leave something alone. In business, the government would not interfere to allow profits to increase

Lend Lease Arrangement for USA to supply weapons to Europe during the Second World War but not expect payment until after the war was over

Lynched Killed by a mob without trial

Mass production Making items quickly and on a big scale so making them cheaper

McCarthyism To make accusations of treason (for example communism) without full evidence

Medicare and Medicaid Kennedy's policies to improve health care for poor people in the USA

MIA Montgomery Improvement Association. Founded in 1955 and led by Martin Luther King, it organised the Bus Boycotts in the same year

Migrated Moving for jobs

Model T The first mass produced car. Made by Henry Ford in 1908

NAACP The National Association for the Advancement of Colored People

Nation of Islam A black nationalist group led by Malcolm X

National Organization of Women Campaigned for gender equality

New Deal Roosevelt's policies to improve to relieve poverty, reduce unemployment and bring economic recovery

Non-violent direct action The style of protest preferred by Martin Luther King

Production line A new way of making goods developed by Henry Ford

Quota A limited or fixed number of people or things

Red Scare The fear of Communism in the 1920s

Repeal To remove or reverse a law

Roe vs Wade A court case that ended with abortion being legal in the first three months of pregnancy

SCLC Southern Christian Leadership Conference. Set up in 1957 by Martin Luther King, it took part in many Civil Rights protests

Sit-in A protest of sitting at lunch counters to end segregated seating

SNCC Student Non-Violent Coordination Committee set up in 1960. It led the sit-in protests

Speakeasy Illegal bar during prohibition

Speculator An investor of money for the hope of gain, but also risking loss

Stock market The buying and selling of shares in a company

Tariff A type of tax charged on imports

Teenager A new term used in the late 1950s for the rebellious youth

Temperance Movement A Christian group that campaigned for Prohibition

Unconstitutional Breaking the highest laws of America

Volstead Act (1919) The law that started prohibition in 1920

Voting rights The legal protections that allow people to vote

Wall Street Crash The 1929 slump on the stock market in New York. People lost a lot of money and it led to the Great Depression of the 1930s

War Bonds People bought bonds from the government boosting the government budget for war

How the Wider World Depth Study will be examined

Overview of the Period Study

A study of a short period (20–30 years), focusing on international conflict and tension in that period.

In this book we cover:

- Conflict and tension, 1894–1918
- Conflict and tension, 1918–1939
- Conflict and tension between East and West, 1945–1972
- Conflict and tension in Asia, 1950–1975.

Wider World Depth Studies are about understanding international conflict and tension in depth:

- Each study focuses on the **reasons for international conflict and tension**, why tension was difficult to resolve and how conflicts were ended.
- Each study asks you to understand a **complex international situation** with a range of **linked causes**.
- You will investigate the role of **key people and groups**.
- You will need to understand what created or reduced tension in this period, and how these **causes** link together.
- You will also need to understand how these situations **changed** over time.
- You will also need to **understand and evaluate sources** in the context of the period.

There are a number of key skills you will need for the Wider World Depth Study

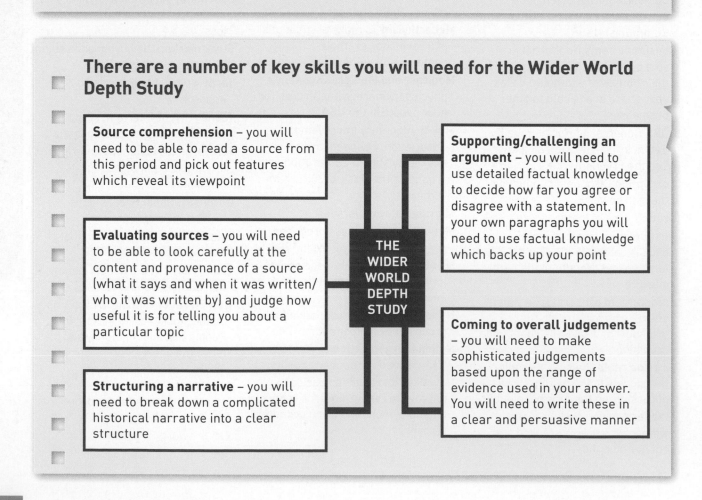

Source comprehension – you will need to be able to read a source from this period and pick out features which reveal its viewpoint

Evaluating sources – you will need to be able to look carefully at the content and provenance of a source (what it says and when it was written/ who it was written by) and judge how useful it is for telling you about a particular topic

Structuring a narrative – you will need to break down a complicated historical narrative into a clear structure

THE WIDER WORLD DEPTH STUDY

Supporting/challenging an argument – you will need to use detailed factual knowledge to decide how far you agree or disagree with a statement. In your own paragraphs you will need to use factual knowledge which backs up your point

Coming to overall judgements – you will need to make sophisticated judgements based upon the range of evidence used in your answer. You will need to write these in a clear and persuasive manner

There are four main question types in the Wider World Depth Study

This is Section B of Paper 1. It is worth 44 marks in total. You will be asked the following types of question.

1 Source analysis *(4 marks)*

You will be given a source and the viewpoint of the source will be explained. You will need to read or look at the source carefully and identify **how** the source represents the viewpoint you have been given.

2 Source usefulness or utility *(12 marks)*

You will be given two further sources and you need to give a supported judgement about how they are useful for a given purpose enquiry. You will need to consider the content, provenance and context of each source.

3 Write an account of ... *(8 marks)*

You will write an analytical, narrative, account of an event or development in the period you have studied. This will need to be structured clearly and contain a wide range of specific factual knowledge.

4 Essay: how far you agree with a statement *(16 marks + 4 SPaG)*

You will need to form and support your own judgement about the issue in a sustained manner.

How we help you develop your exam skills

- The **revision tasks** help you build understanding and skills step by step.

  For example:

  Improve the paragraph or eliminate irrelevance will improve your writing skills practicing the most common question types.

  Support or challenge? will help you use evidence to reach your own judgements which is a key skill for the high mark questions.

  Flow chart activities such as **key events** and **getting from A to B** will help you to write a narrative account of events and see the links between events.

  Develop the explanation or **turn description into explanation** will help you to get better at explaining causes or impacts.

  Considering usefulness will help you to evaluate written and visual sources for utility.

- The **practice questions** give you exam-style questions.
- **Exam focus** at the end of each chapter gives you model answers for each question type.

Plus:

There are **annotated model answers** for every practice question online at www.hoddereducation.co.uk/myrevisionnotes or use this QR code to find them instantly.

4.1 The alliance system

By 1914 **Germany** had become one of the most powerful states in Europe

- Germany had only united from a collection of smaller states in 1870.
- This followed a successful war against France, which also led to Germany taking control of **Alsace-Lorraine** (an important industrial area of France).
- German industry grew rapidly. By 1914 it was outproducing Britain.
- Germany formed an alliance with Austria-Hungary (1872) and Italy (1882).
- By 1892, Germany had become worried about being 'encircled' by France and Russia, who had also become allies.

> **Key point**
>
> Tensions between the major powers of Europe led to the creation of two powerful rival alliances.

Austria-Hungary and Italy joined Germany to form the **Triple Alliance**

- This was a secret agreement that each of the countries in the alliance (also known as the **Central Powers**) would defend each other from attack.
- Austria-Hungary was a huge empire. It contained a number of different nationalities and ethnic groups.
- Some of these groups, such as Czechs and Serbs, had been seeking their independence from the Austro-Hungarian Empire.
- Serbia, which had recently become an independent country on the border with Austria-Hungary, was getting more powerful and posed a threat.
- Serbia was also supported by Russia.
- Italy was not a major military power, but had joined the alliance in the hope of building an empire of its own.

France and Russia formed a secret alliance in 1892

- Russia and France were concerned about the growing power of Germany.
- In response, France had been building up its industry and military.
- France wanted to regain Alsace-Lorraine, which it had lost to Germany.
- Russia was the largest power in Europe and was building a huge army.
- Russia was economically backward and very **agrarian** (its economy was based on farming).
- France lent money to Russia to help build up its industry.
- Russia was keen to defend the Serbs as both were part of an ethnic group called **Slavs**. This caused tension between Russia and Austria-Hungary.

By 1907, Britain, France and Russia formed the **Triple Entente**

- France and Russia had long been the biggest threats to Britain, but this had begun to change.
- Germany was increasingly seen as a threat as the **Kaiser** (the Emperor of Germany) wanted to build up a German navy and empire.
- Russia had been weakened by war with Japan. France and Britain had ended conflict over their colonies in North Africa.
- Britain signed an agreement with France in 1904 and with Russia in 1907.

 Test yourself

1 Why was Germany seen as a threat by France and Russia?
2 Why did Germany feel threatened by the situation in Europe?
3 Why did Britain form alliances with France and Russia?
4 How did the Moroccan and Bosnian crises increase the tension in Europe?

Crises in Morocco and the Balkans had already threatened war in Europe

1905: Morocco	The Kaiser made a speech in Morocco supporting Moroccan independence.	This angered France who planned to take control of Morocco.	A conference to settle this dispute in fact caused more tension. Germany felt ignored and worried by the way France and Britain supported each other.	This crisis was one of the reasons why Britain, France and Russia formed the Triple Entente.

1908: The Balkans	The Balkans was an area influenced by two rival empires (Austria–Hungary and Russia) which was unstable as countries were becoming independent.	In 1908, Austria took control of Bosnia. This angered Serbia and Russia.	Germany supported Austria which forced Russia and Serbia to back down.

1911: Morocco	Germany sent a gunboat to the port of Agadir in response to France moving to take over Morocco.	Again war was avoided, but Britain and France came to a further agreement to use their navies to contain the German navy.

✎ Topic summary

Complete the pyramid below to summarise the key points:

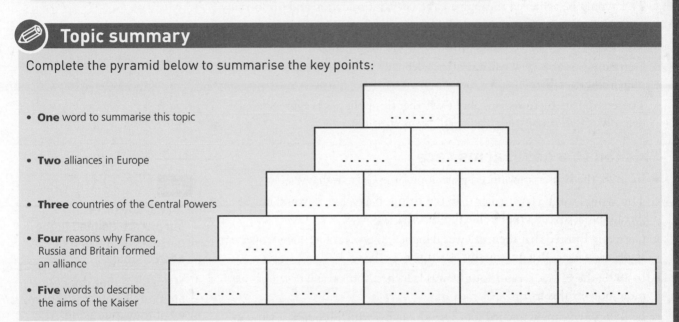

- **One** word to summarise this topic
- **Two** alliances in Europe
- **Three** countries of the Central Powers
- **Four** reasons why France, Russia and Britain formed an alliance
- **Five** words to describe the aims of the Kaiser

✎ Spot the opinion in a source

The first question on your depth study paper will be based on a source. You will be told what its viewpoint is and you have to explain how you know that.

Study Source A. Source A is supporting the formation of the Triple Entente. How do you know? (4 marks)

Annotate the cartoon to show how this message is conveyed.

La triple détente.

Source A *A French cartoon from 1907 showing a figure representing Kaiser Wilhelm being kicked by France, Russia and Great Britain.*

4.2 Anglo-German rivalry

Britain had followed a policy of **splendid isolation**

- Britain had the largest Empire and navy in the world.
- Its approach to **foreign policy** was known as 'splendid isolation'. This meant avoiding getting dragged into alliances in Europe.
- Germany was Britain's main trading partner outside the Empire.
- The monarchy in Britain and Germany was also linked by blood (i.e. they were family relatives).
- However, Britain would oppose any attempt by Germany to gain colonies or develop its navy.

> **Key point**
>
> Tensions between Britain and Germany led to a huge build up of naval power at the same time as the powers in Europe built up their armies.

Germany developed a more **aggressive foreign policy**

- Wilhelm II wanted Germany to have a more important role in world affairs.
- He wanted Germany to build up an Empire and have influence in Europe.
- This would be achieved through a large navy, intimidation and **diplomacy** (negotiation with other countries).
- This policy was known as **Weltpolitik** (world politics).
- Germany was also very **militaristic** (celebrated military strength) and held huge military rallies.
- There is debate by historians about whether this policy was aggressive or defensive (as Germany felt 'encircled' by its enemies).

This led to a **naval arms race**

- In 1898, the Kaiser announced plans for a large German navy.
- This would still be far smaller than the British Navy, but it would not be spread out across an empire like the British Navy was.
- Germany insisted that the navy was designed to protect Germany's overseas trade. However, Britain saw this as a threat.
- In 1906, the **HMS Dreadnought** was launched. This was a new class of more powerful warship.
- In 1908, Germany launched four Dreadnoughts which brought it close to Britain's total.
- By 1914, Germany had 17 Dreadnoughts and Britain had 29.

> **TIP**
>
> All the key terms in **purple** are defined in the glossary at the end of each chapter.
>
> Make sure that you can spell the key terms, know what they mean and aim to use them in your written work.

The European powers were also building up **large armies** and making **plans for war**

- As a result of the alliance system and tensions in Europe, many countries began to think that a war was unavoidable.
- All of the major powers increased the size of their armies.
- By 1910, France, Britain, Russia and Germany all had armies of nearly one million men or more.
- The powers also developed war plans in preparation for conflict.
- The German **Schlieffen Plan** prepared for a fast strike on France before turning their forces on Russia who would be slow to **mobilise** (have their army ready for battle).
- The French **Plan 17** also planned for a quick war, with the army marching rapidly into the centre of Germany.
- Britain also prepared to send a well-trained **British Expeditionary Force** of 150,000 men to France to fight Germany if they attacked.

 Test yourself

1 What was Weltpolitik?
2 Why was there a naval arms race between Britain and Germany?
3 How were the European powers preparing for war?

Develop the explanation

Complete the table to explain why each of the following increased the tension in Europe.

General statement	Supporting detail
The Kaiser encouraged a policy of Weltpolitik.	This meant that Germany would try to build up its navy and empire.
The Kaiser announced that Germany would build a large navy.	
Britain launched the first Dreadnought in 1906.	
Each power developed a war plan.	
The powers built up their armies.	

Improve the paragraph

The highest mark question in the depth study exam will be an essay writing task like this:

'German foreign policy was the main reason for the increasing tension in Europe by 1914.'

How far do you agree with this statement? (16 marks)

This needs well argued, clear paragraphs full of supporting evidence.

Below is a paragraph answering this question. It is missing one key feature. Work out what is missing and rewrite the paragraph to improve it.

> German foreign policy was one of the main reasons for tension. The German ruler wanted Germany to be more powerful and made speeches about this. To become more powerful, Germany would have to build up weapons. This threatened other countries, and so other countries grouped together and built up their armies. This made a war much more likely.

4.3 The outbreak of war

Austrian **Archduke Franz Ferdinand** was **assassinated** by **Serbian nationalists**

- Franz Ferdinand was visiting Sarajevo, the capital of Bosnia, which was under Austrian control.
- The assassination was carried out by a group called the **Black Hand Gang**. They were Serbian nationalists who wanted Bosnia to be free from Austria and join with Serbia.
- The first attempt to throw a bomb at the royal car was unsuccessful. However, this led to a change in the planned route and later in the day the Archduke's driver got lost.
- The car stopped just metres away from one of the assassins, **Gavrilo Princip**, who shot the Archduke and his wife. Both were killed.

> **Key point**
>
> The pre-existing tensions in Europe caused the assassination of Franz Ferdinand to escalate into a full European war.

Existing **tensions in the Balkans** dragged other European powers into the conflict

- Austria-Hungary decided to deal harshly with Serbia following the assassination.
- Serbia had increased in power due to a series of wars in the Balkans. It was now the most powerful country in the region.
- It also had the support of Russia, who had become increasingly aggressive after being forced to back down in 1909.
- Austria was keen to reduce the power of Serbia and strengthen their control in the Balkans. Germany was keen to show that it had a strong influence in Europe.
- Austrian nationalists also saw Serbs as inferior.

The **July crisis** escalated the conflict

- On 23 July, Austria sent an **ultimatum** to Serbia. This was a list of demands that Serbia had to accept or face war.
- The demands were very harsh, however, Serbia was keen to avoid war and accepted nine out of ten demands.
- However, they were unwilling to accept Austria interfering in the Serbian justice system to punish the assassins.
- Serbia offered to allow the matter to be settled at the International Court, but Austria refused.
- On 28 July, Austria declared war against Serbia. On 30 July, Russia mobilised its forces against Austria and Germany, and Germany declared war on Russia on 1 August.
- However, at this stage the conflict was only in Eastern Europe.

Key dates: 1914
28 June: Franz Ferdinand assassinated
28 July: Austria attacks Serbia
30 July: Russia mobilises its army
1 August: Germany declares war on Russia
2 August: Britain prepares its warships
3 August: Germany declares war on France
4 August: Germany invades Belgium; Britain and Belgium declare war on Germany
6 August: Austria declares war on Russia
12 August: Britain and France declare war on Austria

The **Schlieffen Plan** dragged Western Europe into the conflict

- Germany had to act quickly to carry out their plan to defeat France before facing Russia.
- As a result, the German Army began a planned invasion of France, hoping for victory in six weeks.
- The German plan involved attacking France through Belgium. A treaty in 1839 had promised that Belgium **neutrality** (its right to stay out of conflicts) would be respected.

Quick quizzes at **www.hoddereducation.co.uk/myrevisionnotes**

- German troops invaded Belgium on 4 August. Britain sent an ultimatum to Germany ordering them to withdraw.
- This did not happen and so at midnight on the 4 August, Britain declared war on Germany. Austria then declared war on Russia on 6 August.

The war quickly became a **stalemate**

- Strong resistance meant the German Army took longer than expected to move through Belgium.
- Russia also managed to mobilise more quickly than expected which forced the Germans to move 100,000 troops East, and the British Expeditionary Force managed to slow the German advance.
- A combined British and French force managed to hold the Germans at the **Battle of the Marne** and even succeeded in pushing back the German Army.
- By early September, both sides were digging trenches to defend the lands they held.
- Throughout October, both sides tried to **outflank** the enemy (manoeuvre around their lines) in the 'race to the sea', but neither side succeeded.

 Test yourself

1 Why did Austria issue a harsh ultimatum to Serbia?
2 Why did Russia and Germany become involved in the conflict?
3 Why did the war spread to Western Europe?

 Structure the detail

Question three in your depth study exam will ask you to write an account. For example:

Write an account of the events of June–August 1914 to show how these led to the outbreak of a European war. **(8 marks)**

Below are a number of key events in 1914. Put these in order and structure them into three paragraphs to answer the exam question.

A Austria declared war on Serbia.

B Russia mobilised to defend Serbia.

C Archduke Franz Ferdinand was assassinated by Serbian nationalists.

D Germany enacted the Schlieffen Plan and began an invasion of Belgium.

E Austria sent a harsh ultimatum to Serbia.

F Britain declared war on Germany.

G Britain sent Germany an ultimatum.

H Serbia refused one of the ten demands.

TIP

When you write an account, you don't write everything you know about a topic. You have to select carefully and refer everything back to the focus of the question. In this case how the events led to the outbreak of war.

 Develop the explanation

Explain why each of the following led to the war becoming a stalemate by the end of 1914.

Factor	Explanation
Belgian resistance	*This slowed the German advance and gave more time for the British and French to prepare defences.*
The British Expeditionary Force	
Russian mobilisation	
The Battle of the Marne	
Trenches	

4.4 Tactics and technology on the Western Front

Both sides on the Western Front dug **trenches**

- By the end of 1914, a network of trenches ran from the sea to the Alps.

- There were **front line trenches** for fighting troops and reserve and support trenches further back which allowed troops to rest and be resupplied.

- The trenches were an effective defensive tactic. They protected troops from snipers and artillery attacks.

- Trenches reduced the effectiveness of cavalry and so **infantry charges** (attacks led by foot soldiers) became the main form of attack.

- Major infantry charges were known as 'going over the top'. They were usually preceded by an artillery barrage. It was hoped that these would eventually wear down the enemy's defences.

- Infantry tactics improved throughout the war. The use of artillery became better coordinated and troops were protected by camouflage and steel helmets (introduced in 1916).

Key point

Fighting was characterised by trench warfare and infantry charges. However, new tactics and technologies were developed throughout the war.

Trench conditions could be very unpleasant

- Large-scale attacks were not common. Soldiers spent a lot of time digging or repairing trenches or moving equipment.

- They also performed **sentry** duty (watching for enemy attacks).

- **Sappers** tried to mine under enemy trenches.

- There were also regular small attacks called **trench raids**, which would attempt to capture prisoners or gather information.

- Trench conditions could be appalling, especially in the early stages of the war. In the summer the smell in the trenches was awful.

- In winter they would become waterlogged, leading to problems such as **trench foot**.

- Rats and lice were also a serious problem.

However, many soldiers found ways to cope with these conditions

- Most soldiers believed the war was justified and were **patriotic** and proud to fight for their country.

- For some, the war gave a sense of adventure. It was often soldiers' first experience of travel.

- Soldiers were also given a lot of leisure time. Troop rotation meant that soldiers would spend about 10 days per month in the trenches and as little as three days in front line trenches.

- **Comradeship** was also very important to soldiers, many signed up in 'Pals' battalions' with people they knew and many developed close friendships with their fellow soldiers.

- Soldiers' morale was also kept up by letters from home, good food (particularly in the British Army) and by luxuries like chocolate and cigarettes.

- However, troops also knew that there were serious punishments for breaking rules in the army. Soldiers could be **court-martialled** (tried in an army court) and even executed.

TIP

Remember that all sources are useful for something. It all depends on what you are using them for. Never dismiss a source as useless because it is one-sided or incomplete. It will be still be very useful for finding out about the attitudes of the person who made it.

Technology developed significantly during the war

- Although trench warfare continued on the Western Front until 1918, new tactics and technology meant that the fighting changed.
- The biggest development was artillery, which became crucial to any successful infantry charge. By 1918, barrages were carefully timed to protect the infantry and allow them to attack successfully.
- Each country produced thousands of shells per month for use on the Western Front.
- Machine guns offered a huge defensive advantage from the start of the war. By 1918 most platoons had their own machine guns.
- Poison gas was first used in 1915. Although gas masks were quickly developed to protect troops, more effective poison gas continued to be developed throughout the war.
- Planes were used for **reconnaissance** (spying on enemy troops). By 1915, planes were also fitted with machine guns and used for attack.
- Tanks were developed towards the end of the war, but were unreliable.

 Test yourself

1 What was trench warfare?
2 What was life like for soldiers in the trenches?
3 How did technology change throughout the war?

Part 2: The First World War – stalemate

 Evaluate the usefulness of sources

The second question in your exam will be about the usefulness of sources. For example:

Study Sources A and B. How useful are these sources to a historian studying life in the trenches? (12 marks)

Read through the sources and complete the table below to summarise their usefulness.

	Content (what it says)	Provenance (who made it)
Source A	*This is useful because it describes some of the jobs soldiers might have done, it says…*	
Source B		

Source A *Private Stanley Terry of 15 North End, East Grinstead, wrote a letter to his family in November, 1915. The letter was not censored.*

We have just come out of the trenches after being in for six days and up to our waists in water. While we were in the trenches one of the Germans came over to our trench for a cigarette and then back again, and he was not fired at. We and the Germans started walking about in the open between the two trenches, repairing them, and there was no firing at all. I think they are all getting fed up with it.

Source B *Photograph of soldiers unloading shells from a train Third Battle of Ypres.*

4.5 Key battles on the Western Front

In 1916, Germany launched a huge offensive at Verdun

- Neither side was able to break the stalemate in 1915. Britain, France and Germany had all faced heavy losses in attempts to break through enemy lines.
- Falkenhayn, the German commander, developed a strategy of **attrition**. This involved repeated large-scale attacks which would eventually break down enemy resistance.
- The German plan was to launch a huge attack at Verdun, an area surrounded by strong French forts.
- The attack began in February 1916. The French managed to hold on but both sides suffered appalling casualties.
- These casualties were fairly even, so attrition was not working. However, the German Army had more resources and could hold out for longer.
- By July 1916, over 700,000 men had been killed and the French Army was close to collapse.

> **Key point**
>
> Both sides launched major offensives across 1916 and 1917 in an attempt to break the deadlock, suffering extremely high casualties.

In July 1916, Britain launched an offensive at the Somme

- Before the attack at Verdun, Britain and France had been planning a joint offensive along the River Somme.
- The British were forced to launch the attack in July to relieve the pressure on the French Army.
- The British were led by Douglas Haig. He warned the government in advance that the offensive would result in huge casualties.
- In an attempt to minimise losses, the attack was preceded by a huge artillery bombardment lasting a week.
- However, this failed to destroy German barbed wire and deep German dug-outs meant soldiers were generally well-protected.
- When the bombardment ended, German soldiers rushed to set up machine gun positions. The British advanced against these defences, suffering 57,000 casualties on the first day.
- Fighting on the Somme lasted until November and casualties on both sides were around 1.25 million men.
- The British did manage to push back the German Army.

> **TIP**
>
> The examiners want you to use relevant and detailed knowledge in your answers. In your revision you should try to remember a specific piece of information associated with each general idea.

Huge losses continued in 1917 at Passchendaele

- The Battle of Passchendaele (or the Third Battle of Ypres) began in July 1917.
- The British detonated mines under German artillery positions at Messines and caused huge casualties.
- However, heavy rain had made the ground extremely boggy and the British infantry struggled to advance. The British again suffered heavy losses.
- Tanks were used in November in an attempt to break the deadlock, but without infantry support they were not able to hold gained ground.
- British and French losses were over a quarter of a million, and for Germany the losses were even greater.

 Test yourself

1 What was attrition?
2 Why were casualties so high in 1916?
3 What were the key events of the Battles of Verdun, the Somme and Passchendaele?

Topic summary

Complete the mind map below to summarise the key battles of 1916–17.

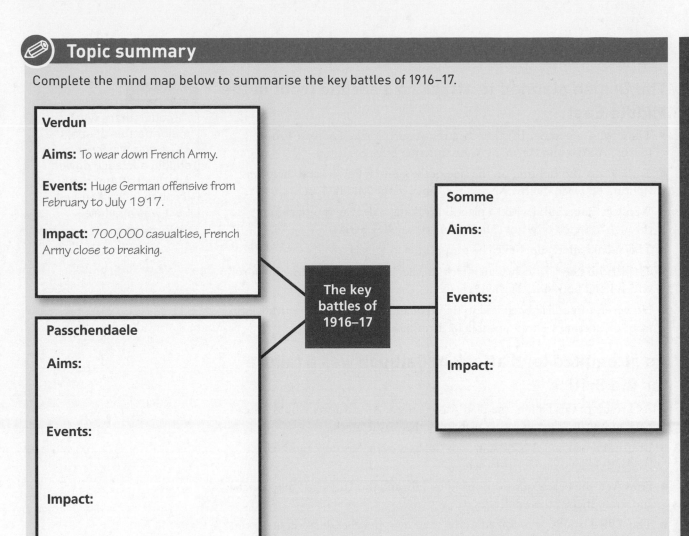

Verdun

Aims: To wear down French Army.

Events: Huge German offensive from February to July 1917.

Impact: 700,000 casualties, French Army close to breaking.

Passchendaele

Aims:

Events:

Impact:

The key battles of 1916–17

Somme

Aims:

Events:

Impact:

Improve the paragraph

Write an account of the key battles of 1916 to show why there were such high casualties on the Western Front. (8 marks)

The paragraph below answers the exam question. However, it is missing one key feature of a good answer. Work out what is missing and rewrite the paragraph to improve it.

The attack on the Somme was another example of war by attrition. The British Army bombarded the German trenches for a week before the advance. They also set off huge mines under German positions. On the morning of 1st July 1916 British soldiers went over the top. There were 57,000 casualties on the first day. The fighting on the Somme continued until November 1916, with over 1.25 million casualties on both sides.

4.6 The war on other fronts

The British planned to attack on a second front in the Middle East

- There were a number of other theatres of war. On the **Eastern Front**, Russia, Austria and Germany were suffering huge casualties.
- Turkey was also fighting on the side of the Central Powers and there was fighting between the British and the Turks in the Middle East.
- Winston Churchill devised a plan to break the stalemate by attacking through a stretch of water called the **Dardanelles Strait**.
- This would allow supplies to be transported to Russia.
- The British Navy launched an attack in March 1915, bombarding the forts which lined both sides of the Dardanelles.
- However, mines had been laid in the strait and this combined with shell fire from the forts made it impossible for British ships to advance.

An attempted land attack at **Gallipoli** was a failure for the British

- As a result of this failure, the plan was changed. A land army would instead have to capture the peninsula before another naval attack.
- British, French and **ANZAC** troops (soldiers from Australia and New Zealand) landed on Helles Beach.
- However, the beach was overlooked by hills and the Turks had dug trenches and strengthened their defences.
- The Allied troops were forced to dig their own trenches, but conditions in the heat were dreadful and disease spread quickly.
- A second attempted attack on another beach also failed and by the winter it was clear that the operation had failed.

There were very few major **naval battles** during the war

- Before the war, both sides had developed huge navies to prepare for a war at sea.
- Naval tactics continued to develop during the war. Radios were improved to allow ships to communicate and torpedoes were developed.
- Submarines were also developed and used particularly effectively by the Germans.
- However, the only major sea battle of the war was at **Jutland** in 1916.
- Germany lost 13 ships in this battle. The British lost 14 ships and in general these were larger, more powerful ships.
- However, it was the last time the German fleet was able to fight and so Britain controlled the sea for the rest of the war.

However, control of the sea was crucial for **supplies**

- The main aim of the British Navy was to prevent supplies reaching Germany by creating a **blockade**.
- This was particularly successful after Jutland. By 1918, many Germans were starving and there was a **mutiny** (rebellion against the leadership) in the German Navy.

> **Key point**
>
> Although there were no major battles at sea, the naval war was crucial for supplies to each power. An Allied attempt to break through in the Middle East was a failure.

 Test yourself

1 Why did the British launch an attack on the Dardanelles?

2 Why was the Gallipoli campaign a failure?

3 What was the importance of the Battle of Jutland?

- The German response was to use **U-boats** (submarines) to sink ships bringing supplies to Britain.
- This strategy eventually helped to bring the USA into the war, as American ships were also attacked by the Germans.
- The British also developed the **convoy system** to protect their ships. Large ships were supported by fast destroyers and other anti-submarine defences.

TIP

In your exam you have about a minute writing time per mark! So don't waste time on the low-tariff questions. Save time for the 12-mark questions.

Topic summary

Complete the summary pyramid below to summarise the main fighting on other fronts.

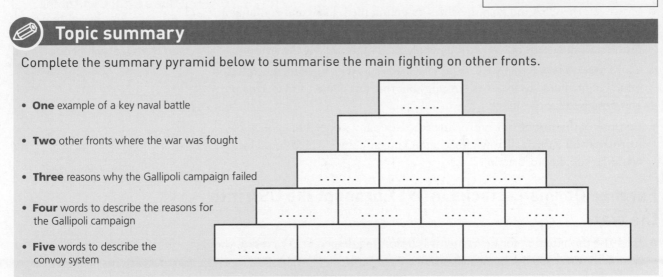

- **One** example of a key naval battle
- **Two** other fronts where the war was fought
- **Three** reasons why the Gallipoli campaign failed
- **Four** words to describe the reasons for the Gallipoli campaign
- **Five** words to describe the convoy system

Spot the opinion in a source

Source A is suggesting that the Gallipoli invasion was a disaster for the Allies. How do you know?   **(4 marks)**

Complete the sentence starters below:

- In the source there is a figure representing the Turkish Army. His size is supposed to represent...
- He is sweeping away soldiers. This is supposed to show that...
- From my own knowledge, the Gallipoli invasion failed because...

Source A *A cartoon commenting on the Gallipoli invasion. The figure with the broom represents the Turkish Army.*

4.7 Changes in 1917

The USA had supported the Allied war effort throughout the war

- The USA was neutral at the start of the war. Most people in America did not support the USA getting involved in the conflict.
- However, the USA did help the allies by giving them loans and equipment.
- In 1915, a German U–boat attack on a passenger ship called the *Lusitania* resulted in the death of over 1,000 people; 128 of these were Americans.
- The *Lusitania* was actually carrying war materials (which led to an explosion which contributed to its quick sinking) but this was denied and Germany was criticised for the attack.
- Because of the risk of war with America, Germany stopped the policy of **unrestricted submarine warfare** (attacking any ships which could be bringing supplies to Britain).

Further German attacks in 1917 brought the USA into the war

- By 1917, the situation for Germany was becoming desperate. As a result, they resumed unrestricted submarine warfare.
- This was very effective in the short term and severely limited supplies to Britain.
- In early 1917, the **Zimmerman telegram** was discovered which showed that Germany planned to form an alliance against the USA with Mexico.
- This, and attacks on American ships, led to the USA joining the war on the Allied side in April 1917.
- The US Navy was the third largest in the world and now supported British ships crossing the Atlantic. More loans were also made to Britain.
- However, it would take a long time to train US troops and produce equipment.
- By the summer of 1918 around one million US troops had landed in Europe, making a huge contribution to the Allied war effort.

Russia left the war after revolutions in 1917

- Russia had been badly affected by the war, and in March 1917 these problems contributed to a revolution.
- The Tsar (the Russian emperor) was overthrown and replaced by a temporary government.
- The government found it hard to organise the war effort and a further offensive in June was a disaster. Germany began to inflict heavy defeats on Russia.
- In November there was second revolution led by the **Bolsheviks** (a Russian Communist party). They immediately ended the war.
- Russia was forced the sign the harsh **Treaty of Brest-Litovsk** which gave Germany control of huge areas of land which could supply important raw materials to their army.
- More importantly, the Germans could now transfer hundreds of thousands of troops to the Western Front.

> ### Key point
> Changes in 1917 led to the USA joining the war on the Allied side. However, the end of the Russian war effort had a more immediate impact on the Western Front.

 Test yourself

1 What was unrestricted submarine warfare?
2 Why did the USA join the war?
3 What was the impact of Russian withdrawal from the war?

Develop the explanation

Complete the table to explain how each of the following affected the war in 1917.

Factor	Explanation
Unrestricted submarine warfare	Led to attacks on American ships which were one reason for US involvement in the war.
The Zimmerman telegram	
USA joining the war	
The abdication of the Tsar	
The Treaty of Brest-Litovsk	

 ## Structure the detail

Write an account of the events of 1917 to show how they changed the situation on the Western Front.

(8 marks)

Below are some key events in the development of the war through 1917. How would you structure these into paragraphs for the question above?

You will need to think about the following:

● Which order these events occurred in.

● How you could divide them into paragraphs. This could be key turning points or periods or themes (for example, 'the war at sea').

● How you could link these to the changing situation on the Western Front.

What other details you might want to include or develop.

A	The US Navy helped to protect British shipping.
B	Food and supplies were running short in Germany.
C	The Tsar was forced to abdicate.
D	Russia was ruled by a temporary government.
E	Russia withdrew from the war.
F	Germany sent hundreds of thousands of extra troops to the Western Front.
G	Germany made a secret deal with Mexico to attack the USA.
H	The USA joined the war.
I	The Bolsheviks took power in Russia.
J	The Treaty of Brest-Litovsk was signed.

TIP

Remember you are not only telling a story. Your account needs to explain the issue in the question. So, to check you are doing that make sure that every paragraph has a clear link back to the issue in the question.

And remember to use words like 'because', 'therefore', 'this meant that' or 'so' to remind you to explain rather than just describe.

4.8 The war in 1918

The German Army gambled on an all-out attack in 1918

- With the surrender of Russia, the Germans had an opportunity to divert troops for a huge final attack on the Western Front.

- However, they knew they had to win a quick victory as 50,000 US troops were arriving in Europe every month. American tanks and artillery were also being shipped to France in huge numbers.

- The blockade had been very successful and the German Army lacked equipment. Worse still, food was running out for both civilians and soldiers.

- The British Royal Flying Corps was also successfully using airplanes against German submarines.

- Military tactics had developed a great deal, with a new focus on attack. This was supported by better tanks and improved artillery.

- The German Army had also developed highly trained **storm troopers** who specialised in making rapid, penetrating attacks against enemy lines.

- The plan was named the **Ludendorff Offensive** (or Spring Offensive) after the German General Ludendorff. It was launched in March 1918.

> **Key point**
>
> In 1918, the German Army launched an all-out attack to end the war. This ran out of steam and an Allied counter-attack forced the Germans into retreat.

 Test yourself

1 Why did the German offensive fail?
2 Why was the Allied counter-attack successful?

Despite initial success, the offensive ultimately failed

- The Germans launched a huge artillery bombardment, which was much more concentrated and shorter than previous attacks.

- Small groups of storm troopers then attacked along the entire line, which prevented the Allies from building up their defences in any one place.

- The German Army broke through Allied lines and made rapid progress, advancing 64 km. German artillery was now in range of Paris.

- However, casualties were huge (around 400,000 German soldiers) and supplies couldn't keep up with the advance.

- Many German soldiers stopped to loot food and discipline was poor.

- By May the advance had stopped.

The Allies launched a huge and successful counter-attack

- By August the Germans had still made no more progress and it was clear their attack was over.

- The Allies were now strengthened by US troops and supplies and their armies were well-fed, well-trained and well-equipped.

- A counter-attack was launched on 8 August which used the latest tactics to break the German lines. It was planned jointly by French commander **Foch** and British commander **Haig**.

- Artillery was used in a **creeping barrage** which slowly moved forward to provide a smokescreen for the infantry advance.

- At the same time, tanks punched holes in German lines and aircraft launched attacks behind the lines.

- This became known as the German Army's 'Black Day'.

- By October, the German Army was in full retreat.

Key events

Complete the flow chart below to summarise the key events on the Western Front in 1918.

| Germany wanted a quick victory as US troops were arriving in Europe. | ▶ | | ▶ | | ▶ | | ▶ | | ▶ | |

 ## Support or challenge?

'New tactics were the main reason why the German Army was defeated in 1918.' How far do you agree with this statement? **(16 marks)**

Look at the statement in the exam question. Decide if each of the points in the table supports or challenges this statement.

Points	Support	Challenge
German troops stopped to loot food.		X
There were major food shortages in Germany.		
Supplies could not keep up with the German advance.		
Allied forces used creeping barrages to protect infantry advances.		
Tanks were used to penetrate German lines.		
50,000 US troops were arriving in Europe every month.		

Essay plan

The secret of writing a good essay is good planning. Here is a plan for answering the question above.

Read through the advice then map out what you say in each of the paragraphs. Then either write a full essay or just practice writing a conclusion.

Paragraph	Purpose/points to include
Introduction	You state your view on how far you agree or disagree. This sets your essay off on a positive track and gives you an argument to hold on to throughout your answer. The question asks 'how far you agree …' so words and phrases such as 'mostly', 'partly', 'totally' will be useful.
Paragraph 1 Reasons to agree.	Explain how the issue mentioned in the statement (new tactics) helped lead to Germany's defeat. This helps ensure you stay focused on the actual statement. Make sure you support everything you say with detailed and precise knowledge.
Paragraph 2 Reasons to disagree.	Explain at least one other factor that led to Germany's defeat (for example the success of the naval blockade). It's better to explain one cause thoroughly than more than one superficially. You only have 20 minutes for this whole essay. Link these reasons if you think they linked.
Conclusion	Restate your judgement as to how far you agree or disagree and give one key argument as to why. This should be easy if you have kept your focus through the essay. SPaG: check your work and correct it if necessary.

TIP

Candidates find it hard to give time to planning in an actual exam which is why it is very important to practise it before the exam so that it becomes instinctive.

4.9 German surrender

The **impact of the blockade** put pressure on Germany to surrender

- As well as the collapse of the German military, there were huge problems on the home front.
- Over half a million German civilians died of starvation or starvation-related diseases in 1917 and 1918.
- Supplies of even basic foodstuffs had run out by early 1918.
- In Berlin there were riots and protests in response to the food shortage.
- At the German naval base of Kiel there was a mutiny.

The **Kaiser abdicated** in November 1918

- As riots spread through German cities and the military situation collapsed, there was increasing pressure for the Kaiser to **abdicate** (step down).
- While the Kaiser was in power, he was involved in the negotiations for German surrender.
- Many politicians felt that they would be in a better position to lead negotiations.
- The largest German political party, the **Social Democrats**, threatened to resign from the government.
- As a result, the Kaiser abdicated and Germany became a **republic** (a country without a monarchy).

Germany agreed to allied demands and signed an armistice

- There were different views about the terms of any **armistice** (peace agreement).
- The US President Woodrow Wilson drew up a list of **Fourteen Points**, which he believed were a fair settlement which would avoid a future war.
- Germany hoped to sign an agreement which was based on the Fourteen Points.
- However, Germany was presented with a list of much harsher demands. Many of these were designed to prevent Germany from resuming fighting:

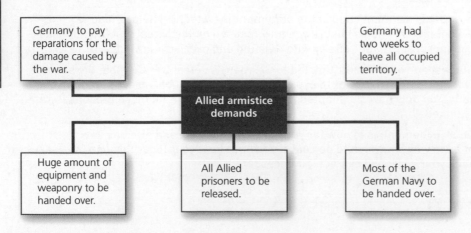

- On 11 November, the armistice was signed. The war was over.
- In January 1919 full peace negotiations started. These eventually produced the **Treaty of Versailles**.

> **Key point**
>
> The German Army and home front collapsed and in November 1918, Germany was forced to sign an armistice.

> **Test yourself**
>
> 1 Why did the Kaiser abdicate?
> 2 What were the Fourteen Points?
> 3 What were the terms of the armistice?

> **TIP**
>
> A possible writing frame for an answer to a 'usefulness of sources' question will be in four paragraphs, two for each source (one on provenance and another on content).
>
> In your exam you won't actually be asked to compare the two sources but you can write about how they are more useful together than separately.

Key events

Complete the flow chart below to summarise the key events leading up the signing of the armistice in November 1918.

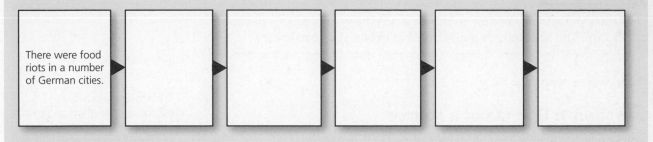

| There were food riots in a number of German cities. | | | | | |

 ## Evaluate the usefulness of sources

Study Sources A and B. How useful are these sources to a historian studying the reaction to the armistice in Britain? **(12 marks)**

Source A *The front page of the* Daily Mirror *12 November 1918.*

Source B *An extract from the diary of Michael McDonagh written on 11 November 1918. McDonagh was an Irish journalist living in London during the First World War.*

I was stunned by the news [but] I felt no joyous exultation. There was relief that the War was over, because it could not now end, as it might have done, in the crowning tragedy of the defeat of the Allies. I sorrowed for the millions of young men who had lost their lives; and perhaps more so for the living than for the dead – for the bereaved mothers and wives whose reawakened grief must in this hour of triumph be unbearably poignant. But what gave me the greatest shock was my feeling in regard to myself. A melancholy took possession of me when I came to realize, as I did quickly and keenly, that a great and unique episode in my life was past and gone, and, as I hoped as well as believed, would never be repeated.

Complete a table like this to summarise the usefulness of the two sources. Then use your table to answer the exam question.

	Content	Provenance
Source A	This is useful because it suggests the mood of the country was…	
Source B		

Study Source A on page 87.

Question 1: Opinion of a source

Source A is suggesting that the Gallipoli invasion was a disaster for the Allies. How do you know? **(4 marks)**

> Source A is suggesting that the Gallipoli invasion was a disaster as the Allies had no chance of defeating the Turkish army and taking control of the Strait. In the source a large figure representing the Turks is sweeping away the Allied forces, suggesting it was easy for them to defend the peninsula. This was the case as the Turkish forces had dug a complex network of trenches at Helles Beach which bogged down Allied forces in stalemate causing heavy losses and eventual withdrawal.

> The answer opens by addressing the question directly. This shows the examiner that you have read and understood the question but it also helps to remind you to focus your answer on the question.

> The answer refers to a detail in the source and explains what this suggests.

> The answer uses a range of contextual knowledge to explain the details in the source.

Study Sources B and C on page 83.

Question 2: Usefulness of sources

Study Sources B and Source C. How useful are these two sources to a historian studying life in the trenches? **(12 marks)**

> Source B is useful for giving a sense of conditions in the trenches. The author describes having been 'six days up to our waists in water' which suggests very poor conditions. Early in the war (this letter was written in 1915) conditions in the trenches could be very poor, and heavy rains could cause heavy waterlogging. This could also lead to conditions such as trench foot. However, later in the war trenches were built with better drainage and hygiene improved considerably. The author also mentions that he is coming out of the trenches after 6 days which shows how regular troop rotation was used to make sure troops did not spend too long at the front. Troops on average spent about 60% of their time out of the trenches. As this letter was uncensored it gives a useful soldier's view of conditions without army interference, but many troops self-censored their letters to avoid upsetting relatives and friends.
>
> Source C is also useful as it shows us some of the jobs which troops had to do. In this image a group of soldiers are building a footbridge over a river. Much of troops' time away from the front lines would be spent building or repairing trenches (as mentioned in Source B) and other constructions. Soldiers would also spend much of their time moving supplies and equipment. The source is useful as it is a photograph which appears to have been taken spontaneously as none of the soldiers are posing. The image does not particularly glorify the war effort, and so it is unlikely to be a propaganda photograph. Instead, it is a good example of an image of the more routine aspects of trench life and therefore is particularly useful for understanding what troops spent much of their time doing.

> This answer opens by directly addressing the question. This shows the examiner that you have understood, but will also help you to focus your answer as you write.

> In these sections the answer references a range of details from the source content and explains what they can tell us by linking clearly to the question.

> Here the answer uses contextual knowledge to test the claims made in the sources.

> Here the answer refers to the provenance of the sources and uses this to judge their utility.

Question 3: Write an account

Write an account of the events of June–August 1914 to show how these led to the outbreak of a European war. (8 marks)

On 28 June 1914, Archduke Franz Ferdinand was assassinated in Sarajevo. The assassination was carried out by the Black Hand Gang, a Serbian nationalist group who hoped to gain independence for Bosnia from the Austro-Hungarian Empire and unite Bosnia into a Greater Serbia. As Serbia had been growing in power in a series of Balkan Wars and now represented a threat to Austrian dominance in the region, Austria saw this as an opportunity to deal with Serbia. Germany promised to support Austria, and as a result Austria issued a harsh ten-point ultimatum which Serbia would have to agree to in order to avoid war.

Although Serbia agreed to 9 of the 10 demands, they were not willing to allow Austria to carry out a criminal investigation in Serbia. On 28 July, Austria declared war on Serbia, sparking a chain of events which would eventually lead to a European War. Russia soon began to mobilise its forces, and as a result Germany declared war on Russia on 1 August. However, at this stage the war was concentrated in the East.

What spread the conflict to the rest of Europe was the German Schlieffen Plan. Germany wished to avoid a war on two fronts at all costs, and so began to implement its war plan. This involved an invasion of France, hoping to knock France out of the war before Russia could fully mobilise. In order to do this, the German Army marched through Belgium which violated a treaty guaranteeing Belgian neutrality. When Germany refused to withdraw, Britain declared war on Germany on 4 August. By 6 August, all of the alliance powers had joined the conflict and the war had spread throughout Europe.

> Here the answer is giving precise knowledge. It is crucial that you use as much relevant detailed knowledge as possible to show your grasp of the topic.

> This is an example of linking together developments. This is necessary to make your answer more analytical. Wherever you can you should show your understanding of the causes or consequences of developments.

> Here the answer explicitly links to the issue raised in the question.

Question 4: How far do you agree? (Essay)

'New tactics were the main reason why the German Army
was defeated in 1918.' How far do you agree with this
statement?   (16 marks + 4 SPaG)

New tactics were one reason why the Allies were able to defeat Germany in 1918.
During the Hundred Days, the Allied counter attack combined new tactics and
technologies to devastating effect. One of the key developments was the use of
artillery and the creeping barrage to create a smokescreen to cover the infantry
advance. In 1918, the infantry advance was also supported by aircraft who bombed
enemy positions, and by cavalry and tanks who could support the infantry in punching
through enemy lines. Waves of infantry were also used to relieve troops who had
advanced. With these tactics, the Allied counter attack routed the Germany Army on
the 8th August, causing a collapse on many parts of the line which became known as
the German Army's 'Black Day'.

However, one of the reasons this attack was so successful was the fact that the
German Army had become overstretched. The German Ludendorff Offensive, which had
begun in March 1918, had made very quick initial progress, with the Germans in some
places advancing 64 km. However, by 1918 the German Army was poorly supplied and
many troops were underfed. The rapid advance put extra pressure on supplies and so
many troops stopped to loot food from French villages or Allied trenches. This ended
the German advance and created the opportunity for a counter attack, as the Germans
had abandoned their defensive positions for the advance.

The pressure on supplies, and the growing pressure on German politicians to consider
surrender was also caused by the Allied blockade. Particularly following the Battle
of Jutland, the Royal Navy had control over the English Channel and North Sea, and
German ports were blockaded by British ships. This had prevented supplies from
reaching Germany, which led to shortages. By 1918, many people in Germany were
starving and there were even mutinies in the German Navy. This made it harder for the
German Army to continue fighting and encouraged Germany to consider a ceasefire.

The blockade was the key reason for the success of the Allied offensive in 1918. The
German Army came very close to breaking through and capturing key objectives which
might have won the war before the huge impact of the USA joining the war was fully
felt. Although new tactics helped the Allies, Germany had also used tactics like storm
troopers very effectively during the Ludendorff Offensive. It was the blockade which
weakened the German Army and halted the advance, allowing the counter offensive to
be so successful.

The answer opens by directly addressing the statement in the question.

Each paragraph opens with a clear argument which is focused on the question.

The argument in the paragraph is then supported by a range of detailed, specific knowledge.

Here the paragraph links the evidence to the question.

Here the answer fulfills the requirement to form a complex explanation by linking reasons together before coming to an overall judgement.

Abdication A king or emperor stepping down from their role.

Agrarian Based on farming.

Alsace-Lorraine An area of France which had been captured by Germany in the Franco-Prussian War.

Armistice A peace agreement.

Attrition A strategy which focuses on wearing down the enemy with repeated attacks.

Balkans An area of high tension in the southeast of Europe.

Black Hand Gang A group of Serbian nationalists who assassinated Archduke Franz Ferdinand.

Blockade Preventing supplies from reaching an enemy by blocking ports.

Bolsheviks A Russian Communist Party.

British Expeditionary Force A small, well-trained force of British soldiers who were prepared to support France against German attack.

Comradeship A feeling of loyalty and friendship with fellow soldiers.

Court-martialled Being put on trial in a military court.

Creeping barrage An artillery tactic which slowly moves the fire forward to provide a smokescreen for the infantry.

Diplomacy Negotiation between countries.

Eastern Front The area of fighting between Russia, Austria and Germany.

Foreign policy One country's aims and dealing with other countries.

Fourteen Points US President Wilson's plan for a peace agreement to end WW1.

Front line trenches The trenches closest to the enemy.

Infantry Soldiers who fight on foot.

Jutland The main naval battle of World War One.

Kaiser The Emperor of Germany.

Ludendorff Offensive A major German offensive in 1918.

Mobilisation Preparing an army for war.

Mutiny A rebellion by soldiers or sailors against their leaders.

Outflank To move an army around the enemy to gain an advantageous position to fight.

Patriotic Proud of one's country.

Reconnaissance Spying on enemy troops.

Republic A country without a monarchy.

Sappers Soldiers who were specially trained to mine under enemy trenches.

Sentry duty Watching for enemy attacks.

Slavs An ethnic group which united some Russians with people living in the Balkans.

Stalemate A conflict in which neither side can win or make significant progress.

Storm troopers Highly trained troops who specialised in breaking through enemy lines.

Treaty of Brest-Litovsk A treaty signed by Russia to end the war with Germany.

Treaty of Versailles The final peace agreement which ended war with Germany.

Trench raids Small attack on enemy trenches to try to gain information.

Triple Alliance/Central Powers A military alliance made up of Germany, Italy and Austro-Hungary.

Triple Entente A military alliance made up of Britain, France and Russia.

U-boats German submarines.

Ultimatum A list of demands with consequences for not agreeing.

Unrestricted submarine warfare The German policy of attacking all shipping across the Atlantic.

5.1 The armistice and the aims of the peacemakers

REVISED ☐

The **big question** at the Paris Peace Conference was **how to treat Germany**

- A peace treaty is a set of agreements that deal with the complicated issues left after war. The aim is to bring lasting peace.
- Germany was dealt with by the Treaty of Versailles.
- The discussions about this treaty were led by the leaders of the victorious countries (the **Big Three**).
- Germany was not invited to the peace talks at all.

President **Wilson** wanted a **fair settlement** to be based on his **Fourteen Points**

- Wilson wanted a settlement that allowed for the development of a more peaceful world.
- To show how to achieve this, Wilson had drawn up and published his **Fourteen Points** in January 1918 to guide the future peacemaking.
- The Fourteen Points included:
  - **self-determination**: the principle that **nationalities** should be able to rule themselves – that is, not be inside another country's 'empire'
  - **disarmament** for all countries
  - a **League of Nations** to ensure peace in the future.
- Wilson was seen as an **idealist** – seeing hope for the future and ignoring some of the harsh realities of the time.
- Wilson wanted to be fair towards Germany to help keep peace in Europe.

Clemenceau wanted a **harsh settlement** that would cripple Germany

- French Prime Minister, Georges Clemenceau, was 77 years old in 1919. Twice in his life he had seen France invaded by Germany – in 1870 and in 1914. He was determined that this should never happen again.
- He had seen the great suffering caused by the war. Two-thirds of French soldiers who fought in 1914–18 had been either killed or injured.
- So Clemenceau wanted a harsh treaty to weaken Germany (so it could not attack France again) and punish Germany (because France had suffered so much in the war).
- His views reflected French public opinion.

Lloyd George often took a more **middle ground**

- British Prime Minister David Lloyd George knew that British public opinion was hostile to Germany. He had just won a general election promising to 'make Germany pay'.
- He wanted to see Germany punished, but not to an extent that would cause revenge.
- He wanted things that would help Britain, for example for Germany to lose its colonies and its navy because they threatened the British Empire.

> **Key point**
>
> The leaders of the USA, France and Britain met at the Paris Peace Conference in 1919 to agree a treaty to end the First World War. They disagreed significantly about how to deal with Germany.

> **TIP**
>
> All the key terms in **purple** are defined in the glossary at the end of each chapter.
>
> Make sure that you can spell the key terms, know what they mean and aim to use them in your written work.

- Lloyd George wanted Germany to be able to recover internally as Germany had been one of Britain's most important trading partners. Prospering German industries would provide jobs for those involved with British trade.

 Test yourself

1 What is the difference between an armistice and a peace treaty?
2 List three things that each Allied leader wanted from the peace settlement in 1919.
3 Why would none of the three be able to get everything he wanted in the treaty?

 Spot the opinion in a source

The first question on your depth study paper will be based on a source. You will be told what its viewpoint is and you have to explain how you know that.

The source below was published in a British magazine in February 1919, during the negotiations at the Paris Peace Conference.

How do you know that this source supports Britain and opposes Germany? Annotate the highlighted features to show how the message is conveyed. One has been done for you.

SOURCE A *Cartoon from* Punch *magazine, 1919. The title was, 'Giving him rope?', and the caption reads: 'German criminal (to Allied police): "Here, I say, stop! You're hurting me!" [Aside] "If I only whine enough I may be able to wriggle out of this yet."'*

Facial expression of criminal

Body of criminal Although beaten, Germany is shown as solid and dangerous, not weak

British policeman

Criminal's words

GIVING HIM ROPE?

German Criminal (to Allied Police). "HERE, I SAY, STOP! YOU'RE HURTING ME! [Aside]
IF I ONLY WHINE ENOUGH I MAY BE ABLE TO WRIGGLE OUT OF THIS YET."

 Practice question

Write an account of how the Armistice of November 1918 led to disagreements among the Allied leaders during the Paris Peace Conference.

(8 marks)

> **TIP**
>
> In answering this type of question, the key thing is to remember you are not only telling a story. Your account needs to explain the issue in the question.

5.2 The Versailles settlement

German representatives were forced to sign the treaty in June 1919

- As the defeated country, Germany was not invited to the peace conference.
- Despite this, the German government had reasons to expect a fair treaty:

The Kaiser – the leader who had taken Germany into war – had gone	Germany had a new democratic constitution and new leaders	The new government needed all the help it could get to stabilise Germany and prevent a Communist revolution	The most powerful of the Allied leaders, Woodrow Wilson, wanted the treaty to be fair on Germany

- For months, the victorious countries argued over how to treat Germany.
- When the terms were made public in May 1919, Germans were appalled. They complained it was very harsh.
- However, they ignored the fact that Germany had imposed a far harsher settlement on Russia at the Treaty of Brest-Litovsk in March 1918.
- The leaders of the new German government could not negotiate. It was a *diktat*. They had to sign – or face renewed attacks by the Allies.
- The treaty was publicly signed in humiliating circumstances at Versailles in June 1919.

Germany lost a lot of its land and population

- Germany lost 10 per cent of its land, 12.5 per cent of its population, 16 per cent of its coal fields and almost half of its iron and steel industry.

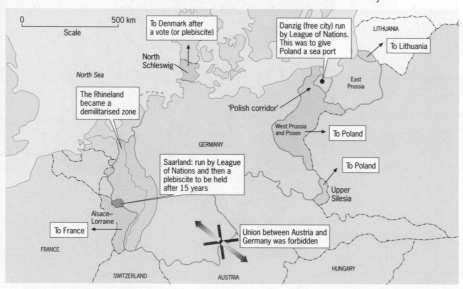

- Germany's overseas colonies became mandates ruled by victorious countries (mainly Britain or France) on behalf of the League of Nations.

Severe limits were put on Germany's armed forces

- The army was limited to 100,000 troops.
- Soldiers had to be volunteers. No **conscription** was allowed.
- Germany could have no tanks, submarines or military aircraft.
- The navy could have only six battleships.
- The Rhineland (the border with France) was **demilitarised**, that is, Germany was not allowed to have troops in that area.

Key point

The Treaty of Versailles punished Germany more than Germans expected because they had assumed that the terms would have been guided by the Fourteen Points of Woodrow Wilson.

Test yourself

1 List three territorial losses and three military restrictions imposed on Germany by the Treaty of Versailles.

2 What are reparations?

3 What argument could the Allies use to justify making Germany pay reparations?

Quick quizzes at www.hoddereducation.co.uk/myrevisionnotes

Germany was **blamed for the war** and was told to **pay reparations**

TIP

In your exam you will be asked to evaluate two sources. You won't actually be asked to compare the usefulness of the sources but you will be able to comment on how they are more useful together than separately.

- The **War Guilt Clause** blamed Germany for starting the war and for the damage caused by it.
- This was even more unpopular in Germany than the loss of territory. Germans disagreed that their actions had been the main cause of the war.
- Because of war guilt, Germany had to agree to pay **reparations** for war damage.
- In 1921, reparations were fixed as £6.6 billion. Germany would be paying until 1984.

Topic summary

Copy and complete this table to show which country (France, USA or Britain) would be most pleased with a particular aspect of the Treaty of Versailles. And why?

Aspect of the Treaty	Most pleased (France, USA or Britain)?	Explain why they would be pleased
Reducing the German navy	Britain	Because Britain wanted to preserve the superiority of the British navy
Reducing the German army		
Preventing Germany putting troops in the Rhineland		
Creating the League of Nations		
Germany's overseas territories controlled by League of Nations		

Challenge: Which aspect do you think would be most disliked by the following groups? And why?

a German army leaders   b German business leaders.   c German politicians.

Evaluate usefulness

The second question in your exam will be about the usefulness of sources.

How useful is Source B to a historian studying German reactions to the Treaty of Versailles?

Make notes using the grid below of what you might use in your answer.

Provenance	Content
a Who made it, when and why? **b** How does this affect its usefulness?	**a** What does it say about German reactions? **b** From your knowledge of these events is this accurate? **c** How does this affect its usefulness?

SOURCE B *Cartoon from the British magazine* Punch, *23 April 1919. 'The Reckoning'. 'German: "Monstrous, I call it. Why, it's fully a quarter of what we should have made them pay, if we'd won."'*

THE RECKONING.

PAN-GERMAN. "MONSTROUS, I CALL IT. WHY, IT'S FULLY A QUARTER OF WHAT WE SHOULD HAVE MADE *THEM* PAY, IF WE'D WON."

5.3 Reactions to the Versailles settlement: strengths and weaknesses

The Big Three who agreed the treaty were not totally happy with it

- In France, Clemenceau was criticised because many people thought the treaty was not harsh enough. In 1920 he was voted out of office.
- In contrast, Lloyd George was greeted as a hero back in Britain. But he privately feared that German anger would lead to future conflict.
- Woodrow Wilson was the most disappointed as many of his Fourteen Points had been ignored or modified.
- His most important idea was that the League of Nations would ensure lasting peace by solving international disputes by peaceful methods. But the US Congress voted not to join.

> **Key point**
>
> The Treaty of Versailles brought peace to Europe but it also created problems for the future, especially in Germany.

Leader	Liked	Disliked
Clemenceau	• Military restrictions on Germany • Gaining of Alsace-Lorraine • Reparations	• League of Nations • Saar only gained for fifteen years
Lloyd George	• Punishment of Germany • Mandates for ex-German colonies • Naval restriction	• Not enough recognition that Britain and Germany needed to re-establish trade links
Woodrow Wilson	• Creation of League of Nations	• Reparations payments • Failure to agree on disarmament • Failure to implement principle of self-determination

Almost all Germans hated the treaty and it contributed to great instability in Germany

- The Weimar government was seen as weak for signing the treaty.
- Germany's problems over the next few years were blamed on the treaty.
- There was political chaos in Germany with attempted revolutions by both Communists and Nazis.
- Germany's failure to pay reparations in 1922 led France and Belgium to invade the **Ruhr**. This led to economic chaos and hyperinflation in 1923.
- The atmosphere of chaos and weak government encouraged the growth of extremist political parties – including the Nazis.

The treaty had strengths and weaknesses but some of these were only clear with hindsight

Strengths (seen at the time by victorious countries)	Weaknesses (seen initially by the defeated countries and later by all)
• The treaty brought peace to Europe after four years of terrible fighting • An international peacekeeping organisation, the League of Nations, was set up to prevent future conflict • The terms of the treaty were not as harsh as they might have been. For example, not as harsh as Germany had imposed on Russia at the Treaty of Brest-Litovsk in 1918 • Some had wanted to split Germany into separate countries but Germany was preserved as a large democratic country of 60 million people as a barrier against possible Communist expansion from Russia	• Germans felt bitter about unfair treatment – which extremist parties exploited • Reparations payments crippled the German economy • The treaty punished Germany enough to want revenge but not enough to stop it from recovering and acting against the Allies in the future • Woodrow Wilson placed too much faith in the League of Nations

Quick quizzes at **www.hoddereducation.co.uk/myrevisionnotes**

- However, historians now mostly agree that the negotiators did their best in a limited time while facing an almost impossible task.
- The international situation in 1919 was so complex, and countries had such competing priorities, that it would have been impossible to reach a set of agreements that pleased everyone and guaranteed future peace.

Test yourself

1 What did the French public think of the Treaty of Versailles?
2 Why did France invade the Ruhr in 1923?
3 List three reasons why the peace settlement was likely to lead to future problems for Europe.

Develop the detail

Each of the following statements is vague and general. Add further details to show that you understand the general point being made. One example has been done for you. This will help with most questions as it is important throughout your exam to use 'detailed, accurate and relevant knowledge'.

General statement	Supporting detail
The treaty made war less likely in the future	Germany was restricted in its power and had no chance of starting a war in the near future. The League of Nations was a serious attempt to maintain world peace.
Germany remained one country	
Reparations had bad consequences for Germany	
Woodrow Wilson was disappointed by the Treaty of Versailles	

Support or challenge?

Your final question in the depth study exam will be an essay writing task like this:

'The main weakness of the Treaty of Versailles was the decision to impose reparations on Germany.' How far do you agree with this statement? Explain your answer. (16 marks)

To prepare for the essay write notes in two columns on a separate piece of paper.

Support	Challenge

Start off with these statements. Which column should each go in?

A Reparations assumed Germany was to blame for the war. Germans resented this.

B France wanted reparations to cripple the German economy.

C In peace treaties, the victors almost always demanded reparations from the losers.

D The level of reparations was not set at the time. A separate commission was set up to work out what would be a reasonable figure that Germany could pay.

E Germany most resented the reduction in their armed forces.

5.4 The formation, organisation and membership of the League of Nations

REVISED

The League of Nations was **Wilson's idea** to **prevent future wars**

- The League of Nations was created as part of the post-war peace treaties. It had to enforce the terms of the post-war treaties.
- All countries joining the League had to sign the **Covenant of the League of Nations**. This involved promising to protect other member nations.
- The League would provide **collective security** – each member country would feel protected by the others who had signed the Covenant.
- The headquarters was to be in Geneva, Switzerland.
- Most people in Europe supported the creation of the League in principle as they did not want another war.

Key point

The League was set up at a time when the horror of war was very fresh in people's minds. The ambitious plans suited the atmosphere at the time. It was all an experiment, but with good will it seemed that it could work to keep world peace.

The League had a cleverly planned but **complex organisation**

- **Assembly** – every member country sent a representative. They met once a year. Decisions had to be unanimous.
- **Council** – a smaller group that made decisions and met several times a year. It consisted of permanent members (Britain, France, Italy and Japan) and several non-permanent members elected for three years. The Council could make decisions, but they had to be unanimous.
- **Secretariat** – kept records, prepared reports, translated documents, and fulfilled a range of other administrative functions.
- **Permanent Court of International Justice** – based at The Hague, in The Netherlands. It was intended to settle disputes between countries and provide advice to the Assembly and the Council.
- **Commissions** – committees that dealt with major economic or social issues, such as refugees and epidemics.

The League had around 50 **members** – but the **USA never joined**

- The League started with 42 members. These were all countries that had fought for or supported the Allies in the war.
- The US Congress voted not to join. Congress did not want the USA to get dragged into European disputes. This was important as the USA in the 1920s was by far the most powerful and wealthy country in the world.
- At first, defeated countries were not allowed to join, although Germany was admitted in 1926.
- The USSR was not let in until 1934 because of fear of Communism.
- Some members later withdrew, for example Japan and Germany in 1933.

The League had **powers** set out in the Covenant, but in practice they were **limited**

- The Council of the League could, in a dispute between nations, decide who was in the wrong and tell the country to stop. (**Moral condemnation.**)
- The Council could tell member countries not to trade with the 'guilty' country. (**Economic sanctions.**)
- The League did not have an army but the Council could instruct its members to provide troops to fight together against the aggressor.
- The League relied on persuasion, in the 1920s this seemed to be working.

Test yourself

1 List the main differences between the Assembly and the Council.

2 What could the League do if one country invaded another?

3 List possible reasons why the League might not be able to stop an invasion.

Quick quizzes at **www.hoddereducation.co.uk/myrevisionnotes**

Topic summary

A common angle in questions on the League is about strengths and weaknesses. You might be asked to write an account of the strengths and weaknesses or asked to analyse them as part of the essay question. Whichever it is, you need to have a firm grasp of the content.

	Strengths	Weaknesses
Membership	Many countries were members	Defeated countries excluded, as was Russia. USA decided not to join
The Assembly		
The Council		
The International Court		
The League's powers to act		

 ## Evaluate usefulness

How useful is Source C for studying attitudes towards the League of Nations in 1919?

SOURCE C *A cartoon from* Punch, *10 December 1919. The figure in the white top hat represents the USA.*

THE GAP IN THE BRIDGE.

Make notes in this grid to plan your answer.

Provenance	Content
Who made it, when and why?	What does it say about the League of Nations?
	From your knowledge of these events is this accurate?
How does this affect its usefulness?	How does this affect its usefulness?

TIP

Remember that all sources are useful for something. It all depends on what you are using them for. Never dismiss a source as useless because it is one-sided or incomplete. It will be still be very useful for finding out about the attitudes of the person who made it.

5.5 Successes and failures of the League in the 1920s

The League **successfully sorted out** various international **disputes in the 1920s**

- In 1921, the League solved a dispute between Poland and Germany over part of Upper Silesia. The League asked the people to vote which country they wanted to be in and divided it in line with the vote.
- In a similar disagreement over the Aaland Islands in 1920, the League decided Finland should have it. Sweden accepted this.
- The League was successful in these disputes because they did not involve the most powerful countries or ambitious dictators.

The League's **Commissions** did important **humanitarian work**

- These were the most lasting aspects of the work of the League.

The Refugees Commission	The Health Commission	The Mandates Commission
Resettled hundreds of thousands who had been displaced by the war. It also helped ex-prisoners of war	Was more long term (its work has since been taken over the United Nations). It aimed to reduce deaths from dangerous diseases and educated people about good sanitation	Britain and France were put in charge of Germany's former colonies as **mandates**. The Mandates Commission tried to ensure that Britain and France were not acting in their own selfish interests

There were also **signs** that the League was **potentially weak**

- Countries sometimes ignored the League. As early as 1920 Poland invaded Vilna, the capital of Lithuania, and the League was ignored.
- Mussolini, the new leader of Italy, invaded the Greek island of Corfu in 1923. Italy was clearly in the wrong, but the League sided with him.
- This showed how the League was not willing to stand up to an aggressor, even though that country had a permanent seat in the Council!

The **League was helped** in its peacemaking role by other **international agreements**

- The Locarno Treaties (1925) were important signs of goodwill between Germany and France. They promised not to invade each other. Germany promised to keep troops out of the Rhineland.
- After this agreement, Germany was allowed to join the League in 1926.
- The Kellogg–Briand Pact of 1928 was signed by 61 countries who all promised not to go to war to solve disputes.
- These agreements were not the work of the League but they helped its work because they showed that countries were prepared to work peacefully with former enemies.
- That situation changed quickly with the onset of the Great Depression.

> **Key point**
>
> The League had successes in the 1920s, but it was limited in its scope, and some important international decisions were already taking place without using the League.

 Test yourself

1. What did the League do when Mussolini invaded Corfu?
2. What was the role of the League's Health Commission?

Quick quizzes at **www.hoddereducation.co.uk/myrevisionnotes**

Develop the explanation

Read the six statements below.

1 Decide if the statements are correct or not. Correct them if necessary.

2 Then for each statement add your own explanation of how this affected the power of the League in the 1920s. The first one is done for you.

Statement	Correct?	Explanation
The League was successful in the 1920s because no aggressive dictators wanted to upset the Treaty of Versailles	Correct	This made it appear that the League was more powerful than it actually was
Germany won the dispute over land in Upper Silesia		
The Aaland Islands were divided between Sweden and Finland		
The Mandates Commission looked after colonies which had been German		
The Locarno Treaties ignored French fears of a future German invasion		
The Kellogg–Briand Pact of 1928 made sure that no war would ever happen again		

Spot the mistakes

People find it easy to criticise the League. Many students focus only on its weaknesses but for the essay questions you need to give a balanced answer. You also need to be aware of its strengths. This paragraph attempts to describe the strengths of the League. Cross out anything that you think is inaccurate or should not be in this answer because you think it was not a strength. Rewrite the passage making the necessary corrections.

The League of Nations had lots of members including all the important countries in the world. It was likely to succeed because in the early 1920s memories of the First World War were fresh in people's minds. The League also had an imposing organisation. For example, its Assembly consisted of all the member countries and everyone's voice could be heard. The Council could make decisions, and make sure they were carried out. The International Court of Justice could rule on international cases and make sure that everyone followed its decisions. The first time that the League was shown to be weak was when it faced a powerful country who ignored it.

Essay plan

'The main reason for the League to be seen as weak in the 1920s was the absence of the USA.' How far do you agree? Explain your answer. (16 marks)

Note down a list of things you would write in each section of this essay.

Essay plan

Introduction: You state your view on how far you agree or disagree

First main paragraph: The USA's absence was important – give some reasons

Second and third paragraphs: two other major reasons for the League being seen as weak

Conclusion: your judgement on whether the absence of the USA was the main reason

TIP

When writing an essay some people try to say too much. You only have about twenty minutes to write this essay. It is much better to write well about less than to have a long list of undeveloped points. The best answers see connections between points – what the mark scheme calls complex thinking.

5.6 The collapse of the League in the 1930s

The Wall Street Crash followed by the Great Depression caused problems for the League in the early 1930s

- The USA recalled its loans and wanted less to do with Europe.
- The British economy suffered badly meaning less enthusiasm for spending money on the League.
- Italy faced huge economic problems. Mussolini was keen to divert attention by building an overseas empire.
- Japan had less money to buy food and raw materials.
- Germany was in turmoil leading to Hitler becoming Chancellor. He criticised the League for enforcing the terms of the Treaty of Versailles.

> **Key point**
>
> In the 1930s, international tensions rose because of the Great Depression. The League was powerless to prevent invasions by Japan and Italy.

The Manchurian Crisis of 1931–33 showed the weaknesses of the League

September 1931: Japan invades Manchuria	1931–2: the League investigates	March 1933: Japan ignores the League
Japan wanted Manchuria for its raw materials. Japan knew that Chinese control was weak	China appealed to the League for help	The Lytton Commission found in favour of China
The Japanese already had mining rights and controlled railways in the area	It sent Lord Lytton on a fact-finding mission	The League ordered Japan to leave Manchuria
An incident on the railway line at Mukden was used as an excuse for a Japanese invasion	Meanwhile Japan completed its invasion	The Japanese ignored this and left the League
		Japan invaded more of China

The Abyssinian Crisis of 1935–36 confirmed how ineffective the League had become

- Mussolini invaded Abyssinia because of its mineral wealth.
- The Abyssinian Emperor, Haile Selassie, appealed to the League for help.
- The League condemned Italy and imposed economic sanctions. However, the sanctions did not include oil. Italy continued to trade with the USA.
- Britain and France were desperate not to anger Mussolini (which they feared might drive him closer to Hitler).
- The Hoare–Laval Pact was a proposed secret deal with Italy. It caused outrage when it was leaked to the public.
- Italy completed its invasion, then left the League.

These events also showed the reasons why the League of Nations was powerless to stop aggressors

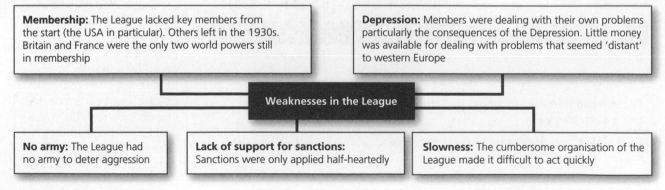

Membership: The League lacked key members from the start (the USA in particular). Others left in the 1930s. Britain and France were the only two world powers still in membership

Depression: Members were dealing with their own problems particularly the consequences of the Depression. Little money was available for dealing with problems that seemed 'distant' to western Europe

Weaknesses in the League

No army: The League had no army to deter aggression

Lack of support for sanctions: Sanctions were only applied half-heartedly

Slowness: The cumbersome organisation of the League made it difficult to act quickly

Quick quizzes at www.hoddereducation.co.uk/myrevisionnotes

Test yourself

1 How did the Depression affect Britain's attitude to the League?
2 Why did Japan invade Manchuria?
3 How did the League try to force Mussolini out of Abyssinia?

TIP

It is always useful to have a structure in mind to help you in the rush of the exam. For this question think of two short paragraphs on each source: one focused on provenance, the second on content.

 Evaluate usefulness

In the exam, question 2 will be based on two sources. For example:

How useful are Sources D and E to a historian studying the failure of the League of Nations over Abyssinia?
Explain your answer using Sources D and E and your contextual knowledge. (12 marks)

You will need to think about the following:

● Provenance: who made it, when and why?
● Content: is it useful for its content and does your knowledge agree?

Annotate each source to show the points you are going to make about provenance and content.

Challenge: write up your notes as a full answer using the writing frame suggested in the tip above.

SOURCE D *A cartoon from* Punch *magazine 1935. Punch was usually very patriotic towards Britain; it rarely criticised British foreign policy.*

THE AWFUL WARNING.

FRANCE AND ENGLAND (*together ?*).

"WE DON'T WANT YOU TO FIGHT,
BUT, BY JINGO, IF YOU DO,
WE SHALL PROBABLY ISSUE A JOINT MEMORANDUM
SUGGESTING A MILD DISAPPROVAL OF YOU."

SOURCE E *From a speech by Anthony Eden, who became British Foreign Secretary after the resignation of Sir Samuel Hoare, explaining to Parliament why sanctions should be ended, June 1937.*

There was a very good reason for the League to enforce the particular sanctions they chose, because with an incomplete membership they were the only ones they could impose and which by their own action alone they could hope to see effective. Oil could not be made effective by League action alone.

I think it is right that the League should admit that sanctions have not realised their purpose and should face that fact.

5.7 Hitler's early actions, 1933–35, and the development of tension

Hitler had **clear aims for his foreign policy** that would lead to tension in Europe

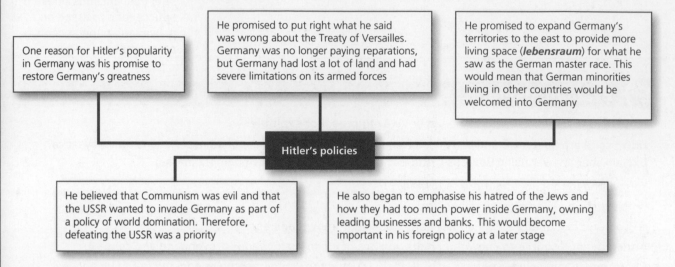

One reason for Hitler's popularity in Germany was his promise to restore Germany's greatness

He promised to put right what he said was wrong about the Treaty of Versailles. Germany was no longer paying reparations, but Germany had lost a lot of land and had severe limitations on its armed forces

He promised to expand Germany's territories to the east to provide more living space (*lebensraum*) for what he saw as the German master race. This would mean that German minorities living in other countries would be welcomed into Germany

Hitler's policies

He believed that Communism was evil and that the USSR wanted to invade Germany as part of a policy of world domination. Therefore, defeating the USSR was a priority

He also began to emphasise his hatred of the Jews and how they had too much power inside Germany, owning leading businesses and banks. This would become important in his foreign policy at a later stage

At home Hitler started to **build up Germany's military strength** as soon as he came to power

- In 1933, Hitler began rearming Germany in secret, ignoring the terms of the Treaty of Versailles.
- From March 1935, he openly started a policy of conscription (that is, forcing young men to join the armed forces for a number of years).
- He held massive rearmament rallies in Germany in 1935 to show off his power to European countries. He withdrew Germany from the League of Nations.
- He announced in 1935 that he had a peacetime army of 550,000 – more than five times what he was allowed.
- An air ministry trained pilots and started building hundreds of aircraft.
- He also wanted to build a bigger navy (see page 111).

> **Key point**
>
> From the start, Hitler made clear his aims to expand Germany and restore German pride. When he acted in these first years (1933–35), he saw clearly that Britain and France would in reality do very little to stop him – just as they had not stopped Japan in Manchuria.

In foreign policy Hitler successfully increased German influence without meeting much resistance

- In 1934, Hitler tried to take over Austria – but this was too ambitious at this time.
- There was open violence in Austria. This included the killing of Chancellor Dollfuss.
- Hitler thought of invading in support of some Austrian Nazis who had been killed, but Mussolini wanted to establish friendship with Austria, and Hitler could not afford to lose Mussolini's support.
- In 1935, Hitler was able to reunite the Saar with Germany. Over 90 per cent of the people of the area voted that this was what they wanted (they had been under the League's control for fifteen years). This was good for Hitler's confidence in his future ambitions.

- In 1935, Britain, France and Italy signed an agreement aimed at stopping Germany from doing any more against the Treaty of Versailles. It was of very limited effect, as Mussolini invaded Abyssinia later in the year, and Britain compromised with Germany over its navy.
- The Anglo-German Naval Agreement of 1935 allowed Germany to increase its navy to up to 35 per cent of the size of the British navy. Hitler had again been shown that Britain would compromise over the exact terms of the Treaty of Versailles rather than risk fighting.

 Test yourself

1 When did Hitler start rearming Germany?

2 Why did Hitler not invade Austria in 1934?

3 What was the Anglo-German Naval Agreement of 1935?

 ## Write an account

Write an account of how Hitler's foreign policy made Germany stronger by the end of 1935. (8 marks)

According to the mark scheme what the examiners look for in a 'write an account' question is as follows:

- relevant, detailed and accurate knowledge ...
- well organised into an orderly account ...
- which answers the question!

So that means you need:

- To know things.
- To plan your answer so it all connects to the question and has a clear structure.
- To select from your knowledge the things that belong in your orderly account. This is not everything you know about Hitler's policies but how they made Germany stronger. Every fact you use needs to be relevant and accurate and support your narrative.
- And each paragraph needs to include a clear reference back to the question.

Link the annotations to the features in this first paragraph.

> Germany had become stronger by the end of 1935 because Hitler had ignored some of the details of the Treaty of Versailles – and Britain and France allowed this to happen. He started a policy of rearmament, manufacturing more weapons, and recruiting more men into the army. He was ignoring the limit of 100,000 troops stipulated in the Treaty of Versailles and by 1935 boasted that he had more than five times that number – 550,000. He also started a policy of conscription at that time, and this guaranteed that his armies consisted of fit and trained personnel.

A Clear opening statement.

B Identifies one overall reason.

C Supports the reason with examples – displaying relevant detailed knowledge.

D Connects the reason back to the focus of the question.

Challenge: write a second paragraph on another reason (for example, the Anglo-German Naval Agreement) with the same model. Annotate your own paragraph in the same way.

TIP

A probable structure for an account is chronological – but that is not the only way. In fact writing an account in chronological order might tempt you to just describe things rather than answering the question. This example takes a thematic approach looking at each feature in turn and identifying how it made Germany stronger.

5.8 The escalation of tension, 1936–38, and the role of appeasement

REVISED

In **March 1936** Hitler sent German troops into the **Rhineland** facing no opposition from the League of Nations

- This was a calculated risk for Hitler as he was openly breaking the terms of the Treaty of Versailles.
- It was risky because if the French army had prevented them the German troops were not strong enough to resist.
- The Germans claimed that they were only putting troops in part of their own country to defend the area from possible French attack in the future.
- Britain and France did nothing as Hitler's reasons seemed believable. Plus the focus of attention was on Italy's actions in Abyssinia.

> **Key point**
>
> Britain and France tried to avoid war with Germany through appeasement – giving Hitler what he wanted. The most famous example is the Munich Agreement which gave the Sudetenland to Germany.

By 1937 Hitler had formed an **anti-Communist alliance** with **Italy** and **Japan**

- Hitler was keen to ally himself with Italy led by Mussolini (the other **Fascist** dictator in Europe).
- Mussolini had successfully invaded Abyssinia. The League of Nations had not stopped him.
- Hitler also had much in common with the expansionist government in Japan. Japan had taken over Manchuria and was advancing further in Chinese territory.
- In 1936–37, Germany, Italy and Japan signed the **Anti-Comintern Pact**. This was an alliance against Communist USSR. But it also acted as an alliance against leading democratic nations.

 Test yourself

Explain what these words mean:

1 Conscription.
2 *Lebensraum.*
3 Appeasement.

In **March 1938 Austria united with Germany** – with the approval of most Austrian people

- A union (*Anschluss*) between Austria and Germany was forbidden under the Treaty of Versailles but Hitler was determined it should happen. Many in Austria supported it.

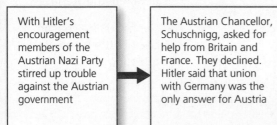

With Hitler's encouragement members of the Austrian Nazi Party stirred up trouble against the Austrian government	The Austrian Chancellor, Schuschnigg, asked for help from Britain and France. They declined. Hitler said that union with Germany was the only answer for Austria	Schuschnigg decided on a **plebiscite** (referendum) asking the Austrian people. Before the referendum could be held, Hitler's troops marched in. 99.75 per cent voted in favour of union with Germany	Britain and France accepted Hitler's action. The League of Nations did nothing. The Treaty of Versailles was being torn up by agreement

Britain and France followed a policy of appeasement for logical reasons but it played into Hitler's hands

Reasons to appease	Reasons not to appease
• Neither Britain nor France wanted war. They had major economic problems. They still remembered the horrors of the First World War. Their armies and navies were not ready for a war • Many politicians believed that the Treaty of Versailles was flawed and they should not go to war to defend it • Hitler was standing up to Communism – to be encouraged!	• **Appeasement** encouraged Hitler to make demands • It made Britain and France seem weak

In September 1938 Hitler was given the Sudetenland in return for a promise to make no further demands

- The **Sudetenland** area of Czechoslovakia consisted largely of 3 million German-speaking people who had been inside the Austro-Hungarian Empire before 1919.
- Hitler wanted this area for its industry and raw materials.

The leader of the Nazis in the Sudetenland, Henlein, stirred up trouble (encouraging protests against the government), and demanded that the area become part of Germany	The Czech leader, Beneš, was frightened and asked for help from Britain and France	The British Prime Minister, Neville Chamberlain, consulted with other European leaders, and flew to Germany to discuss with Hitler	On Chamberlain's third visit at the end of September 1938, he met Hitler, Mussolini and Daladier (France) in Munich. Hitler promised this was his last territorial demand. They decided to give Hitler what he wanted. The Czechs were excluded from the talks	Hitler's troops marched into the Sudetenland on 1 October 1938

This flow chart shows how the crisis developed.

- War had been avoided and a line had been drawn. Hitler had promised that this was his last territorial demand. If he demanded or took more, he was proving right the critics of the Munich Agreement – that Hitler could not be trusted and had to be stopped.

Key events

One secret of writing an account of something is to have a clear sense of the chronology – how each stage led to the next. Fill in the missing details in the chart below.

1933	Hitler started to make Germany stronger in Europe by … (clue: soldiers and weapons)
1935	Hitler forced chosen young men to join the army by …
1935	The Saar …
1936	The Rhineland …
March 1938	Austria …
Sept 1938	The Sudetenland …

Essay plan

'Appeasement was the best way to deal with Hitler's Germany in 1938.' How far do you agree? Explain your answer. (16 marks)

Note below your ideas for each section of your essay. Then write a full conclusion.

Essay plan	Your ideas
Introduction: show that you understand what appeasement was and state your view on how far you agree or disagree	
First main paragraph: list reasons that will help you to support the notion that appeasement was a good policy	
Second (and third) paragraphs: list reasons why you could challenge this and argue that appeasement was a bad policy	
Conclusion: outline whether you support the quotation – or wish to challenge it	

5.9 Events in 1939 leading to the outbreak of war in September

In **March 1939** Hitler invaded the rest of **Czechoslovakia** ignoring the **Munich Agreement**

- The invasion made Germany more powerful. It gained control of additional territory and Czech raw materials and industries.
- The invasion showed Britain and France that Hitler's promises at Munich were worthless.
  - They accepted that appeasement had failed to stop Hitler's aggression.
  - His likely next move would be to invade Poland so they said they would defend Poland if that happened.

In **August 1939** Germany signed the **Nazi–Soviet Pact** although the USSR was Germany's greatest enemy

- Nazis were anti-Communist. Hitler had said he intended to take *lebensraum* in eastern Europe and the USSR.
- Communism was anti-Nazi and the USSR aimed (in the long term) to conquer Europe as part of its policy of exporting Communism.
- Despite these differences, on 23 August 1939 they signed the **Nazi–Soviet Pact**. They agreed not to go to war against each other and to divide Poland between them.
- They both benefited:
  - Germany could now risk war in western Europe without having to worry about being invaded from the east. No war on two fronts!
  - The USSR was secure from invasion by Germany. It also gained part of Poland as well as Estonia, Latvia and Lithuania.
- News of the pact astonished Europe. It meant war was virtually certain. Preparations for war were put into action immediately. For example: Britain started evacuating children from cities at risk of bombing on 1 September – just one week after the pact.
- German troops entered Poland on 1 September 1939. Britain and France said they would declare war on Germany if its troops were not withdrawn. On 3 September, Britain and France declared war on Germany.

The **main cause** of war was **Hitler's aggression** but other factors contributed

How other factors contributed to the outbreak of the Second World War:

- The weak response of Britain and France at critical moments gave Hitler confidence. For example, after he sent troops to the Rhineland in 1936, he later said that if he had met resistance he would have drawn back.
- The harshness of the Treaty of Versailles. Leading British politicians believed that the treaty was flawed. So they saw some of Hitler's demands as reasonable.
- Fear of Communism. Western politicians saw Communist USSR as a greater threat than Germany. Some saw Germany as the buffer between the Communist USSR and western Europe. They wanted Germany to be strong enough to stand up to Soviet aggression.

 Test yourself

1 How did Hitler's invasion of Czechoslovakia change British policy towards Germany?
2 Why did a) Hitler and b) Stalin sign a Pact in August 1939?
3 Why was the Pact unlikely to last?

- The Nazi–Soviet Pact: Stalin's pact with Hitler was the final act that allowed Hitler to invade Poland.
- The League of Nations had become powerless and ignored by 1939.
- The USA pursued a policy of isolation from Europe and did not want to get involved.

 Essay plan

The most valuable question in your depth study exam will be an essay question like this.

'The main reason for the outbreak of war in September 1939 was Hitler's aggression.' How far do you agree with this statement? Explain your answer. (16 marks + 4 SPaG)

The secret of writing a good essay is good planning. Here is a plan.

Plan	Purpose/points to include	Comment
Introduction	You state your view on how far you agree or disagree	This sets your essay off on a positive track and gives you an argument to hold on to throughout your answer
		The question asks 'how far you agree …' so words and phrases such as 'mostly', 'partly', 'totally' will be useful
Paragraph 1	Reasons to agree. Explain how the issue mentioned in the statement ('Hitler's aggression') helped lead to war	This helps ensure you stay focused on the actual statement
		Make sure you support everything you say with detailed and precise knowledge
Paragraph 2	Reasons to disagree. Explain at least one other factor that helped lead to war (for example the Treaty of Versailles)	This is your chance to shine. Whether you write about one other cause or more than one depends how quickly you think and write. But it's better to explain one cause thoroughly than more than one superficially
		You can link these reasons back to Hitler's aggression if you think the two things are linked
		Once again make sure you support everything you say with detailed and precise knowledge
Conclusion	You state your judgement as to how far you agree or disagree and give one key argument as to why	This should be easy to write if you have kept your focus through the rest of the essay
		There are four marks for spelling, punctuation and grammar so use your final minutes to check your work and correct it if necessary

- Step 1: in note form write down two reasons to agree with the statement, and two reasons to disagree.
- Step 2: decide on your argument – based on your notes in step 1. How far do you agree or disagree? Stick with that conclusion when you write your essay.
- Step 3: (in the exam) this step would be to write your full essay, but for this task just practise writing your conclusion.

TIP

Candidates find it hard to give time to planning in an actual exam which is why it is very important to practise it before the exam so that it becomes instinctive.

Study Source A on page 99.

Question 1: Opinion of a source

How do you know that Source A supports Britain and opposes Germany?   (4 marks)

The source is from a British magazine and shows Germany wriggling to try and avoid being punished. The Germans are shown as dangerous people. The British person appears to be shown as a policeman keeping order. It is warning British people that Germany would protest about its punishment – but that the protest should be ignored.

> Identifies relevant features
> Uses knowledge to explain

Study Sources D and E on page 109.

Question 2: Usefulness of sources

How useful are Sources D and E to a historian studying the failure of the League of Nations over Abyssinia? Explain your answer using Sources D and E and your contextual knowledge.   (12 marks)

Source D (the cartoon) is useful because it shows the view of a famous British magazine at the start of the crisis in 1935. It is intended to remind the British public how weak the mechanisms of the League are, and quite probably intended to encourage the British government into more explicit action.

> This answer opens by directly addressing the question. This shows the examiner that you have understood, but will also help you to focus your answer as you write

Its title 'The Awful Warning' reflects the situation at the time. Mussolini was not likely to stop his aggressive policies just by threats of sanctions at some time in the future. The League lacked an army; and it had few allies by 1935 as Germany and Japan had both left the League. The USA was still neutral. Therefore, the cartoon is excellent for highlighting the weaknesses of the League which led to its failure over Abyssinia the following year.

> Uses contextual knowledge to test the details or the claims made in the source

Source E comes from a speech at the end of the crisis, and its purpose was to tell both Parliament and the British public that they have to be realistic. Sanctions did not work; they were an inadequate weapon against an enemy who continued the invasion before sanctions could possibly have any effect.

> Here the answer refers to the provenance of the source and uses this to judge its utility

The failure of sanctions was recognised by the British and French governments during the crisis with an attempted compromise (the Hoare–Laval Pact). When this secret proposal became public knowledge, the weakness of the League was openly recognised. The secret deal would have by-passed the League altogether. It shows how irrelevant the League had become by 1937 for dealing with aggressive dictators and keeping world peace.

> Here the answer uses contextual knowledge that links back to the question

Question 3: Write an account

Write an account of how Hitler's foreign policy made Germany stronger by the end of 1935.

(8 marks)

Germany had become stronger by the end of 1935 because Hitler had ignored some of the details of the Treaty of Versailles – and Britain and France allowed this to happen. He started a policy of rearmament, manufacturing more weapons, and recruiting more men into the army. He was ignoring the limit of 100,000 troops stipulated in the Treaty of Versailles and by 1935 boasted that he had more than five times that number – 550,000. He also started a policy of conscription at that time, and this guaranteed that his armies consisted of fit and trained personnel.

Germany was also potentially stronger by the end of 1935 because of the Anglo-German Naval Agreement of that year. This allowed Germany to increase the size of its navy to up to 35 per cent of the size of the British navy. This reflected the fact that Britain had agreed that Germany could ignore a key clause in the terms of the 1919 treaty.

Germany also become stronger industrially when it regained the important area of the Saar in 1935. The 1919 treaty had given the area to the League of Nations for fifteen years, after which the people of the area could vote for which ruler they wanted. In a plebiscite over 90 per cent voted to return to Germany.

Hitler had also made Germany stronger by forging alliances. He saw the importance of the Fascist dictator Mussolini and he aimed to increase Nazi support in Austria with the intention of absorbing that country into Germany. Although his first attempt in 1934 failed, a large proportion of Austrians would have been in favour of it happening then – and were certainly in favour in 1938 when it happened.

> The answer opens with a statement which is directly relevant to the question

> Here the answer uses precise knowledge. It is crucial that you use as much relevant detailed knowledge as possible to show your grasp of the topic

> Use of different phrases to show the importance of each development

> Each paragraph opens with a clear link back to the question. This helps make sure your account is analytical

Question 4: How far do you agree? (Essay)

'The outbreak of war in September 1939 was due to the actions of Hitler.' How far do you agree with this statement? Explain your answer.

(16 marks + 4 SPaG)

It is easy to argue that Hitler was largely responsible for the outbreak of war in September 1939, but it is important not to forget other contributory factors which aided him in his ambitions.

> The answer opens by directly addressing the statement in the question

The actions of Hitler caused war because he was the aggressor. It was he who ordered the invasion of Czechoslovakia in March 1939 and Poland in September 1939, and ignored all agreements that he had made. In particular, he totally ignored the fact that he had signed the Munich Agreement less than a year before.

> Each paragraph opens with a clear argument which is focused on the question

It was also Hitler's responsibility because he signed the Nazi–Soviet Pact in August 1939 with the explicit intention of ensuring that when he attacked western Europe he would not be attacked from the east. In other words, he could avoid the war on two fronts that had largely been responsible for Germany's defeat in the First World War. This cynical signing of the pact with his long-term enemy showed the degree of cunning he was willing to use in order to build up his Third Reich bit by bit in the next few years showing that he must be given responsibility for starting the war.

> The argument in the paragraph is then supported by a range of detailed, specific knowledge

> This links the evidence to the question

On the other hand, Hitler was aided by circumstances in Europe at the time, some of which stemmed back to the end of the First World War and others to the economic consequences of the Wall Street Crash.

It was the injustices of the Treaty of Versailles that gave Hitler the opportunity to summon such widespread support in Germany for an aggressive policy. If Germany had not been punished so much, the German nation would not have been so susceptible to propaganda about righting the injustices of 1919. In particular, war guilt was deeply resented by almost all Germans.

The policy of appeasement followed by Britain and France led Hitler to believe that those countries were weak and would do anything to avoid war. Hitler had gambled several times and won – and thought he could continue doing this when he invaded Poland. Indeed, he was mildly surprised when Britain actually declared war over Poland on 3 September 1939. He believed that Britain and France would continue to buy time by not declaring war.

Hence Hitler was clearly responsible; it was his Panzer divisions that started warfare on 1 September 1939. Yet only because of other circumstances was he confident of success – the alliance with the USSR, the weaknesses of Britain and France, and the backing of a German nation believing that Germany's greatest time as a nation was about to be fulfilled.

> The answer fulfils the requirement to form a complex explanation by linking reasons together before coming to an overall judgement

Glossary: Conflict and tension, 1918–1939

Anti-Comintern Pact An alliance in 1936–37 between Germany, Italy and Japan against Communist USSR

Appeasement The policy followed by Britain and France in the 1930s towards Hitler, giving him what he wanted to keep peace

Assembly of the League of Nations The part of the League where all member states were represented equally

Big Three Woodrow Wilson (President of the USA); Georges Clemenceau (Prime Minister of France); David Lloyd George (Prime Minister of Britain)

Collective security Cooperation between allies to strengthen security for each of them

Commissions In connection with the League of Nations, agencies with particular responsibilities, for example refugees

Conscription A system whereby people are forced to join the army or navy

Council In connection with the League of Nations, the body where a few countries (including Britain, France, Italy and Japan) could make detailed decisions

Covenant of League of Nations A document which all members of the League had to sign guaranteeing to carry out the League's policies

Demilitarised An area without armed troops or weapons

Diktat Term used in Germany to describe the Treaty of Versailles because Germany had no say in the terms of the treaty

Disarmament Getting rid of military forces and weapons

Economic sanctions Deciding not to trade with a country as a punishment

Fascist Extreme right-wing supporters, such as the Nazis in Germany and Mussolini's party in Italy

Fourteen Points The proposals for a peace settlement made by President Wilson in January 1918 before the end of the First World War

Idealist Someone who hopes for the future and ignores the harsh realities of life

League of Nations The international organisation set up in 1919 intended to prevent future wars by solving disputes peacefully

Lebensraum Additional territory believed to be necessary by a country for its natural development, for example Germany in the 1930s

Mandates Authority given by the League of Nations to one of its members to rule a territory on behalf of the League

Moral condemnation Shaming a country into seeing that it is in the wrong

Nationalities Groups of people with a common language or culture, and often their own government

Nazi–Soviet Pact The alliance between Germany and the USSR in August 1939 which made the Second World War almost inevitable

Permanent Court of International Justice International court at The Hague intended to adjudicate on international disputes

Reparations Compensation paid by Germany to France, Belgium, Britain and other states as a result of the First World War

Ruhr Area of Germany that is very industrial; occupied by France in 1923

Secretariat of League of Nations The huge number of clerical workers at all levels who were tasked with the job of maintaining the machinery of government of the League

Self-determination Where the people of an area decide their own political future

Sudetenland Area of Czechoslovakia where most people spoke German

War Guilt Clause Clause 231 of Treaty of Versailles which blamed Germany and its allies for the First World War

Chapter 6 Conflict and tension between East and West, 1945–1972

6.1 The end of the Second World War and relations between the superpowers

The **USA and USSR** had been **hostile to and suspicious** of each other before the war

- The USA (**capitalist**) and USSR (**Communist**) were the leading **superpowers**.
- They had been allies against Hitler but had differing **ideologies**.

The USA was capitalist	The USSR was Communist
• **Business and property** owned by individuals, who make profits • **Inequality** between rich and poor • **Parties:** many political parties • **Personal freedom:** individual rights such as free speech or a free press valued	• **Business and property** owned and run by the government • **Greater equality** between rich and poor • **One-party state:** all candidates are from the Communist Party • **Control:** individual rights were seen as less important than the needs of the state. Personal freedom was limited

- The USA had deported thousands of suspected Communists in the 1920s.
- The policy of **appeasement** in the 1930s made the USSR mistrust Britain.

At **Yalta**, the USA and USSR seemed to **negotiate and compromise** successfully

- In February 1945, the leaders of the USSR, the USA and Britain (Stalin, Roosevelt and Churchill) met at Yalta to agree what should happen after the war was over.

Agreements at Yalta	Disagreement
• Stalin would join the war against Japan when Germany surrendered • They would divide Germany into zones run by USSR, USA, Britain and France • They would hunt down and prosecute Nazi war criminals • They would join the new **United Nations Organisation** • Countries of Eastern Europe would hold free elections once they were freed from Nazi occupation. • However they also agreed that Eastern Europe would be a **Soviet sphere of influence** (an area which the USSR had some control over)	The only real disagreement was about Poland. Stalin wanted to move the border of the USSR further into Poland. The USA and Britain did not like this, but felt they had to agree

Five months later (July 1945) at **Potsdam**, many things changed leading to a number of **disagreements**

- Britain and the USA had new leaders, Attlee and Truman. Truman was more anti-Communist than Roosevelt had been.
- Stalin's armies controlled much of Eastern Europe.
- Stalin had set up a Communist government in Poland and wanted to set up pro-**Soviet** governments throughout Eastern Europe. Truman saw this as evidence that Stalin wanted to build up a Soviet Empire.
- Stalin wanted to cripple Germany but Truman disagreed. Stalin demanded $10 billion compensation from Germany.

> **Key point**
>
> There were ideological differences between the USA and USSR, but these were made worse by disagreements about what Europe should look like after the end of the war.

> **TIP**
>
> All the key terms in **purple** are defined in the glossary at the end of each chapter.
>
> Make sure that you can spell the key terms, know what they mean and aim to use them in your written work.

> **Test yourself**
>
> 1 List three ideological differences between the USA and USSR.
> 2 List three agreements at Yalta.
> 3 List three reasons for disagreement at Potsdam.

The **USA** developed an **atom bomb** which deepened the **mistrust** between the two sides

- The USA developed this weapon in secret, even though it was an ally of the USSR in the war.
- Truman told Stalin about the atom bomb at the Potsdam Conference.
- On 6 August 1945, the USA dropped the first atom bomb on Japan. Some historians believe this was done partly as a warning to Stalin.

 Develop the detail

The diagram below gives reasons for growing tension between the USA and USSR. Add supporting detail. One example has been done for you.

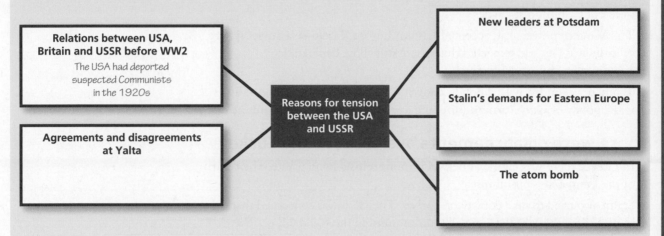

Relations between USA, Britain and USSR before WW2
The USA had deported suspected Communists in the 1920s

Agreements and disagreements at Yalta

Reasons for tension between the USA and USSR

New leaders at Potsdam

Stalin's demands for Eastern Europe

The atom bomb

 Spot the opinion in a source

The first question on your depth study paper will be based on a source. You will be told what its viewpoint is and you have to explain how you know that. For example:

Source A is criticising the British. How do you know? Explain your answer using Source A and your contextual knowledge. (4 marks)

Complete the sentence starters below to plan an answer to the question above.

A Churchill has a sword in his belt. This suggests that he is …

B Churchill's sign says that 'the Anglo-Saxons must rule the world'. This suggests that he wants …

C One of the flags has an atom bomb attached. This suggests that Britain is threatening the USSR by …

D Churchill's shadow is turned into Nazi leaders Hitler and Goebbels. This implies that …

SOURCE A *A Soviet cartoon from 1946. One of Churchill's flags says 'the Anglo-Saxons must rule the world', the other threatens an 'Iron Curtain'.*

6.2 The Iron Curtain and the evolution of East–West rivalry

Soviet expansion in Eastern Europe caused increased tension between the USA and USSR

- By 1946, there were Communist governments in Poland, Albania, Hungary, Romania and Bulgaria. They were all loyal to Stalin.
- Churchill described the border between these countries and Western Europe as an **Iron Curtain**.
- Stalin used secret police to tighten his control over countries in Eastern Europe. In 1947, **Cominform** was set up to co-ordinate the work of the different Communist Parties.
- The Western powers had accepted Eastern Europe should be a Soviet sphere of influence, but had expected this would still allow democratic governments in Eastern Europe.
- Truman responded with a policy known as the **Truman Doctrine**. This was a policy of **containment** (stopping any further spread of Communism).

> **Key point**
>
> The period from 1946 to 1949 saw increased tension over Soviet control in Eastern Europe. The USA began to take action to stop the spread of Communism.

There were disagreements over Greece and Turkey

- In Greece there was civil war between **monarchists** (who wanted the return of the king) and Communists.
- Stalin also tried to take control of Turkey. The USA was concerned that this would allow the USSR to spread Communism in the Middle East. The Americans were also concerned as Turkey was important for its oil reserves.
- Truman persuaded the US Congress to grant $400 million aid to Greece and Turkey. This made Turkey an ally of the USA and helped the monarchists in Greece. However, it harmed relations with the USSR.

Marshall Aid aimed to stop the spread of Communism

- Truman sent General Marshall to assess the post-war situation in Europe. He found ruined economies and extreme shortages.
- His **Marshall Plan** proposed $17 billion aid to help rebuild Europe. Marshall believed tackling poverty would make it harder for Communism to spread.
- In 1947, Truman tried to get Congress to approve this aid. He failed.
- In 1948, however, the Communists took control in Czechoslovakia. This shocked Congress who granted the aid (known as Marshall Aid).
- Stalin was suspicious of Marshall Aid. He banned Communist states from applying for it. Stalin set up his own version, called **Comecon**.

> **TIP**
>
> In your exam you have about a minute writing time per mark! So don't waste time on the low-tariff questions. Save time for the 16-mark essay questions.

The Berlin Blockade brought the two sides close to war

- In 1948, Britain, France and the USA combined their zones into one to allow the German economy to recover more quickly.
- Stalin worried that Germany was being built up deliberately. His response was the Berlin Blockade.
- Berlin was deep in the Soviet zone (see the map on page 123). In June 1948, Stalin closed links between Berlin and the West which left West Berlin without supplies.
- To use tanks to move the roadblocks would be seen as an act of war. Instead, the allies flew supplies to Berlin (the **Berlin Airlift**).

 Test yourself

1. How did Stalin begin to take control of Eastern Europe?
2. What was the Truman Doctrine?
3. What was the Marshall Plan?

Quick quizzes at **www.hoddereducation.co.uk/myrevisionnotes**

- There was a fear that the Soviets would shoot down planes which would start a war. But this never happened.

- Although there were shortages, the airlift kept West Berlin going. After eleven months Stalin reopened the links.

- After the blockade, Germany was formally divided into two countries: the **Federal Republic of Germany** (West Germany) and the **German Democratic Republic** (East Germany, under Soviet control).

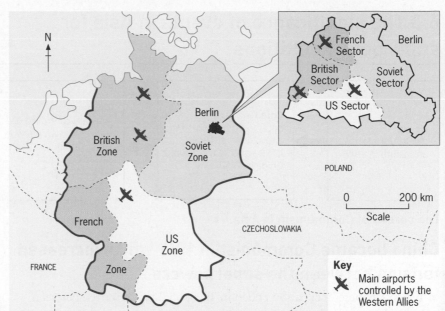

Germany in 1948.

 ## Spot the opinion in a source

Source B is criticising the USSR. How do you know? Explain your answer by using Source B and your contextual knowledge. (4 marks)

SOURCE B *An American cartoon published in the 1940s commenting on Stalin's takeover of Eastern Europe.*

Copy and complete the sentence starters below.

A Hat shows that ...

B Sharp teeth and claws show that ...

C The bear is drooling which suggests that ...

D The bear is reaching around the whole globe which suggests that ...

E This cartoon is reacting to (what events – use your own knowledge) ...

 ## Key events

Write an account of how tension in Europe developed between the USA and USSR 1946–1949. (8 marks)

What the examiner is looking for in a 'write an account' question is

- relevant, detailed and accurate knowledge ...

- well organised into an orderly account ...

- which answers the question!

So that means you need to know things, and you need to have a clear structure in your head. This task helps you with structure.

Make a flow chart to show how the events of 1946–49 increased tension between the USA and the USSR. You will need at least three boxes.

Stalin controlled Eastern Europe in 1946
Germany was divided into two zones: the FDR and the GDR

 ## Practice question

'The main reason for the development of the Cold War, 1945–48, was the occupation of Eastern Europe by the USSR.' How far do you agree with this statement? Explain your answer. (16 marks)

6.3 The significance of events in Asia for superpower relations

REVISED

Korea –
divided into North and South in 1948

China –
became Communist after a revolution in 1949. USSR signed a treaty with China in 1950

Vietnam –
originally controlled by France who withdrew in 1954. Communist forces gained control of North Vietnam

The spread of Communism in Asia.

China became Communist in 1949 which increased tension between the superpowers

- When Japanese occupation ended in 1945, civil war restarted between Nationalists and Communists in China.
- The USA backed the Nationalists, although they were unpopular and poorly led.
- By 1949, the Communists led by Mao Zedong triumphed. The most populous country in the world was now Communist.
- In February 1950, the USSR signed a treaty of friendship with China.
- In America, this led to an even greater fear of Communism. Truman's policy of containment seemed to have failed in Asia.
- Under US influence the **United Nations** (UN) refused to recognise the new Communist leadership. Instead the ousted leader Chiang Kai-Shek in exile in Taiwan represented China.
- The USSR protested by **boycotting** (refusing to take part in) the UN Security Council. This proved very important in what happened next!

The USA and its allies were dragged into a war in Korea

1948: Korea divided into two countries	June 1950: Invasion	July 1950: UN Resolution	September 1950: UN invasion
North Korea was a Communist **dictatorship** supported by the USSR and China South Korea was anti-Communist and supported by the USA. It was not run very democratically either	Both North and South Korea claimed the whole country. In 1950, North Korea invaded South Korea. Most of the South was quickly taken over	The Americans proposed that the UN intervene to help South Korea. This would have been vetoed by the USSR but they were boycotting the UN. The resolution passed without opposition	A UN force (mostly American troops, but supported by other countries including Britain) was sent to fight against Communist North Korea. The UN forces were led by the American General MacArthur

The Korean War worsened the relationship between the USSR and the USA and led the USSR to distrust the UN

- The Korean War was the first time the divisions between East and West were played out in a physical conflict.
- Both sides used the conflict to test out new weapons such as advanced jet aircraft and faster tanks.
- The war quickly became a **stalemate** (neither side could win). A peace treaty was signed in 1953.
- The UN had proved it could take effective action, although it could only do this because the USSR had not been present.
- The USSR returned to its seat at the UN Security Council and was careful not to miss any other important votes.

The outbreak of **war in Vietnam** further **divided the** superpowers

- From 1945 to 1954, Vietnam was ruled by France, but a group of Communist fighters called the **Viet Cong** fought against French rule.
- The USA provided financial aid to France to fight the Communists.
- In 1954, the French withdrew. Vietnam was temporarily divided into North and South Vietnam.
- The USA continued to send aid to the South (which was anti-Communist). The North was supported by the USSR and China.

 Test yourself

1 When did the Korean War start and finish?
2 Why did the USA become involved in Vietnam?
3 What was 'containment'?

 Develop the detail

Below are some correct statements about the Cold War in Asia but each one is too vague for an exam answer. Use your own knowledge to add relevant supporting details. The first has been done for you.

Vague statement	Developed with detailed knowledge
UN troops fought in Korea	A UN resolution was passed to intervene to defend South Korea. A UN force was sent to South Korea, although it mostly consisted of American troops and was led by US General MacArthur
China and the USSR signed a treaty	
The USA and USSR were both involved in the Vietnam War	
Korea was divided into North and South	

 Improve the paragraph

Write an account of how events in Asia between 1949 and 1960 affected the development of the Cold War. (8 marks)

When you write an account you don't write 'everything you know about ...' a topic. You have to select carefully and refer everything back to the focus of the question: in this case 'how events in Asia affected the development of the Cold War'.

The paragraph below contains relevant information but could be improved. Rewrite it to make it better by:

- giving it structure
- linking everything back to the question.

Events in Asia involved the USA and USSR. Vietnam had been controlled by the French. There was a Communist group called the Viet Cong which were fighting against the French. The USA was giving them financial aid. The USSR and China supported North Vietnam. This is similar to Korea. In Korea the country was divided between North and South along the 38th parallel. The North invaded the South in 1950. The UN sent troops to support the South. The USSR had boycotted the UN Security Council so it couldn't oppose the proposal to send the troops. General MacArthur led the UN forces and there were soldiers from other countries including Britain. Also China had become Communist in 1949.

6.4 Military rivalries between the superpowers

Both superpowers created **military alliances** which **increased tension** between the USA and USSR

- During the **Berlin Blockade** Truman saw how easily Soviet troops could invade Western Europe while the USA would have to send troops across the Atlantic. He wanted European bases for US troops.
- In April 1949, some Western powers formed the **North Atlantic Treaty Organisation** (NATO). It allowed the USA to base troops in Europe. Members agreed to defend each other if they were invaded.
- The USSR was furious that the USA had developed a **military bloc**.
- The Soviets were more alarmed in 1955, when West Germany joined NATO and was allowed its own army.
- In response, the new leader of the USSR, Khrushchev, created a military bloc called the **Warsaw Pact** in 1955. This included all Communist countries in Eastern Europe except Yugoslavia.

> **Key point**
>
> In the 1950s, the superpowers developed powerful military alliances and spent huge amounts of money competing to have the best military and space technology.

From 1949 the USA and USSR were locked in an **arms race** to develop more powerful nuclear weapons

- The USA dropped the first atom bomb in 1945.
- By 1949, the USSR had its own atom bomb. This shocked the USA who thought it would take the USSR longer to develop its own atom bomb.
- The USA boosted its spending on defence and military technology. Forty per cent of US defence spending went to the air force during the Cold War.
- In 1952, the USA developed a **hydrogen bomb** (H-bomb) – 1000 times more powerful than the atom bomb. In 1953, the USSR did the same.
- In 1954, the USA developed an H-bomb which could be dropped from a plane. The USSR did the same just a few months later.

Superpower rivalry also led to a 'space race'

- In 1955, Eisenhower announced US plans to make a satellite (which could orbit the Earth from space).
- In 1957, the USSR beat the Americans to it when it launched the satellite *Sputnik*. In 1957, the USSR also sent a second, larger satellite called *Sputnik II* into space. This time it carried a dog.
- The USA increased funding for space programmes. In 1958, it launched its *Explorer I* satellite and **NASA** was set up.
- In 1961, the USSR shocked the USA again by sending the first man into space, Yuri Gagarin.
- President Kennedy set up the **Apollo** programme which aimed to put a man on the moon. By July 1969 this was achieved.

> **TIP**
>
> A possible writing frame for a question 2 answer will be in four paragraphs, two for each source (one on provenance and another on content).
>
> In your exam you won't actually be asked to compare the two sources but you can write about how they are more useful together than separately.

Space technology led to more dangerous missiles

- The technology that sent rockets into space could also launch nuclear missiles. This was one reason why the superpowers spent so much on their space programmes.
- Khrushchev built a top-secret rocket base called Baykonyr.
- In 1957, the USSR tested the world's first **intercontinental ballistic missile** (ICBM) which could be fired into space and then brought down on a target anywhere in the world.

> ✏️ **Test yourself**
>
> 1 When were NATO and the Warsaw Pact formed?
>
> 2 What developments in the arms race occurred in 1949, 1952 and 1953?
>
> 3 What was a) *Sputnik* and b) ICBM?

- In 1959, the USA developed its own ICBM system. In 1960, the Americans developed Polaris missiles which could be fired from submarines (which made them harder to detect).
- In 1960, the media in the USA reported a '**missile gap**' between the USA and USSR which caused panic. President Eisenhower knew there was no missile gap because of secret intelligence but he couldn't reveal this information to the public.

✎ Evaluate usefulness

Question 2 of your exam will ask you to consider the usefulness of two sources. For example:

Study Sources C and D. How useful are these two sources to a historian studying American attitudes towards the space race at the beginning of the 1960s? Explain your answer using Sources C and D and your contextual knowledge. (12 marks)

You will need to think about:

- Provenance: who made the source, when and why?
- Content: what it says. Does it agree with what you know? What do you know about this topic that it does not mention?

Next to the sources are points that you might make or features you need to notice. Draw lines and add notes.

SOURCE C *The logo of the Apollo 11 mission, 1969.*

A This is a bald eagle. In the source it looks …

B The eagle is landing on the moon. This is because the aim of the mission was …

C The eagle is holding an olive branch (a symbol of peace). However, the space race was not entirely peaceful because rocket technology could be used for …

D The source is a logo produced by NASA, so it might emphasise …

SOURCE D *Extracts from a speech by US President John F. Kennedy. Kennedy became President in January 1961.*

First, I believe that this nation should commit itself to achieving the goal, before this decade is out, of landing a man on the Moon and returning him safely to the Earth. No single space project in this period will be more impressive to mankind, or more important in the long-range exploration of space; and none will be so difficult or expensive to accomplish.

A Kennedy says that the reason for trying to land on the moon is …

B However, another reason for the moon landings was …

C Because this speech is by the US President, he might focus on …

Challenge: write up your notes as a full answer.

6.5 The thaw, reforms in Hungary and the U-2 crisis

The new Soviet leader, Nikita Khrushchev, was very different from Stalin

- Stalin died in 1953. He was a hero to millions of people, and it took two years for Khrushchev to emerge as the new leader of the USSR.
- Khrushchev talked about peaceful **coexistence** (living together peacefully) with the West.
- He planned to reduce the USSR's spending on its military.
- He followed a policy of **de-Stalinisation**.

> **Key point**
>
> Under Khrushchev there was some reduction in the conflict between the USSR and USA, but crises in Hungary and over the U-2 incident continued to keep the tension high.

Rebellion against Soviet rule in Hungary led to an attempt to reform Communism

- Khrushchev's apparent relaxation of control in the USSR led to opposition to the Communist regime in Hungary.
- Many Hungarians hated having Soviet troops in their country, and the restrictions imposed by their hard-line Communist leaders.
- In October 1956, at a huge student protest in Budapest, a statue of Stalin was pulled down.
- The USSR allowed a new government to form under the control of a moderate leader Imre Nagy. The Soviet army began to withdraw from Hungary. Local councils were set up to replace Soviet power. Thousands of Hungarian soldiers joined the rebels.
- Nagy announced publicly that he planned to leave the Warsaw Pact, to reintroduce private ownership of farms and to declare Hungary neutral in the Cold War.

Relaxed the USSR's control on Eastern Europe

Removed Soviet troops from Austria

Criticised Stalin in a speech in 1956, especially the **purges**

Released political prisoners

De-Stalinisation under Khrushchev

Closed down Cominform

Improved relations with Marshal Tito in Yugoslavia

Dismissed Molotov (Stalin's controversial Foreign Minister)

Khrushchev crushed the uprising once Nagy threatened to leave the Warsaw Pact

- To start with, Khrushchev seemed to accept the changes in Hungary. However, he was not willing to let Hungary leave the Warsaw Pact.
- In November, Soviet troops and tanks moved into Budapest.
- Hungarians fought back, but they were defeated in two weeks. Thousands were killed. 200,000 Hungarians fled into Austria. Nagy and other Hungarian leaders were executed. A new leader, Kádár, took over and arrested 35,000 people for anti-Communist activities.
- Khrushchev sent extra troops to Hungary and forced the Hungarians to pay for them.
- The Western powers were too distracted by the **Suez crisis** to do much more than condemn the actions of the USSR in Hungary.

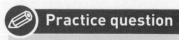 **Practice question**

Write an account of how events in Hungary in 1956 affected the Cold War.

(8 marks)

The **capture of a US pilot** led to the U-2 crisis in 1960

- Since 1950, the USA had flown spy planes over the USSR to gather **intelligence** (secret information) about their nuclear weapons.
- Their **U–2** spy planes flew very high but carried powerful cameras which could read a newspaper on the ground from 23 km.
- The USSR knew about these flights but they flew so high that they did not have the technology to shoot them down.
- In 1960, the USSR managed to shoot down one of the planes and capture its pilot, Gary Powers. This happened just before a major meeting between the USSR and the Western powers at the Paris Peace Summit.
- The USA eventually admitted that Powers was on a spying mission and Khrushchev pulled out of the conference.
- Powers was jailed but he was soon swapped for a captured Soviet spy.

 Test yourself

1 List three reforms made by Imre Nagy which were accepted by Khrushchev.
2 What reform did Khrushchev object to?
3 What was a U–2?

 Develop the explanation

The top marks in an exam are always given for the ability to explain.

Column 1 of this table lists some key events from this topic. Complete the second column by explaining the consequences of this event for superpower relations. The first one is done for you.

Event	Consequence for superpower relations (the response or outcome or importance)
Khrushchev became the new leader of the Soviet Union	He introduced a policy of de-Stalinisation which aimed to reduce the hostility with the West and give more freedom to Eastern European countries under Soviet control
Imre Nagy became the new leader of Hungary	
Nagy said he intended to take Hungary out of the Warsaw Pact	
Gary Powers was shot down over the USSR	

 Support or challenge?

The most valuable question on your exam will be worth 16 marks and will ask you how far you agree with a statement. For example:

'Under Khrushchev the tension between the superpowers decreased.' How far do you agree with this statement? (16 marks + 4 for SPaG)

For each of the events below, decide whether it agrees or disagrees with the statement in this question.

Challenge: Add one more piece of evidence on either side.

Evidence	Support	Challenge
Khrushchev talked about peaceful 'coexistence' between the USA and USSR		
He closed down Cominform		
Soviet tanks were sent to crush the uprising in Hungary		
Soviet troops were removed from Austria		
Nagy and other Hungarian leaders were executed		

Part 2: The development of the Cold War

6.6 The Berlin Wall and Kennedy's response

Berlin had been a key area of conflict between the Western powers and the USSR since the end of the Second World War

- Berlin was divided between East Berlin (part of the USSR) and West Berlin which was a free, capitalist state. However there were also US troops in West Berlin.
- The Western powers had poured a lot of money into West Berlin. Many people in East Berlin thought that standards of living were much better in the West.
- East Germany was ruled by Walter Ulbricht. He was a hard-line Communist and many hated his rule.
- After the Hungarian uprising was crushed by Khrushchev, many people realised that there was no way to end Soviet control of their countries.
- Because of these issues, many East Germans travelled to West Berlin, where they could then travel on to West Germany and escape Soviet control.
- Lots of the people who left were skilled workers which had a significant economic impact on East Germany. It also made life under Communism look bad compared to life under capitalism.

Key point

Berlin was always a key area in the Cold War struggle, but in 1961 the building of the Berlin wall nearly caused a war between the USA and USSR over the border between East and West Germany.

In 1961, Khrushchev built the Berlin Wall to divide East and West Berlin

- This wall began as a barbed wire fence. It stopped anyone from travelling from East Berlin to West Berlin.
- It was soon replaced with a thick concrete wall and guarded by soldiers. These soldiers had orders to shoot anyone who tried to cross the wall.
- There was now only one place (called **Checkpoint Charlie**) where people could cross between East and West Berlin.
- Many people were divided from their families, or from their workplaces.

The building of the wall nearly led to armed conflict between US and Soviet tanks

- After the building of the wall, US diplomats (government representatives who deal with other countries) and soldiers had continued to cross into East Berlin.
- However, in October 1961, Soviet tanks blocked Checkpoint Charlie and refused to allow anyone to cross the border.
- US tanks then pulled up to the border and for eighteen hours there was a real risk that one of the tanks would fire and cause a war.
- Eventually, the tanks slowly retreated. As a result the wall stayed, and did not come down until 1989.

TIP

Remember that all sources are useful for something. It all depends on what you are using them for. Never dismiss a source as useless because it is one-sided or incomplete. It will be still be very useful for finding out about the attitudes of the person who made it.

Test yourself

1 Why did people from East Germany choose to cross into West Berlin?
2 When was the Berlin Wall constructed?
3 How did the building of the wall nearly lead to a conflict between the USA and the USSR?

Develop the explanation

Complete the diagram below to explain why each of these reasons led people from East Germany to cross into West Berlin.

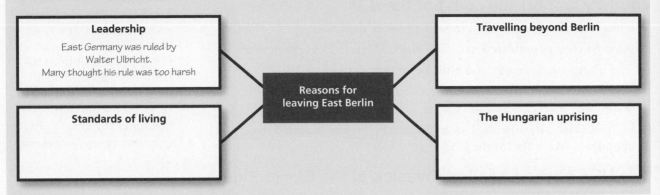

Leadership East Germany was ruled by Walter Ulbricht. Many thought his rule was too harsh	**Travelling beyond Berlin**
Reasons for leaving East Berlin	
Standards of living	**The Hungarian uprising**

 Support or challenge?

'The Space Race was the main reason for developing tension between the superpowers from 1957 to 1961.' How far do you agree with this statement? Explain your answer. (16 marks +4 SPaG)

You should use information from the last five pages to decide whether each of the statements below supports or challenges the statement in the question.

Evidence	Support	Challenge
In 1957, the USSR launched the first man-made satellite called *Sputnik*		
Soviet tanks were used to crush the Hungarian uprising		
In 1960, US U-2 pilot Gary Powers was shot down over the USSR		
In 1961, the USSR sent the first man into space, Yuri Gagarin		
The USA developed Polaris missiles which could be fired from submarines and were very hard to detect		
Khrushchev tightened Soviet control over Warsaw Pact countries after the Hungarian uprising		

 Practice question

Look at Sources E and F. How useful are these two sources to a historian studying the reasons for the construction of the Berlin Wall? Explain your answer using Sources E and F and your contextual knowledge.

(12 marks)

SOURCE E *Extracts from a speech by President Kennedy in June 1963.*

[There are] a few who say that it is true that Communism is an evil system, but it permits us to make economic progress. Let them come to Berlin. Freedom has many difficulties and democracy is not perfect, but we have never had to put a wall up to keep our people in, to prevent them from leaving us.

SOURCE F *A Soviet cartoon produced in 1959. The caption reads 'The socialist stallion far outclasses the capitalist donkey'.*

6.7 The causes and impact of the Cuban Missile Crisis

In 1959 the Cuban revolution created a Communist country just off the coast of the USA

- Cuba is an island just 160 km from the coast of the USA.
- Rich Americans holidayed in Cuba. The USA also had warships there.
- The USA gave economic and military support to Cuba.
- The Cuban leader Batista was corrupt and unpopular. In 1958 his army was defeated by rebels led by Fidel Castro.
- In 1959, Castro became the Cuban leader. He arrested or **exiled** many opponents. Many fled to the USA.

The USA backed a failed invasion at the Bay of Pigs

- Initially, the USA recognised Castro as the new leader of Cuba. Over the next two years the relationship between the USA and Cuba got worse, particularly when Castro took over American-owned businesses in Cuba.
- Cuban exiles in the USA pressurised the President to act.

June 1960	Summer 1960	January 1961	April 1961
President Eisenhower gave the **CIA** permission to try to overthrow Castro. They funded Cuban exiles who were trying to get rid of Castro The USA also investigated ways to damage the Cuban economy, for example damaging Cuban farms	Castro promised to protect Americans living in Cuba and to allow the USA to keep its naval base However, by the summer of 1960 he had signed an agreement with the Soviet Union	President Kennedy broke off **diplomatic relations** (official cooperation) with Cuba. He was determined to overthrow Castro Some argued for a US invasion. But instead the USA supplied weapons and equipment to 1400 Cuban exiles to invade Cuba	The exiles invaded at the **Bay of Pigs**. It was a disaster. They faced 20,000 Cuban troops with tanks. All the exiles were captured or killed. It was a major embarrassment for the USA and for Kennedy

Tension rose in 1962 when the USSR supplied weapons to Cuba

- In May 1962, the USSR announced it was supplying weapons to Cuba.
- By September, Cuba had the best-supplied military in the region. This included missiles, tanks, jet fighters and 5000 Soviet technicians.
- The US seemed willing to allow **conventional** (non-nuclear) Soviet arms on Cuba, but they were very worried about the possibility of the USSR placing nuclear missiles on Cuba.

Tension turned into crisis when USSR sent nuclear missiles to Cuba in October 1962

- In October 1962, an American spy plane photographed nuclear missile sites being built in Cuba. They also reported Soviet ships on their way to Cuba carrying nuclear missiles.
- Some of Kennedy's advisors proposed an invasion of Cuba, or air strikes to destroy the missile sites.
- Kennedy decided instead on a **naval blockade** (stopping the Soviet ships from bringing the missiles to Cuba).
- There was a serious fear this could lead to a nuclear war. However, the ships did not try to break the blockade.
- After four tense days, Khrushchev agreed to remove the missiles from Cuba. Secretly Kennedy agreed to remove US missiles from Turkey.
- The relationship between the superpowers improved after this (see page 136).

Key point

The Cuban Missile Crisis was the closest the Cold War came to an all-out nuclear war, but both the USA and USSR worked hard to avoid this. It led to reduced tension between the superpowers.

TIP

The examiners want you to use relevant and detailed knowledge in your answers. In your revision you should try to remember a specific piece of information associated with each general idea.

✎ **Test yourself**

1 How did the USA respond to Castro's takeover of Cuba?

2 What happened at the Bay of Pigs?

3 What was a naval blockade?

Develop the detail

Write an account of how the Cuban revolution led to a crisis between the USA and the USSR in 1962. (8 marks).

The statements below are accurate but they are too vague. Add some supporting detail to develop them further in answer to the question above.

Statement	Developed with detail
General Batista was replaced by Castro	The revolution was led by Fidel Castro and his Communist-influenced guerrilla movement. He became the new leader of Cuba and the country became sympathetic to Communism
Relations between the USA and Cuba got worse	
The USA tried to get rid of Castro	
The USSR supplied weapons to Cuba	
The crisis brought the world to the brink of nuclear war	

Eliminate irrelevance

'The main reason for escalating tension in the Cold War from 1960 to 1962 was the Bay of Pigs incident.' How far do you agree with this statement? (16 marks + 4 SPaG)

In a timed exam make sure everything you write in an essay is relevant. The paragraph below comes from an answer to the question above. Cross out anything which you think does not help answer this question.

The Bay of Pigs incident was a US-supported attempted invasion to replace Castro as the leader of Cuba. Before this the USA had looked at other ways of overthrowing Castro. The CIA had been given this job. They had come up with a range of ideas such as disrupting plantations in Cuba. There were also economic sanctions which stopped trade with Cuba. Castro had taken over in a revolution in 1959 and the USA did not like having a Communist-leaning country so close to its coastline. Because the invasion was not fully supported by Kennedy it was a disastrous failure and this showed that the USA was not willing to get directly involved in Cuba. This also led to further Soviet support for Cuba which included installing Soviet weapons on Cuba, leading to the later Cuban Missile Crisis.

Practice question

Study Source G. Source G is critical of the USA. How do you know?   (4 marks)

SOURCE G *A 1960 Soviet cartoon. The notice held by the US Secretary of State says to Castro in Cuba: 'I forbid you to make friends with the Soviet Union'.*

6.8 The impact of the Prague Spring (1968) on Cold War relations

The 1960s saw **growing opposition** to Communist rule in **Czechoslovakia** leading to the **Prague Spring**

- Czechoslovakia was one of the most important countries in the Warsaw Pact. It was in the centre of Eastern Europe and it had the most developed industry.
- In December 1967, the old Communist leader resigned. In January 1968, he was replaced by a reformer called Alexander Dubček.
- Dubček wanted to create 'socialism with a human face'. He promised Brezhnev (the new Soviet leader) that Czechoslovakia would not try to leave the Warsaw Pact.
- Dubček reduced censorship and reduced the role of the secret police.
- This led to increasing criticism of Communism by people in Czechoslovakia. Communist leaders were questioned in newspapers and on TV.
- This period became known as the **Prague Spring** (Prague was the capital of Czechoslovakia) because of the new mood and ideas.
- By the summer of 1968, there were plans to allow another political party, the Social Democratic Party, to oppose the Communists in elections.

> ### Key point
> The Soviet response to the Prague Spring showed that the USSR would not tolerate any attempts to reform Communism in Warsaw Pact countries.

Brezhnev responded increasingly harshly to events in Czechoslovakia

- The leaders of other Warsaw Pact countries put pressure on Brezhnev to stop the changes taking place in Czechoslovakia.
- Soviet troops threatened Czechoslovakia by performing training exercises on the border.
- The USSR also considered taking economic action against Czechoslovakia such as cancelling wheat supplies the Czechs depended on.
- In July 1968, at a meeting of all the Warsaw Pact countries, the other leaders called on Czechoslovakia 'to maintain stability'.
- Dubček agreed not to allow the new Social Democratic Party but he kept on with his other reforms. It seemed that he was going to be allowed to do this.
- However, on 20 August 1968, without any warning, Soviet tanks moved into Czechoslovakia. There was no fighting or armed resistance.

After the Prague Spring, Brezhnev set **clear rules for Communist governments** in Eastern Europe

- These rules were called the **Brezhnev Doctrine**. Communist countries had to have **one-party system** (no other political parties were allowed) and be members of the Warsaw Pact.
- Dubček was removed from power. Although he was not killed, he was taken from Czechoslovakia and images of him as a leader were censored.
- This led to more tension between the Western powers and the USSR. There was also increasing hatred of Communism in Czechoslovakia.

 Test yourself

1 What changes did Dubček try to make to Communism in Czechoslovakia?

2 How did the USSR initially deal with Czechoslovakia?

3 What was the Brezhnev Doctrine?

Key events

Below are the events which started and ended the crisis in Czechoslovakia. Complete the four boxes to show how the situation in Czechoslovakia developed.

In 1967 the old Communist leader of Czechoslovakia was replaced by Alexander Dubček					The Brezhnev Doctrine laid down clear rules for Communist countries in the Warsaw Pact

 Structure the detail

Write an account of the Czech crisis to show how this led to the development of tension between the USA and USSR. (8 marks)

Below are some key events in the Czech crisis. How would you structure these into paragraphs for the question above? You will need to think about the following:

● Which order these events occurred in.

● How you could divide them into paragraphs, usually by key turning points or periods (for example, '1967 and the change of leadership')

● How you could link these to the development of tensions between the USA and USSR.

● What other details you might want to include or develop.

A	Dubček considered allowing a new party, the Social Democratic Party
B	Other Warsaw Pact countries wanted Brezhnev to stop reforms in Czechoslovakia
C	The new atmosphere in Czechoslovakia was called the 'Prague Spring'
D	Brezhnev made clear rules for Communist countries in the Brezhnev Doctrine
E	Soviet tanks entered Czechoslovakia
F	Communist leaders were criticised in the media

 Practice question

Study Source H. Source H is criticising the USSR. How do you know? **(4 marks)**

SOURCE H *A street cartoon in Prague*

 TIP

The key thing to remember when you write an account is that you are not only telling a story. It needs to explain the issue in the question. So refer each development back to the focus of the question – the development of tension.

TIP

Refer to at least two details of a source in your answer. Link everything you say to something in the source.

6.9 Détente and the easing of tension

The Cuban Missile Crisis led to attempts to reduce the threat of nuclear weapons

- Both leaders realised how close they had come to nuclear war. A permanent 'hot line' was created so the leaders of the USSR and USA could contact each other directly.
- In 1963, they signed a treaty to ban further tests of nuclear weapons.
- Cuba remained highly armed, and the crisis was seen as a victory for Khrushchev in the Soviet Union.
- In the USA, Kennedy was also respected for his handling of the crisis.

> **Key point**
>
> By the 1970s, tension between the superpowers was reducing. This was helped by agreements to limit the spread of nuclear weapons.

The late 1960s and early 1970s was a period of détente

- **Détente** is a French word meaning a reduction in tension.
- In 1968, the USSR, USA and Britain signed the **Nuclear Non-Proliferation Treaty** to reduce the spread of nuclear weapons.
- There were several reasons for détente:

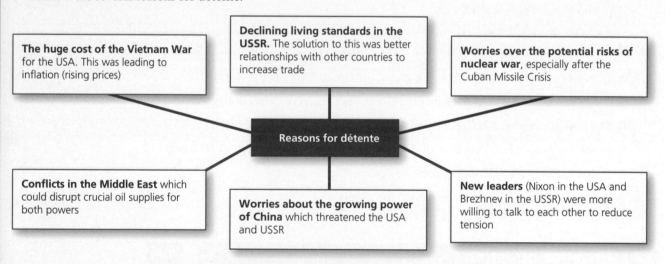

The huge cost of the Vietnam War for the USA. This was leading to inflation (rising prices)

Declining living standards in the USSR. The solution to this was better relationships with other countries to increase trade

Worries over the potential risks of nuclear war, especially after the Cuban Missile Crisis

Conflicts in the Middle East which could disrupt crucial oil supplies for both powers

Reasons for détente

Worries about the growing power of China which threatened the USA and USSR

New leaders (Nixon in the USA and Brezhnev in the USSR) were more willing to talk to each other to reduce tension

The SALT treaties further reduced hostility

- The USA and USSR took part in **Strategic Arms Limitations Talks (SALT)** to agree limits on the number of nuclear weapons.
- After a three-year negotiation, in 1972, the agreement was signed. It limited the ICBMs and anti-ballistic missiles (ABMs) on both sides.
- It also allowed both sides to use spy satellites to check that the other side was keeping to the agreement.
- The agreement lasted five years and was seen as a major achievement.

> **TIP**
>
> Candidates find it hard to give time to planning in an actual exam which is why it is so important to practise it before the exam so that it becomes instinctive.

Test yourself

1 What is the meaning of détente?
2 Why did both sides want to reduce tension?
3 What was agreed at the SALT talks?

Quick quizzes at **www.hoddereducation.co.uk/myrevisionnotes**

Develop the explanation

Below are a series of statements which identify reasons for détente. Develop each one to explain why they reduced tension. The first has been done for you.

Statement	Developed explanation – why it reduced tension and helped détente
The Vietnam War was very costly	There was rising inflation in the USA and declining living standards in the USSR. This encouraged both sides to seek a way out of costly further conflicts and arms development
The Cuban Missile Crisis had brought the world close to nuclear war	
China was becoming more powerful	
Nixon became US President in 1969	

 Essay plan

The question with the most marks in your depth study exam will be an essay question like this.

The main reason for the reduction in tension between the USA and USSR by the early 1970s was the threat posed by nuclear weapons. How far do you agree with this statement? (16 marks +4 SPaG)

The secret of writing a good essay is good planning. Here is a plan.

Plan	Purpose/points to include	Comment
Introduction	You state your view on how far you agree or disagree	You need to open with a clear statement showing your overall answer to the question The question asks 'how far you agree …' so words and phrases such as 'mostly', 'partly', 'totally' will be useful
Paragraph 1	Reasons to agree. Explain how the issue mentioned in the statement (the threat posed by nuclear war) helped reduce tension.	This helps ensure you stay focused on the actual statement Make sure you support everything you say with detailed and precise knowledge
Paragraph 2	Reasons to disagree. Explain at least one other factor that helped reduce tension (for example economic reasons)	You might only write one paragraph here (if that is all you can do in full detail in the time). If you think you can manage to write one or two other reasons in full paragraphs then you should try to do that You can link these reasons back to the threat of nuclear war if you think the two things are linked Once again make sure you support everything you say with detailed and precise knowledge.
A conclusion	You state your judgement as to how far you agree or disagree and give one strong argument as to why	This should be easy to write if you have kept your focus through the rest of the essay There are 4 marks for spelling, punctuation and grammar so use your final minutes to check your work and correct it if necessary

- Step 1: in note form write down two reasons to agree with the statement, and two reasons to disagree.
- Step 2: decide on your argument – based on your notes in step 1. How far do you agree or disagree? Stick with that conclusion when you write your essay.
- Step 3: (in the exam) this step would be to write your full essay, but for this task just practise writing your conclusion.

Part 3: Transformation of the Cold War

Exam focus: Conflict and tension between East and West, 1945–1972

Question 1: Opinion of a source

Study Source B on page 123.

Source B is criticising the USSR. How do you know? Explain your answer by using Source A and your contextual knowledge.　　　　**(4 marks)**

Source B is criticising the USSR by suggesting that they are trying to take over the world. The source suggests that the USSR is a threat to world peace because it is shown as a bear with sharp teeth and claws. The bear is drooling which suggests it is 'hungry' or desperate to control more land. Also the bear is reaching around the whole globe which suggests the USSR is hoping to control more than just Europe. This cartoon is reacting to the fact that the USSR tightened its control over the countries of Eastern Europe in 1947 by setting up the Cominform to coordinate the various Communist parties.

> The answer refers to a number of different details which are shown in the source. It is a good idea to refer to at least two details or sections of a source in your answer

> The answer links these source details to the question and explains them further

Question 2: Usefulness of sources

Study Sources C and D on page 127.

How useful are these two sources to a historian studying American attitudes towards the space race at the beginning of the 1960s? Explain your answer using Sources C and D and your contextual knowledge.　　　　**(12 marks)**

Both of these sources are useful for understanding attitudes to the space race in America, especially in the 1960s. Both sources agree that the moon landing is a key part of the space race, and both openly show that American prestige will be enhanced by a successful moon landing. This is shown by the powerful bald eagle (a bird associated with America) in Source C, and by Kennedy's statement that no achievement would be more impressive. The moon landing was an extremely expensive process for the USA, and a major victory in the space race, but neither source mentions that another reason for the USA pouring all of this money into the moon landing was because the USSR had seemed to be ahead in the space race since 1961 when Yuri Gagarin became the first human in space. The idea that the space race was peaceful, shown by the olive branch in Source C, is inaccurate as both the USA and the USSR also justified the investment in the space race due to the benefits for missile technology which led to the development of the first ICBMs. The sources both share two major limitations to their utility. Firstly, they were both produced in the 1960s which makes them useful for finding out about this highly tense period in the space race but doesn't tell us anything about, for example, earlier attitudes to the space race under Eisenhower. Secondly, both sources are an example of carefully crafted Cold War propaganda and so can only tell us about the attitudes to the space race that the USA wanted to project publicly.

> Here the answer uses contextual knowledge to test the claims made in the sources

> Here the answer refers to the provenance of the sources and uses this to judge their utility

Question 3: Write an account

Write an account of events in Asia between 1949 and 1960 to show how they affected the development of the Cold War. (8 marks)

The rising tension between the superpowers was acted out in global conflicts in the 1950s through their involvement in events in Asia. In 1949, China became Communist when the revolutionaries led by Mao Zedong took over. As China had the biggest population of any country in the world this now meant that a huge number of people were ruled by Communists. Even worse, the US feared that China would now become an ally of the USSR. It did this in 1950 when the USSR and China signed the Treaty of Friendship.

When war broke out in Korea with the invasion of the South by the North the USA found itself supporting the regime of the South against the North Korean invasion which was supported by China. The UN sent troops to fight in Korea (a significant number of whom were American) led by the US General MacArthur. The war lasted three years and ended in stalemate but deepened the distrust between East and West. The USSR, for example, had boycotted the UN Security Council when the decision to send troops to Korea was taken and as a result was sure to be present to oppose further controversial action by the Security Council in future.

By 1960, the USA had been dragged into an even bigger conflict in Vietnam to prevent the spread of Communism there. Again the US was supporting anti-Communist forces with supplies, training and eventually troops who were fighting against the Vietcong supported by the USSR and China. This meant that by the early 1960s the tension between the two sides had developed into conflict (although this was indirect) which further increased the chance of all-out war between superpowers.

> Here the answer is giving precise knowledge. It is crucial that you use as much relevant detailed knowledge as possible to show your grasp of the topic

> Here the answer explicitly links to the issue raised in the question

Question 4: How far do you agree? (Essay)

'The main reason for the development of the Cold War, 1945–1948, was the occupation of Eastern Europe by the USSR.' How far do you agree with this statement? Explain your answer.   (16 marks)

The Soviet occupation of Eastern Europe was one reason why tension between the USA and USSR was heightened, but it was not the only reason why the Cold War developed.

> Each paragraph opens with a clear argument which is focused on the question

By July 1945, the Soviet armies occupied the Baltic States, Finland, Poland, Czechoslovakia, Hungary, Romania and Bulgaria. Stalin claimed that this was in order to create a safe buffer zone for the USSR to protect it from future invasion. The USA, however, saw this as an attempt to build an empire in Eastern Europe. By the time of the Potsdam Conference the US President Harry Truman was determined to get tough on Soviet attempts to control Eastern Europe. This was a major source of disagreement at the conference, but Stalin insisted he had the right to control these areas and that this had been agreed at the Yalta conference. This Soviet zone was increasingly seen as an empire and went against the US desire to hold free elections in liberated countries. These disagreements were the main reason behind the escalation of the Cold War in Europe.

> The argument in the paragraph is then supported by a range of detailed, specific knowledge

> Here the paragraph links the evidence to the question

However, the initial problems which led to the Cold War existed long before the Soviet occupation. The USA was a capitalist society and was committed to democracy, free elections and private control of businesses and property. This ideology was at odds with the Communist ideas of state ownership and a focus on the good of the whole country over individual rights. These disagreements were very hard to overcome and caused suspicion between the powers. Truman was particularly unhappy to see a 'Communist' empire developing in Eastern Europe and so the ideological disagreements meant that the Soviet occupation was very problematic.

The USA also worsened the situation with some of their actions. Most importantly, they developed the atom bomb by July 1945 and Truman used it to put pressure on the USSR. At the Potsdam Conference Truman told Stalin about the bomb, and in August 1945 the USA used the atom bomb against Japan. As this was an immensely powerful weapon, it added to the threat which the USA posed to Soviet security.

Without the ideological differences between the two powers, Stalin would have felt much less threatened and so it would have been easier to find an agreement between the powers. Although the occupation of Eastern Europe became a key issue in the Cold War, the ideological differences were the underlying cause which made some kind of conflict inevitable.

> Here the answer fulfils the requirement to form a complex explanation by linking reasons together before coming to an overall judgement

Glossary: Conflict and tension between East and West, 1945–1972

Apollo The US programme to send a man to the moon

Appeasement The British policy of allowing Hitler to get away with certain foreign policy decisions in order to avoid a war in the 1930s

Bay of Pigs The site of a failed US-sponsored invasion of Cuba

Berlin Airlift The US response to the Berlin Blockade, where supplies were delivered by plane to West Berlin

Berlin Blockade Attempt by Soviet Union to prevent supplies reaching West Berlin

Boycotting Refusing to take part or use something as a form of protest

Brezhnev Doctrine Rules governing the Communist countries in Eastern Europe

Capitalist A political and economic system with democracy and where people can make profit and buy what they choose

Checkpoint Charlie The only place where people could cross between East and West Berlin after the construction of the Berlin Wall

CIA Central Intelligence Agency: the US secret service

Coexistence Two countries living together peacefully

Comecon The USSR's own version of the Marshall Plan

Cominform An organisation to co-ordinate the work of the various Communist parties in different countries

Communist A political and economic system with a strong government which tries to guarantee equality for all people. The USSR was a Communist state

Containment Stopping the spread of Communism. The Truman Doctrine was a policy of containment

Conventional weapons Weapons that are not nuclear

De-Stalinisation The process, begun by Khrushchev, of addressing some of the problems of Stalin's rule

Détente Attempts to reduce tension in the Cold War from the late 1960s

Dictatorship A system of government where one leader has almost total control

Diplomatic relations The relationship between two countries who have representatives to communicate between their governments

Exiled Forced to leave a country as a punishment

Federal Republic of Germany West Germany (not controlled by the USSR)

German Democratic Republic East Germany (controlled by the USSR)

Hydrogen bomb An exceptionally powerful form of nuclear weapon

Ideology Belief about how a country should be run

Intercontinental ballistic missile A missile which can be fired into space and then brought down on a target

Intelligence Secret information

Iron Curtain A term used by Winston Churchill to describe the division of Europe between the free, capitalist West and the area under the control of the USSR

Marshall Plan A US programme to provide loans to rebuild Europe after the Second World War

Military bloc A group of countries whose armed forces work together, for example NATO and the Warsaw Pact

Missile gap The fear in the USA that the USSR had a greater number of nuclear missiles

Monarchist Someone who supports a monarch. In the case of Greece, the monarchists wanted the return of the king

NASA The National Aeronautics and Space Administration which oversees the USA's space programme

Naval blockade Using ships to block access to a port or country or to stop the movement of supplies

North Atlantic Treaty Organisation (NATO) A group of countries including the USA and its allies who promised to support each other in case of an attack

Nuclear Non-Proliferation Treaty An agreement between the USA, USSR and Britain to reduce the spread of nuclear weapons

One-party system Where only one political party is permitted

Prague Spring A period of increasing hostility in Czechoslovakia towards rule by the USSR in 1968

Purges Mass murders of apparent enemies by Stalin's regime

Soviet sphere of influence Used to describe those countries in Eastern Europe which the USSR had some control over after the Second World War

Soviet USSR stood for the Union of Soviet Socialist Republics. The word Soviet was often used to refer to the USSR, for example 'the Soviet armies occupied Eastern Europe'

Sputnik The first man-made satellite, launched by the USSR in 1957

Stalemate A situation where neither side can win

Strategic Arms Limitations Talks Talks between the USA and USSR to agree limits on the number of nuclear weapons on each side

Suez crisis The controversial British attack to defend the Suez Canal in Egypt without consulting its allies

Superpowers Used to refer to the USA and the USSR as two countries with a powerful military and strong economy

Truman Doctrine The policy of the USA trying to stop the further spread of Communism

U-2 A type of spy plane used by the USA

United Nations Organisation A group of countries who would work together to keep peace after the Second World War

Viet Cong Communist fighters in Vietnam who originally fought against French rule

Warsaw Pact A military alliance between the USSR and other countries

Chapter 7 Conflict and tension in Asia, 1950–1975

7.1 Causes of the conflict in Korea

In the 1950s there was a strong fear of Communism in the USA

- The USA was in conflict with the USSR in the 1950s. This conflict was called the **Cold War**.
- One reason for this conflict was that the USSR was **Communist**.
- Both the USSR and USA wanted to avoid direct conflict with each other, but they were willing to take military action to spread their own influence or stop the other **superpower** from becoming more powerful.
- After the Second World War, the USSR had taken control of many countries in Eastern Europe. The USA was committed to stopping the spread of Communism.
- In 1947, US President Truman made it clear that the USA would help countries which might be taken over by Communists. This policy was called the **Truman Doctrine**.
- Because of this, the USA put $2 billion of aid into China to help the **Nationalists** (the anti-Communist government of China). However, in 1949, China became Communist.

North Korea was a Communist state which was in conflict with South Korea

- Korea had been ruled by Japan until 1945. When the war ended the North was freed by **Soviet** troops (troops from the USSR). The South was freed by American troops.
- After the war, the North continued to be Communist led. It had a Communist leader who had been trained in the USSR.
- The leader of North Korea was called Kim Il Sung.
- The South was ruled by Syngman Rhee. He had been elected to power in 1948, but his government was not very **democratic**.
- However, the USA supported Rhee because he was anti-Communist.

In 1950, North Korea successfully invaded the South

- North and South Korea were divided by a line at the **38th parallel**. There was a lot of hostility between the two sides.
- In 1950, Kim Il Sung ordered the invasion of South Korea.
- The North Korean forces were supported by equipment from the USSR. Later they were supplied by China.
- Within four months, the North had taken over almost all of Korea except a small corner in the south-east.

The USA intervened to support the South

- Truman immediately sent warships to South Korea and offered advisers and supplies to the South.
- The USA appealed to the **United Nations (UN)** to stop the invasion. The UN was an international organisation, which had replaced the League of Nations, set up to solve disputes.

Key point

Conflict between the Communist North Korea and the anti-Communist South dragged in the USA (to support the South) and the USSR and China (to support the North).

TIP

All the key terms in **purple** are defined in the glossary at the end of each chapter.

Make sure that you can spell the key terms, know what they mean and aim to use them in your written work.

TIP

When asked to write an account, the key thing is to remember you are not only telling a story. It needs to explain the issue in the question, in this case how and why the USA became involved.

- The USA had blocked China from joining the UN in 1949. In protest, the USSR was **boycotting** (refusing to take part in) the UN.
- The USA put pressure on the UN to send troops to defend South Korea. Because the USSR was not present at the meeting, it could not **veto** (block) this suggestion.
- The UN agreed to send troops to Korea. These troops would be from a number of countries but would include many American troops and be led by an American general called MacArthur.

 Test yourself

1 What was the Cold War?
2 When did China become Communist?
3 How did the USA respond to the outbreak of war in Korea?

 Develop the detail

The diagram below has a number of headings which give reasons for the outbreak of the war in Korea. For each one add supporting detail from these two pages. One has been done for you.

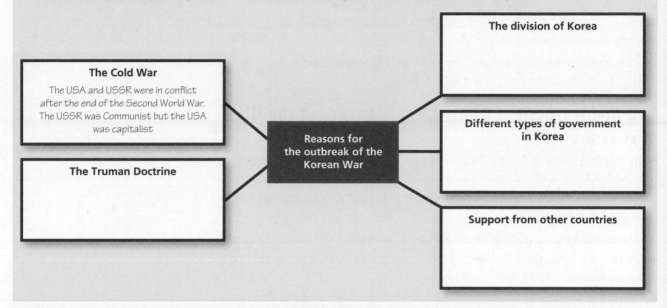

The Cold War
The USA and USSR were in conflict after the end of the Second World War. The USSR was Communist but the USA was capitalist

The Truman Doctrine

Reasons for the outbreak of the Korean War

The division of Korea

Different types of government in Korea

Support from other countries

 Improve the paragraph

Question 3 in your exam will ask you to 'write an account' which means a well-structured narrative which describes what happened but also picks up the angle (the second-order concept) implied in the question. For example:

Write an account of how the outbreak of war in Korea led to the involvement of the USA in the conflict. (8 marks)

The key 'second-order concept' is consequence (you can tell from the underlined phrase) 'how this led to'. Opposite is a paragraph answering the question. What is it missing? Rewrite the paragraph to improve it.

In 1950, the North of Korea, led by the Communist Kim Il Sung, invaded the South. The South was ruled by Syngman Rhee. South Korea was anti-Communist although it also wasn't ruled very democratically. China was also a Communist country (it had been Communist since 1949). There was a lot of hostility between the North and the South because of their different governments, and in June 1950 the North invaded to try to control the whole of Korea. They quickly took over all of Korea except for a tiny corner in the south-east. China supported the invasion by supplying the North with weapons.

7.2 The development of the Korean War

The UN forces quickly won back territory from the North

- Eighteen countries provided troops for the UN force in Korea, but the majority of the troops were American.
- The UN forces landed at Inchon which was near the 38th parallel. At the same time, South Korean forces advanced from Pusan.
- Within weeks, the UN forces had taken control of territory all the way to the 38th parallel which meant that they had met their objective of removing Communism from South Korea.
- However, the UN forces carried on fighting and started to take territory in North Korea. The UN approved a plan to continue the attack in North Korea.
- China's leader, Mao Zedong, warned the UN that China would get involved if the invasion continued.
- This warning was ignored and, by October, US forces were at the Yalu River which was on the border with China.

> **Key point**
>
> The US/UN forces were initially very successful against the forces of North Korea. However, when China got involved the war quickly became a stalemate.

The involvement of China quickly reversed the UN successes

- In October 1950, 200,000 Chinese troops (called **People's Volunteers**) joined the war and launched a very successful attack.
- The Chinese troops were committed to Communism and had been taught to hate the Americans.
- They were also supplied with modern tanks and planes by the USSR.
- By January 1951, the UN forces were driven out of Seoul (the capital of South Korea).
- A few weeks later, after bitter fighting, the US forces pushed the Chinese back to the 38th parallel. The war had become a **stalemate**.

MacArthur disagreed with Truman and was sacked

- President Truman felt that the US forces had achieved enough by freeing South Korea of Communism.
- He was also worried about the threat of the USSR joining the war.
- The UN also wanted to stop the attack and agreed to keep the division of North and South Korea.
- However, General MacArthur wanted to attack China directly. He even considered using nuclear weapons to defeat China.
- In March 1951, MacArthur blatantly ignored the instructions of the UN and his President and openly threatened to attack China.
- In April 1951, Truman removed MacArthur from his position and brought him back to the USA.
- Truman also made it clear that the policy of the USA was **containment** (stopping the spread of Communism, not attacking countries which were already Communist).

 Test yourself

1 What were the Inchon landings?
2 Why did China get involved in the war?
3 Why did the war become a stalemate?
4 Why was MacArthur sacked?

Key events

Use the flow chart below to summarise the key events in the development of the Korean War up to April 1951. The first has been done for you.

In 1950 the UN forces, made up of American troops and troops from seventeen other nations, landed at Inchon.					

 Spot the opinion in a source

Use the sentence starters below to plan an answer to the question.

Study Source A. This source is criticising General MacArthur. How do you know? (4 marks)

SOURCE A *A cartoon entitled 'Not a General's Job' produced in 1951.*

This man is General MacArthur. He is trying to tip a hat which represents ...

If he succeeds, the hat will fall into a space which says 'World War III in Asia'. This suggests that MacArthur's actions could ...

This cartoon is commenting on MacArthur's approach to the Korean War. He wanted to ...

Because of this, in 1951 MacArthur was ...

 Improve the paragraph

Write an account of the UN forces' involvement in Korea to show why the war became a stalemate. (8 marks)

Opposite is an example paragraph answering the question above. What is it missing? Rewrite the answer to improve it.

The UN invaded Korea. They were really successful at first and took back a lot of land. They even started to take land in North Korea. However, they were warned that they would be attacked if they continued and when they got to the border with China the Chinese sent troops to fight them. Once the Chinese got involved they took back a lot of the land the UN had conquered. Neither side could win the war and the UN commander was sacked.

7.3 Ending the Korean War

It took **two years** to conclude **peace talks** in Korea

June 1951	1952	November 1952	March 1953	July 1953
The Korean War reached a stalemate in early 1951. Peace talks began in June 1951 These talks failed to reach an agreement over the exchange of prisoners between North and South Korea	Talks began again in 1952 but again failed to make progress. Fighting in Korea continued	Truman was replaced by Eisenhower as US President. Eisenhower wanted to end the conflict in Korea	The Soviet leader, Stalin, died without an obvious successor. This meant that Soviet policy in future was uncertain and made China and North Korea less confident	Because of this uncertainty, a peace agreement was finally signed in Panmunjom in July 1953

There were **no clear winners** in the conflict

- The UN had demonstrated its power by taking effective joint action in Korea. However, it had only been able to act because the USSR had boycotted the Security Council.
- The USA had lost 30,000 troops in the conflict and increased its defence spending from $12 billion to $60 billion. However, it had successfully stopped Communism from spreading into South Korea.
- China had developed a closer relationship with the USSR and gained the respect of other Asian Communist supporters. It had also secured Korea as a **buffer state**.
- However, China had suffered huge casualties (around half a million) and had made its relationship with the USA much worse, which resulted in a loss of trade and increased support for the rival Chinese government in exile.
- The impact on Korea was disastrous. There were 1.3 million casualties including a large number of civilians. Much of the country's industry and agriculture had been destroyed. Neither side had gained the united Korea which it was fighting for.

The Korean War **extended the Cold War** into Asia

- The USA and UN supported the Nationalist Chinese government (the enemies of Mao's government) who were in exile on the island of Formosa (Taiwan).
- Relationships between the USA, USSR and China were extremely complicated and there was a danger of further conflict.
- In 1954, the **South East Asia Treaty Organisation (SEATO)** was founded. This was like the existing organisation **NATO** which was an alliance of anti-Communist states in Europe.
- This increased the tension between the USA and USSR.

> **Key point**
>
> The Korean War was not a clear victory for either side. However, it extended the Cold War into Asia and increased tensions between the USA and USSR.

> **TIP**
>
> The examiners want you to use relevant and detailed knowledge in your answers. In your revision you should try to remember a specific piece of information associated with each general idea.

Test yourself

1. Why was an armistice eventually signed in 1953?
2. How did the USA and China gain from the conflict?
3. What was the impact of the Korean War on the Cold War?

Support or challenge?

Your final question in the depth study exam will be an essay writing task like this:

'The outcome of the Korean war was more of a victory for the USA than China.' How far do you agree with this statement? Explain your answer. (16 marks + 4 SPaG)

There are many layers to answering this kind of question – but the first layer is to get used to assessing evidence on either side so you can then make an informed judgement. That is the purpose of this task.

Does the evidence below support or challenge this view? Tick the box which you think is most appropriate for each piece of evidence.

Evidence	Support	Challenge
Chinese forces suffered half a million casualties		
Communism was prevented from spreading to South Korea		
US defence spending rose from $12 billion to $60 billion		
US forces suffered 30,000 casualties		
North Korea was secure from UN control or invasion by the South		
China received significant support from the USSR		

 Topic summary

'The Korean War was a war without winners.' How far do you agree with this statement? Explain your answer. (16 marks)

Here is another example of an essay question. It is wide in its scope. To answer this kind of question you need an overview of the topic. You can't get by with just a little knowledge.

Complete this mind map to summarise the gains and losses of the participants in the Korean War. Use specific information from the past six pages or your own knowledge. One example has been done for you.

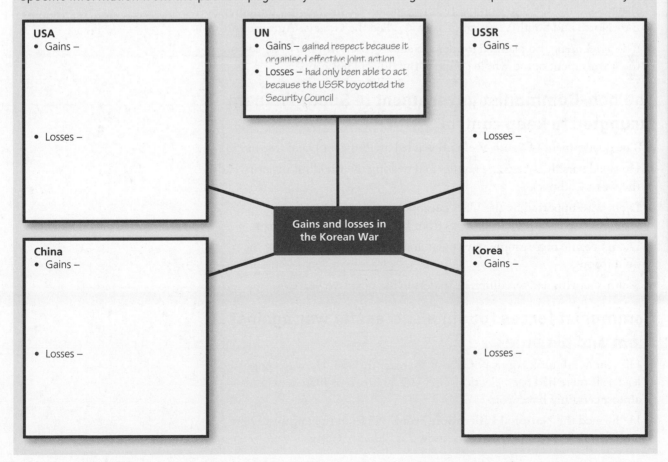

USA
- Gains –
- Losses –

UN
- Gains – gained respect because it organised effective joint action
- Losses – had only been able to act because the USSR boycotted the Security Council

USSR
- Gains –
- Losses –

Gains and losses in the Korean War

China
- Gains –
- Losses –

Korea
- Gains –
- Losses –

7.4 The end of French rule in Vietnam

French rule was collapsing by the end of 1945

- Vietnam (at the time called **Indochina**) was ruled by France before the Second World War.
- French rule was often brutal, and there was growing opposition in Vietnam.
- A strong anti-French group called the **Viet Minh** was formed. This was led by Ho Chi Minh.
- Ho Chi Minh was the leader of the Indochinese Communist Party. He had trained in **guerrilla warfare**.
- By the end of the Second World War, the Viet Minh controlled the north of Vietnam and wanted to take control of the rest of the country.
- In 1945, the Viet Minh tried to take control of Hanoi (the capital of Vietnam) and declared Vietnam independent of French rule.

The Viet Minh defeated the French by 1954

- There were nine years of war between the French and the Viet Minh.
- Ho Chi Minh was supported by China and the USSR.
- France was supported by the USA (which was afraid of Communist rule supported by China). The USA gave $500 million a year to help France control Vietnam.
- Despite this support from the USA, France was unable to hold on to power.
- In 1954, French forces were defeated at the battle of **Dien Bien Phu**. Eight thousand French troops were killed and France surrendered.
- An agreement was made between Vietnam, France, China, the USSR, Britain and the USA to stop the fighting and divide the country temporarily into North and South Vietnam. This was called the **Geneva Agreement**.
- The agreement also planned for democratic elections in 1956 to decide on the government of the whole country. But this did not happen.

The non-Communist government of South Vietnam struggled to keep control

- The government of South Vietnam was led by President Diem from 1954.
- He ruled harshly, arresting enemies and treating the Buddhist majority badly (he was a Catholic).
- Diem was supported by the USA because he was anti-Communist. However, he faced serious protests from Buddhist monks in Vietnam.
- Diem became increasingly unpopular and in 1963 he was killed by his own troops.
- South Vietnam had ten different leaders in the next two years.

Communist forces fought a successful war against Diem and his allies

- Ho Chi Minh took control of North Vietnam in 1954. He was a popular leader. If there had been elections in South Vietnam in 1956 he would almost certainly have won.
- He formed the **National Liberation Front (NLF)** to fight against Diem and the USA. The NLF was also known as the **Viet Cong**.

> **Key point**
>
> The rulers of South Vietnam, despite support from the USA, could not resist the popularity and the military tactics of the Viet Cong. By the 1960s the Viet Cong were gaining control of South Vietnam.

- By 1961, there were 20,000 Viet Cong fighters in South Vietnam.
- They used surprise attacks and traps to fight against their enemies.
- They also moved supplies from north to south using a complex series of trails called the **Ho Chi Minh Trail**.
- The Viet Cong won the support of local populations by treating them well.
- By the 1960s, they had over 100,000 troops and controlled significant areas of South Vietnam.

 Test yourself

1 What were Ho Chi Minh's aims?
2 Why was there opposition to Diem's rule?
3 Why were the Viet Cong so successful?

 Develop the explanation

The secret of getting top marks in any history essay is to write analytically, which means not just describing but explaining.

The statements below identify some general reasons why the Viet Cong were successful. For each one, add one or two more sentences to explain why this made them successful. The first one has been done for you.

Statements	Explanation: why this made the Viet Cong successful
The Viet Cong were committed to ending foreign rule in Vietnam	Vietnam had been under French rule before the Second World War. This was very unpopular. Later the rule of Diem in the South, which was backed by the Americans, was also seen as very harsh. The Viet Cong united lots of people in north and south by promising a free and independent Vietnam
The Viet Cong used guerrilla tactics to fight their enemies	
The Viet Cong were led by Ho Chi Minh	
The Viet Cong transported supplies along the Ho Chi Minh Trail	
The Viet Cong worked with local communities to improve their lives	

 Key events

Use the flow chart below to show the main stages of the emerging conflict in Vietnam 1945–61. The first one is done for you.

By 1945, the Viet Minh had taken control of the north of Vietnam				

 Practice question

Write an account of the rise of Communism in Vietnam between 1954 and 1961 to show how this caused conflict between North and South Vietnam. (8 marks)

TIP

A probable structure for an account is chronological – but that is not the only way. In fact writing an account in chronological order might tempt you to just describe things rather than answering the question. If you do write chronologically every step in your account should refer back to how this caused conflict between North and South Vietnam.

7.5 Increasing US involvement in Vietnam

Eisenhower wanted to stop the spread of Communism in Vietnam

- Eisenhower (US President 1953–60) was convinced that the USSR and China were aiming to spread Communism throughout Asia.

- He worried that if Vietnam fell then Communism would spread, country by country, to Laos, Cambodia, Thailand and perhaps even India. This idea was known as the **Domino Theory**.

- Eisenhower continued to send aid to Vietnam. $1.6 billion was sent to help the South Vietnamese government between 1954 and 1960.

- The USA did not have a clear plan of what to do in Vietnam. Many Americans knew very little about the situation in Vietnam or how unpopular the government of South Vietnam was.

> **Key point**
>
> US involvement in South Vietnam steadily increased. The major escalation came in 1964 after the Gulf of Tonkin incident and President Johnson committed US troops to a full-scale war.

Kennedy increased the US commitment in Vietnam

- Under Kennedy (President 1961–63), 11,000 US military advisers were sent to Vietnam by 1962 to provide training.

- The USA also began the **Strategic Hamlet** programme:

What?	Whole villages (all the people) were moved from areas which were controlled by the Viet Cong into areas controlled by the South Vietnamese government
Why?	The US hoped to prevent the Viet Cong infiltrating villages and gaining more supporters amongst the villagers
How?	The South Vietnam government supplied money, materials and food to villagers to help them build improved farms and homes in the new area. This was paid for by the USA
Consequences	The programme actually increased Viet Cong support: • many peasants did not want to move or to work without pay to build new villages • most Vietnamese peasants did not feel threatened by the Viet Cong. There were also reports of **corrupt** officials who took money which was meant to help the villagers for themselves

US involvement peaked under President Johnson

- In August 1964, North Vietnamese patrol boats were said to have fired on US ships in an area off the coast of Vietnam. This was called the **Gulf of Tonkin incident**.

- Johnson (President 1963–68) persuaded **Congress** (part of the US government) to support him to take action against North Vietnam.

- Congress passed the **Gulf of Tonkin Resolution**. This allowed Johnson to 'take all necessary measures' to protect US interests in Vietnam.

- This meant that Johnson could now involve US forces in a full-scale war.

- In 1965, Viet Cong attacks increased. In response, Johnson approved a massive new bombing campaign called **Operation Rolling Thunder**.

- In March 1965, 3500 US **marines** (combat troops) landed at Da Nang. This marked the start of direct US military involvement.

> **TIP**
>
> A possible writing frame for a question 2 answer will be in four paragraphs, two for each source (one on provenance and another on content).
>
> In your exam you won't actually be asked to compare the two sources but you can write about how they are more useful together than separately.

> **Test yourself**
>
> 1 How was the US involved in Vietnam under Eisenhower?
>
> 2 What were strategic hamlets?
>
> 3 Why did the Gulf of Tonkin incident increase US involvement?

Quick quizzes at **www.hoddereducation.co.uk/myrevisionnotes**

Develop the explanation

The table below summarises the reasons why the USA became increasingly involved in Vietnam. For each one, explain why this increased US involvement.

Reason	Explanation: why this increased US involvement
The end of French rule	France had ruled Vietnam as a colony. When they left Vietnam the North became Communist under Ho Chi Minh. The US was concerned about the whole of Vietnam becoming Communist
The success of the Viet Cong	
Fear of Communism	
Attacks on US forces	

 ## Evaluate usefulness

In your exam, question 2 will be based on two sources. For example:

Study Sources B and C. How useful are Sources B and C to a historian studying attitudes towards the invading US armies in Vietnam? Explain your answer using Sources B and C and your contextual knowledge. (12 marks)

To evaluate usefulness you will need to think about:

● Provenance: who made it, when, and why?
● Content: is it useful for its content and does your knowledge agree?

Annotate each source to show the points you are going to make.

Challenge: write up your notes as a full answer using the writing frame suggested in the Tip on page 150.

SOURCE B *A Chinese poster commenting on the Vietnam War. The text reads 'American imperialism must be driven out of Southern Vietnam!'*

美帝国主义从越南南方滚出去！

SOURCE C *Extracts from a letter written in 1965 by Le Duan, Secretary of the North Vietnamese Communist Party explaining how North Vietnam would react to the arrival of US forces in 1965.*

We need to use the methods most suited for destroying the American troops – guerrilla forces encircling the American troops' bases …

For the next few years, we should kill at least 40–50,000 Americans. This is a new goal which will determine our victory. Along with trying to lessen the Americans' strength, we should try to cause great loss of American aircraft.

We must not neglect the political war. Even though the US brings in more troops to Vietnam, they will fail to weaken our political power. In fact, our political power is likely to be enhanced. The more troops the US brings in, the larger area it occupies, the more sophisticated weapons it uses, the more bombs it drops, the more chemical poisons it uses, the worse the conflict between our people and them becomes, the more our people hate them.

7.6 The war in Vietnam under Johnson REVISED ☐

Key point
The USA had more troops and were better equipped than the Viet Cong. But they were unable to defeat the Viet Cong who made effective use of guerrilla tactics.

The **Viet Cong** used **guerrilla warfare** very effectively

- The Viet Cong and North Vietnamese Army (NVA) had 170,000 troops.
- They were supplied by the USSR and China, but faced a much bigger and better equipped US army.
- The Viet Cong forces could not defeat the US forces in open warfare. Instead they used guerrilla warfare which was very effective:

They were hard to find	Their ambushes and booby traps sapped US morale	They had peasant support	They were supplied from North Vietnam
Viet Cong guerrilla fighters did not wear uniform or have a base. They were very hard to tell apart from the local peasants	They avoided open battle. Instead they would attack US forces quickly and then retreat. They also used booby traps: simple pits filled with bamboo spikes; or explosive devices like the **Bouncing Betty** About eleven per cent of US casualties came from booby traps; 51 per cent came from small ambushes	The Viet Cong worked with local peasants to win their support. However, they could be ruthless: between 1966 and 1971 they killed 27,000 civilians for working with the South Vietnam government. This included teachers and police	40,000 Vietnamese worked to keep the Ho Chi Minh Trail running despite heavy bombing by the USA

American tactics failed to destroy the Viet Cong despite massive spending and effort

Bombing	Search and destroy
Operation Rolling Thunder was the start of a massive bombing campaign lasting until 1972	This involved establishing heavily defended US bases in South Vietnam then launching raids on Viet Cong villages by helicopter to destroy Viet Cong hideouts and discover weapons stores
Targets included towns and cities, as well as the Ho Chi Minh Trail in Vietnam and in other countries	**Search and destroy** raids were effective in locating and destroying Viet Cong strategic locations but they killed and injured a lot of civilians, which probably increased support for the Viet Cong
Bombing damaged the supply lines of the Viet Cong but, even after massive air attacks on North Vietnam in 1972, the Viet Cong were still able to launch a major attack	One of the most infamous examples of this was the **My Lai massacre** in 1968 when 400 civilians were killed by US forces on a search and destroy mission

- The financial cost of these operations was huge: 14,000 US planes or helicopters were shot down. It was estimated that it cost the USA $400,000 to kill one Viet Cong fighter.

The USA also faced other problems which made it increasingly hard to win the war

Geography: the US could not launch attacks into neighbouring countries such as Cambodia and Laos. Viet Cong fighters could retreat into these countries

Low morale: From 1967 an increasing number of American troops were **drafted** (forced to join the army by the government). Many were young men who did not want to fight. There were 500,000 **deserters** (running away and refusing to fight)

Other US problems

Tensions: many of the soldiers lost respect for their officers as conditions worsened. There were incidences of **fragging** (troops killing their own officers)

Losing support: tactics like search and destroy and heavy bombing made many more Vietnamese support the Viet Cong and weakened support back home in the USA

Develop the detail

The diagram lists reasons why the US were not able to defeat the Viet Cong. Complete the diagram with examples of how this helped the Viet Cong or harmed the USA. The first one is done for you.

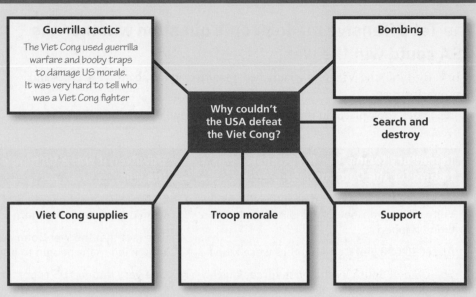

Guerrilla tactics

The Viet Cong used guerrilla warfare and booby traps to damage US morale. It was very hard to tell who was a Viet Cong fighter

Bombing

Why couldn't the USA defeat the Viet Cong?

Search and destroy

Viet Cong supplies

Troop morale

Support

Spot the opinion in a source

Study Source D. Source D supports the Viet Cong. How do you know? Explain your answer by using Source D and your contextual knowledge. (4 marks)

To answer this question you need to spot important details in the source and explain what they suggest. Use the sentence starters below to help you do this.

A The US troops are in open ground and can be clearly seen. This suggests that …

B The Viet Cong are very well hidden in the trees. This suggests that …

C The Viet Cong effectively used guerrilla tactics such as …

SOURCE D *A Viet Cong poster from the 1960s.*

TIP

Question 1 is worth 4 marks so don't overwrite. You will need time for the rest of the questions.

Refer to at least two details of a source in your answer. Make sure you link everything you say to something in the source.

Test yourself

1 What were the tactics used by the Viet Cong?

2 Why were these tactics effective?

3 What tactics did the US forces use?

7.7 Nixon and Vietnamisation

The Tet Offensive made people question whether the USA could win the war

- In early 1968, the Viet Cong launched a massive attack against 100 cities and military targets.
- The attack took place on the Vietnamese Tet (New Year) holiday and so it became known as the **Tet Offensive**.

In military terms, the Tet Offensive was a failure for the Communists	However, it was a turning point in US attitudes to the war
The Viet Cong hoped that people in South Vietnam would rise up and join them but this didn't happen	Before this, most people had believed that the USA was winning the war in Vietnam
About 10,000 Viet Cong fighters were killed	The fact that the Viet Cong could launch such a major attack led many people to question whether this was true
The US and South Vietnamese forces quickly recaptured the lost areas, but there was hard fighting in the capital Saigon and in Hué	One very famous US reporter called Walter Cronkite said he thought the war was unwinnable

President Nixon reopened peace talks and started a process of Vietnamisation

- Peace talks had begun in Paris in May 1968 but they had failed. Nixon became President in early 1969 and said he would continue the war until the US could get 'peace with honour'.
- Nixon's policy was called **Vietnamisation** (to reduce US troops and give the South Vietnam forces more responsibility for the fighting).
- It was clear this policy would probably fail. The North Vietnamese, with support from the USSR and China, would quickly defeat South Vietnam.
- In September 1969, the USA started secret peace talks with North Vietnam (without the support of the South Vietnam government).
- 25,000 US troops withdrew in June 1969 and 35,000 in September.

> **Key point**
>
> Nixon removed US troops from Vietnam, but at the same time he escalated the war in some areas to force North Vietnam to negotiate.

Nixon also increased US involvement

- Nixon did not want to look weak while negotiating with North Vietnam, or allow the North to win quickly as US troops withdrew.
- He ordered US troops to invade Cambodia and attack Viet Cong bases.
- He hoped this would force North Vietnam to negotiate more willingly with the USA. Instead, North Vietnam boycotted the peace talks.
- The USA also supported a disastrous South Vietnamese invasion of Laos.
- Nixon continued to withdraw troops; over 400,000 by the end of 1971.
- He also built stronger relations with China and the USSR.

Bombing of North Vietnam increased again in 1972 to put pressure on the North to make peace

- In March 1972, the North Vietnamese (supported by Soviet tanks) invaded the South. They hoped to win easily as most US troops had left.
- In April 1972, the USA launched a huge new bombing campaign called **Operation Linebacker**. This destroyed roads, factories and supply lines.
- This campaign led to more protests around the world and in the USA.

Develop the explanation

This diagram summarises Nixon's approach to ending the war in Vietnam. Complete the diagram by finding examples for each point and explaining why he did it.

One example has been done for you.

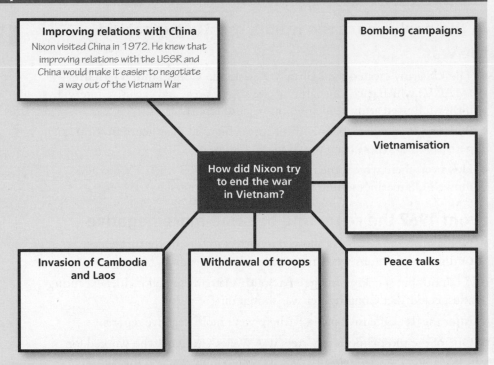

Improving relations with China
Nixon visited China in 1972. He knew that improving relations with the USSR and China would make it easier to negotiate a way out of the Vietnam War

Bombing campaigns

How did Nixon try to end the war in Vietnam?

Vietnamisation

Invasion of Cambodia and Laos

Withdrawal of troops

Peace talks

 ## Improve the paragraph

The most valuable question in the exam will be an essay question like this:

'The Tet Offensive was the main reason why Nixon wanted to end the Vietnam War.' How far do you agree? (16 marks + 4 SPaG)

You will need to consider the role of the factor given in the question and then consider the role of one or two other important factors such as:

- public opinion in America
- the escalating cost of the war
- détente between the superpowers

which are dealt with on the next four pages.

This paragraph tries to explain why the Tet Offensive helped lead to the policy but it includes irrelevant information and it fails to connect to the question. Annotate or rewrite it to improve it.

In 1968 the Viet Cong launched a huge offensive called the Tet Offensive. They took control over a number of cities in South Vietnam for a while. The attack came as a complete surprise. Most Americans thought that they were winning the war, but after the Tet Offensive people began to suggest that the war could not be won. Nixon then tried to get out of Vietnam but he didn't want the North to take over the South so he used Vietnamisation to try to stop this.

 ## Practice question

Write an account to show how the Tet Offensive in 1968 changed American attitudes towards the war in Vietnam. (8 marks)

 ## Test yourself

1. What was the Tet Offensive?
2. What was Vietnamisation?
3. Why did Nixon support the invasion of Cambodia and Laos?
4. What was Operation Linebacker?

7.8 Opposition to the Vietnam War

In the **early years** the media mostly **supported the war**

- The US army created the **Military Assistance Command, Vietnam (MACV)** which gave journalists access to war areas and exclusive interviews if they followed army guidelines on what to report.
- Between 1964 and 1968 only three journalists had their **accreditation** (their permission to report from the MACV) removed.
- However, there were some negative reports in 1965 when TV footage showed US marines setting fire to Vietnamese homes.

From 1967 the reporting became more negative

- New lightweight cameras allowed reporters to film in conflict zones. Ordinary Americans were more exposed to the realities of war.
- A famous but shocking image of a South Vietnamese police chief executing a suspected Viet Cong fighter was shown on TV news.
- After the Tet Offensive of 1968, there were more negative reports.
- One of the most famous reporters was Walter Cronkite who worked for CBS (a US TV channel). In 1968, he said that the war was unwinnable. President Johnson said that this meant he had lost the support of average Americans.
- Many army leaders (for example, General Westmoreland) believed that the media reporting made people in the USA less supportive of the war.
- However, others point out that most news coverage did not criticise the war. Only 76 of 2300 news reports from 1965 to 1970 showed heavy fighting.

The anti-war protest movement grew from 1968

- 1968 saw protests about different issues: for example, poverty and civil rights.
- There was also a huge amount of anti-war protest by college students.
- In many cases, protesters burned the US flag (this was a crime in the USA).
- There were often violent clashes between students and the police. The worst example was the **Kent State massacre** in 1970. Troopers opened fire on student protesters and four students were killed.
- In 1969, information about the My Lai massacre began to leak out and the officer in charge of the mission was put on trial. The atrocity intensified opposition to the war.

Civil Rights leaders criticised the war

- Johnson had promised to reduce poverty as part of his '**Great Society**'. Martin Luther King said he couldn't achieve this because so much money was spent in Vietnam.
- The draft (the way soldiers were called up to fight) was unfair. College students could avoid being drafted. Fewer African-Americans went to college than white people, so 30 per cent of young African-Americans were sent to Vietnam compared to 19 per cent of white Americans.
- The world-famous African-American boxer Muhammad Ali refused the draft and was stripped of his world title.

Key point

Opposition to the Vietnam War increased after 1968. It involved well-known people and a huge number of students. It was also encouraged by information in the media.

Test yourself

1 How had the media reported on the war before 1967?

2 Why did opposition to the war increase after 1968?

3 Which individuals and groups opposed the war?

Nixon's efforts to end the war were overshadowed by the **Watergate scandal** leading to his **resignation**

- In 1972, there was an election in the USA. During the election campaign Nixon was caught up in a scandal called the **Watergate Affair**.
- Watergate was an office building in Washington where the **Democratic Party** (the opposition to Nixon's **Republican Party**) was based.
- There was a break in and a group of men were arrested trying to place listening devices in the office.
- Nixon denied being involved, but over time it became clear that his office was involved in the incident.
- In 1974, Nixon was threatened with being **impeached** (voted out of the presidency) and he resigned.

> **TIP**
>
> Candidates find it hard to give time to planning in an actual exam which is why it is very important to practise it before the exam so that it becomes instinctive.

Essay plan

'The main reason for growing opposition to the Vietnam War was media coverage.' How far do you agree with this statement? (16 marks + 4 SPaG)

The secret of writing a good essay is good planning. Here is a plan.

Plan	Purpose/points to include	Comment
Introduction	State your view on how far you agree or disagree	You should open by briefly stating your overall answer to the question The question asks 'how far you agree ...' so words and phrases such as 'mostly', 'partly', 'totally' will be useful
Paragraph 1	Reasons to agree. Explain how the issue mentioned in the statement (media coverage) helped lead to opposition	This helps ensure you stay focused on the actual statement Make sure you support everything you say with detailed and precise knowledge
Paragraph 2	Reasons to disagree. Explain at least one other factor that increased opposition (for example economic problems)	You can choose to write about one other cause or more than one depending on how quickly you think and write. But it's better to explain one cause thoroughly than more than one superficially You can link these reasons back to media coverage if you think the two things are linked Once again make sure you support everything you say with detailed and precise knowledge
Conclusion	State your judgement as to how far you agree or disagree and give one key argument as to why	This should be easy to write if you have kept your focus through the rest of the essay There are 4 marks for spelling, punctuation and grammar so use your final minutes to check your work and correct it if necessary

- Step 1: in note form write down two reasons to agree with the statement, and two reasons to disagree.
- Step 2: decide on your argument – based on your notes in step 1. How far do you agree or disagree? Stick with that conclusion when you write your essay.
- Step 3: (in the exam) this step would be to write your full essay, but for this task just practise writing your conclusion.

7.9 The end of the war

Peace talks were finally completed in 1973

Secret talks fail	War intensifies	USSR helps	Peace agreement
In 1969, Nixon had asked his National Security Adviser, Henry Kissinger, to begin peace talks in secret with North Vietnam	Public opinion in the USA was turning against the war which made it easier for North Vietnam to put pressure on Nixon to withdraw	Nixon gained the support of the USSR to help negotiate a deal between the USA and North Vietnam	In Paris, in January 1973, the agreement was finally signed by North and South Vietnam and the USA
The North Vietnam government demanded that all US forces immediately withdraw from Vietnam. As a result, the talks did not make much progress	In 1972, North Vietnam launched a major attack on the South but was unable to conquer it	In October 1972, they reached a **provisional** agreement (an agreement that both sides supported but which was not made formal)	Nixon described this as a 'peace with honour' but many people in the USA did not agree with him
			By March 1973 all US forces had been withdrawn from Vietnam

Key point

Once peace talks were completed in 1973, the USA stopped supporting the government of South Vietnam. Within two years the Communists had taken control of the whole country.

In two years the Communists had taken control of South Vietnam

- Nixon had promised to continue to support South Vietnam. However, he was not supported by Congress who refused to give him money to aid Vietnam.
- Many people in the USA now felt that the government of South Vietnam was corrupt and did not have the support of the population.
- To make things worse, Nixon was losing support because of the Watergate scandal.
- After he resigned in 1974, Nixon was replaced by Gerald Ford. However, Ford also failed to get the support of Congress.
- The government of South Vietnam could not resist the Communists without US support.
- In December 1974, North Vietnam launched a major attack. By April 1975, it had captured the capital of South Vietnam, Saigon.

The war had a huge cost for Vietnam and the USA

- The war forced many Vietnamese people out of their homes. Around 5 million people were forced to leave.
- In the late 1970s and early 1980s, thousands of Vietnamese people tried to escape to nearby countries. They were called 'boat people' and 50,000 drowned or were killed by pirates.
- The war also left Vietnam with a lot of corruption and other problems like poverty, prostitution and drug abuse.
- The environment was badly damaged by the use of weapons like **Agent Orange** which destroyed crops and trees.
- Many people were affected by health problems caused by chemical weapons. There were also lots of deaths because of unexploded mines and bombs.
- In the USA, many soldiers found it difficult to settle back into civilian life.
- There was a high rate of drug abuse and stress–related conditions among soldiers who had fought in the war.

 Test yourself

1 Why were peace talks initially unsuccessful?

2 Why was it easier to reach an agreement after 1972?

3 What were the effects of the war on Vietnam and the USA?

Key events

Complete the flow chart below to summarise the main events in American withdrawal from Vietnam using the information on this spread. The first one has been done for you.

Peace talks began in 1969, but they initially did not make much progress.		

 Practice question

Study Sources E and F. How useful are these two sources to a historian studying the reasons for US withdrawal from Vietnam? Explain your answer using Sources E and F and your contextual knowledge.

(12 marks)

SOURCE E
A cartoon published in 1967 in the British newspaper, the Daily Telegraph.

"... AND IN VIETNAM MY PRIMARY OBJECTIVE IS TO WIN THE HEARTS AND MINDS OF THE PEOPLE—OF THE U.S.A."

SOURCE F *Extracts from a speech by civil rights leader Martin Luther King given in 1968.*

The war has put us in the position of protecting a corrupt government that is stacked against the poor. We are spending $500,000 to kill every Viet Cong soldier while we spend only $53 for every person considered to be in poverty in the USA. It has put us in a position of appearing to the world as an arrogant nation. Here we are 10,000 miles away from home fighting for the so-called freedom of the Vietnamese people when we have so much to do in our country.

 Practice question

'The main reason for American withdrawal from Vietnam was the cost of the war.'
How far do you agree with this statement?
(16 marks + 4 SPaG)

TIP

The highest marks in the mark scheme are reserved for candidates who show 'complex thinking'. What this means varies according to the type of question. Complex thinking for this question would be to show you really understand how different causes worked together.

> **Model answers**
>
> Here are model answers for each of the question types on this part of the exam. The annotations highlight what makes it a good answer.

Question 1: Opinion of a source

Study Source D on page 153.

Source D supports the Viet Cong. How do you know? Explain your answer by using Source D and your contextual knowledge. **(4 marks)**

Source D clearly supports the Viet Cong as it is showing how effective its guerrilla tactics were against US troops. In the source, the Viet Cong troops are cleverly concealed in the trees with their guns pointing at the US troops in the middle. This suggests that they were able to use the local environment to ambush US troops. Around 51 per cent of US casualties were caused by ambushes or small fire fights. The US troops also look disorganised which shows how difficult and frightening it is for them to fight against the Viet Cong. The Viet Cong often used booby traps such as spike pits which were terrifying for US troops (eleven per cent of casualties were caused by booby traps) and most soldiers were constantly worried about the threat of ambush.

> The answer refers to a number of different details which are shown in the source. It is a good idea to refer to at least two details or sections of a source in your answer

> The answer links these source details to the question and explains them further

Question 2: Usefulness of sources

Study Sources B and C on page 151.

Study Sources B and C. How useful are Sources B and C to a historian studying attitudes towards the invading US armies in Vietnam? Explain your answer using Sources B and C and your contextual knowledge. **(12 marks)**

Source C is overall more useful than Source B to a historian studying attitudes to invading troops in Vietnam. Both sources agree that there is widespread opposition to US involvement (as shown by the violent response in Source B and the very critical text about US imperialism), but Source C gives us more detail (partly because it is a letter and therefore gives a greater range of detail) about how US involvement in Vietnam is likely to encourage greater support for the Viet Cong. Ho Chi Minh deliberately used this as a way of gaining support for the Viet Cong by encouraging his soldiers to be respectful to the Vietnamese people. They would even help peasants work in the fields. Propaganda (like the poster) then played on this difference to further gain the support of the Vietnamese people. The sources also agree on the guerrilla tactics to be used by the Viet Cong, but again it is Source C which is able to give us greater detail. As the author was close to Ho Chi Minh (who had overall command of the Viet Cong) he is in a position to know about the tactics of the Viet Cong. The Viet Cong used a range of clever tactics to wage guerrilla warfare against the US troops, developing spike pits and other concealed traps as well as a very sophisticated network of tunnels (which ran to an estimated 240 km). Source B is useful, however, for showing us that the negative attitudes in Vietnam were at least to some extent shared in China.

> Here the answer refers to the provenance of the sources and uses this to judge their utility

> Here the answer uses contextual knowledge to test the claims made in the sources

Question 3: Write an account

Write an account of how the outbreak of war in Korea led to the involvement of the USA in the conflict. **(8 marks)**

By 1950, the USA was concerned with developments in Asia. In 1947, the Truman Doctrine had been established which had offered support to countries which were at risk of turning Communist. This had been done originally in Europe, but by 1949 the USSR had gained control of much of Eastern Europe. However, when the Nationalist government of China (the country with the largest population of any in the world) was threatened by Communists the USA had given $2 billion to support the government. By 1949, however, the Communists had taken over China. The USA was extremely concerned about other countries also becoming Communist.

Korea, a country just to the south of China, was divided into North and South after the Japanese were defeated in the Second World War. The North had been freed by the USSR, and had become a Communist country with a leader who had trained in the USSR (called Kim Il Sung). The South was not Communist (it had been freed by US troops) and was ruled by Syngman Rhee. The USA supported Syngman Rhee because he was anti-Communist. However, in June 1950, the South was invaded by the North and very soon almost all of the country was under Communist control.

The USA felt it had to act to stop the spread of Communism and so Truman quickly sent warships and advisers to South Korea. However, the USA also worked hard to get the support of the United Nations. Because the USSR was boycotting the UN, the USA was able to get support for its proposal to send UN troops to South Korea to prevent the North taking over completely. This soon meant that a UN force, which was made up largely of US troops and led by an American general called MacArthur, was involved in the fighting in Korea.

> Here the answer is giving precise knowledge. It is crucial that you use as much relevant detailed knowledge as possible to show your grasp of the topic

> Here the answer explicitly links to the issue raised in the question

Question 4: How far do you agree? (Essay)

'The Korean War was a war without winners.' How far do you agree with this statement? Explain your answer. **(16 marks)**

The Korean War exacted a serious toll from all participants. Although there were no clear winners, Korea was undoubtedly the most seriously affected party. By the end of the war, there had been no change to the border between North and South Korea (which ran along the 38th parallel). However, the war had caused 1.3 million casualties (equally spread between North and South) and including high numbers of civilians. The economic impact of the war was also huge, with industry destroyed and much agriculture ruined. The war had created millions of refugees. There is no doubt that neither North or South gained much from the conflict.

> Each paragraph opens with a clear argument which is focused on the question

> The argument in the paragraph is then supported by a range of detailed, specific knowledge

The USA did not clearly win the Korean war, but it did gain in some sense from the conflict. American losses were small relative to China (30,000 casualties) and it failed to achieve its objective of liberating North Korea from Communist control. However, it is worth noting that this objective was only developed during the war as US forces quickly recaptured territory before the intervention of China. The initial objective, to remove Communists from South Korea (and therefore contain Communism) was in fact met. It was a key victory for the USA to show that the policy of containment worked in Asia as well as in Europe.

The cost of the war for China was extremely high, but in terms of its status among other powers the war could be seen as a victory for China. Chinese casualties were over half a million, and just like the USA the Chinese failed to win South Korea for Communism. However, China did gain an even more secure buffer state on its southern border as a result of the war. More importantly China, which had only emerged as a Communist state in 1949, secured its reputation among Communist supporters in Asia. By standing up to the USA and the UN in Korea, China had demonstrated its power to influence global events and shape the direction of the Cold War. This had most importantly provided China with a close relationship with the USSR (which had supplied weapons and financial aid to the Chinese effort in Korea) and therefore made China a key player in the Cold War.

> Here the paragraph links the evidence to the question

Overall, although the cost for all participants was extremely high, China gained more from the Korean War than any other participant. Because the war did not alter the balance of power in Korea it must be judged instead on its impact on the status of each of the participants. In terms of political standing, China's Communist government (which had only recently formed a state) gained the most from the outcome of the war.

> Here the answer fulfils the requirement to form a complex explanation by linking reasons together before coming to an overall judgement

Glossary: Conflict and tension in Asia, 1950–1975

38th Parallel The dividing line between the areas of Korea occupied by the USA and USSR

Accreditation A journalist's licence to report on a war

Agent Orange A chemical weapon used by US forces in Vietnam

Bouncing Betty A hidden explosive device used by the Viet Cong

Boycotting Refusing to take part or use something as a form of protest

Buffer state A neutral country which separates two hostile countries

Cold War Non-violent conflict between the USA and the USSR from 1945

Communist A political and economic system with a strong government which tries to guarantee equality for all people. The USSR was a Communist state

Congress The law-making branch of the US government

Containment Stopping the spread of Communism. The Truman Doctrine was a policy of containment

Corrupt Someone who abuses their position or power

Democratic A political system where most ordinary people are able to vote to choose their government

Democratic Party One of two main US political parties

Deserter A member of the armed forces who runs away and refuses to fight

Dien Bien Phu A major defeat of French forces in Vietnam in 1954

Domino Theory The US fear that if one state became Communist then other states that it bordered might also become Communist

Drafted Forced to join the army

Fragging Troops killing their own officers

Geneva Agreement A temporary agreement to halt fighting in Vietnam

Great Society President Johnson's policy to solve a number of social problems in the USA

Guerrilla warfare Military tactics which involve small ambushes and the use of traps

Gulf of Tonkin incident An apparent attack on US ships by North Vietnamese boats

Gulf of Tonkin Resolution The act of Congress which gave President Johnson permission to use force in Vietnam

Ho Chi Minh Trail A network of supply routes for Viet Cong forces in South Vietnam

Impeached Voted out of the presidency

Indochina The name of Vietnam while under French occupation

Kent State massacre The killing of protesters on a US university campus by state troopers

Marines Combat troops

Military Assistance Command, Vietnam (MACV) Controlled the access of journalists to information about the Vietnam War

My Lai massacre The controversial murder of 400 civilians by US forces in 1968

National Liberation Front (NLF) The force established by Ho Chi Minh to resist the control of Diem and the USA in South Vietnam

Nationalists In China this was the anti-Communist government which was overthrown by Mao Zedong

NATO (North Atlantic Treaty Organisation) A group of countries including the USA and its allies who promised to support each other in case of an attack

Operation Linebacker A large bombing operation by US forces begun in 1972

Operation Rolling Thunder A heavy bombing operation by the USA in Vietnam

People's Volunteers The name given to the Chinese forces fighting in Korea

Provisional Temporary and not formal

Republican Party One of two main US political parties

Search and destroy Small raids launched by US forces from heavily defended bases

South East Atlantic Treaty Organisation (SEATO) An alliance of anti-Communist states in Asia

Soviet Used to refer to the USSR. For example, Hungary was a Soviet satellite state

Stalemate A situation where neither side can win

Strategic Hamlet A US programme of moving peasant villages into fortified settlements to stop Viet Cong influence

Superpower Used to refer to the USA and the USSR as two countries with a powerful military and strong economy

Tet Offensive A major attack on South Vietnam by Viet Cong forces in 1968

Truman Doctrine The policy of the USA trying to stop the further spread of Communism

United Nations (UN) A group of countries who would work together to keep peace after the Second World War

Veto A President's constitutional right to reject a decision made by a law-making body, for example Congress in the USA

Viet Cong Communist fighters in Vietnam who originally fought against French rule

Viet Minh A group founded to oppose French occupation of Vietnam

Vietnamisation Nixon's policy of training South Vietnamese troops to take over fighting

Watergate Affair A scandal involving the use of listening devices by Nixon's party to spy on their main rival, the Democrats

Section 2A British Thematic Studies

How the Thematic Study will be examined

Overview of the Thematic Study

It covers **a long time-span** (about 1000 years). It is about the **history of Britain** not the wider world.

In this book we cover two thematic studies:
- Health and the people: c1000 to the present day
- Power and the people: c1170 to the present day.

Thematic studies focus on change and continuity over a long period of time:
- The study examines **key developments** which affected Britain – including social, political and economic developments.
- You will consider the **significance** of those different developments for people's health or for who holds power.
- You will identify **similarities and differences** between periods.
- You will assess the **amount of change and continuity** across periods.
- You will consider the **role of factors** in causing or preventing change. Factors include: war, science and technology, individuals, government and religion.
- You will also use lots of **sources** and you will evaluate them for usefulness.

There are various key skills you will need for the Thematic Study

Comprehending and evaluating sources – you will need to be able to look carefully at the content and provenance of a source and use your own knowledge in order to judge its usefulness for understanding a topic

Comparing events – you will need to identify key features of events or developments, from different time periods, and explain how similar or different they are

THE THEMATIC STUDY

Explaining developments – you will need to identify and also explain the impact of a development both at the time and over time

Comparing factors – you will need to use evidence to compare the role of several different factors across time

Coming to overall judgements – you will need to make sophisticated judgements based upon the range of evidence used in your answer. You will need to write these in a clear and persuasive manner

Quick quizzes at **www.hoddereducation.co.uk/myrevisionnotes**

There are four main question types in the Thematic Study

This will be Section A of your Paper 2. It is worth 44 marks in total. You will be asked the following types of question.

1 How useful is this source? *(8 marks)*

You will be given a source and have to study both its content and provenance. You will have to use your own contextual knowledge to explain how useful the source is for understanding the period or topic.

2 Explain the significance of ... *(8 marks)*

You will be given a key event, person, group or development. You will need to identify and explain the importance of this both at the time and in a later period.

3 Compare/in what ways are they similar or different? *(8 marks)*

You will be given two events, developments or individuals/groups – usually from different periods. You will need to identify the features of each and identify ways in which they are similar or different.

4 Essay question on the role of factors *(16 marks + 4 SPaG)*

You will be pointed to one factor which caused or prevented change and will have to judge the importance of this factor in comparison to other factors you have studied. These factors could include war, religion, government, chance, communication, individuals, groups or science and technology. You will need to evaluate at least two factors and come to a judgement on which was more important.

How we help you develop your exam skills

- The **Revision tasks** help you build understanding and skills step by step. For example:

  Role of factors helps you to identify the impact of the key factors

  Activities focused on **comparing periods or events** will help to structure your thinking about similarities and differences over time.

  Flow chart activities will help you to understand the narrative of events and consider the links between them.

  Improve the paragraph style activities will help you to develop your understanding of how to present your ideas for the exam.

  Develop detail/explanation style activities will help you to improve your ability to explain impacts.

- The **practice questions** give you exam style questions
- **Exam focus** at the end of each chapter gives you model answers for each question type.

Plus:

There are **annotated model answers** for every practice question online at www.hoddereducation.co.uk/myrevisionnotes or use this QR code to find them instantly.

Chapter 8 Health and the people: c1000 to the present day

8.1A Key features of British medicine in the Middle Ages

The cause of illness was unknown

- Doctors (at that time called **physicians**) lacked the scientific knowledge required to understand the causes of disease.
- Medical training was to read Church-approved texts such as Galen.

Supernatural beliefs dominated treatments

- The **Doctrine of Signatures** was followed. It taught that God had the power to create illness and guided doctors on treatments.
- Doctors used **zodiac charts** to decide treatment and when to operate.

Some natural treatments were used

- Doctors and women healers had a good knowledge of how to use herbs to treat illnesses. For example with balms made of herbs and honey.
- Breathing problems or eye **infections** were treated with such balms.
- Doctors used **urine charts** to diagnose illness.

> **Key point**
>
> Lack of scientific knowledge and the influence of the Roman Catholic Church during the Middle Ages meant that religious ideas dominated British medicine.

8.1B Main influences on British medicine in the Middle Ages

Hippocrates greatly influenced diagnosis and treatment of illness

- Hippocrates (460–370BC) taught that **clinical observation** (examining and observing your patient and keeping detailed records) was very important. It still underpins medicine today.
- His **Theory of Four Humours** said that the body consisted of four humours (blood, phlegm, black bile and yellow bile) that had to be balanced for good health.
- Many doctors followed this theory. It influenced medicine until the 1800s.
- **Bleeding** was used to prevent or treat illness. It involved opening a vein or applying leeches to draw blood. It was used to balance humours. Monks were bled up to eight times a year.
- The Hippocratic collection of books was used to train doctors for hundreds of years. They were significant as they provided the first detailed account of symptoms and treatments.

Galen's ideas dominated medical training and treatments through to the 1800s

- Galen (AD130–c.210) built on the Theory of the Four Humours.
- To learn about human **anatomy**, Galen **dissected** animals. As a result he made errors. His errors were accepted because the Church banned people questioning his work.
- The Church liked Galen's work because it supported the **design theory** (that God designed humans). Galen called God 'the creator'.

> **TIP**
>
> You will find that events in this course are sometimes more significant in later periods than they were at the time. Galen influenced treatments in Britain right up to the 1800s. Hippocratic methods still influence medical ideas today.

> **Test yourself**
>
> 1 Provide three examples of lack of scientific knowledge limiting progress.
>
> 2 Describe one difference between Islamic and British medicine.
>
> 3 List three influences on British medicine.

The Church played a significant role in medicine

- Christianity taught that God sent illness as punishment for sinful behaviour. To treat illness, people had to repent their sins. As a result, prayer was a popular treatment.
- The Church controlled the universities where doctors trained. Teaching was based on ancient texts written by Hippocrates (c129–c210) and Galen (c460–c370BCE).
- The Church banned medical research and human dissection. Roger Bacon was sent to prison by Church leaders for advocating scientific observation.

Medieval hospitals were small and mainly a place for people to rest and recover from illness

- Hospitals were linked to monasteries or nunneries.
- There were no doctors. Monks and nuns provided nursing care and mainly relied on prayer and herbal treatments.
- Hospital wards had altars where prayers were said regularly.

Islamic medicine and training was significantly more advanced than the Christian West

- Islamic doctors wrote medical encyclopaedias. Their ideas were spread to Britain by crusaders.
- Islamic philosopher and doctor, Avicenna, wrote the *Canon of Medicine*. It remained an important text for medical students until the 1700s.
- Islamic hospitals treated patients and also trained doctors.

Warfare helped surgeons improve their skills

- Improved skill in sealing wounds. Quicker **amputations**.
- New tools, including the arrow cup (designed to remove an arrow-head from the body without causing further damage).
- Improved ointments (for example, John Arderne's painkiller).
- Sharing through manuals or diagrams such as the 'wound man'.

 Support or challenge?

Question 4 of your exam will ask you to explain the role of factors. Read this statement about the role of religion.

The Church prevented medical progress in the Middle Ages.

Decide whether each piece of evidence below supports or challenges the statement. The first has been done for you.

Task: add at least one extra piece of evidence for each side.

Evidence	Support	Challenge
The Church established universities that trained doctors		X
Church supported the work of Galen		
Christianity taught followers to care for the sick		
Church leaders imprisoned those who advocated dissection		

 **Eliminate irrelevance**

Question 2 of your exam will focus on significance. For example:

Explain the significance of the work of Hippocrates on the development of medicine. (8 marks)

In the paragraph below cross out sentences or phrases that do not help explain significance. Having deleted irrelevant elements, justify your deletions with Post-it notes.

He taught medicine and influenced many people. His work is significant because he developed medicine based on nature, observation and logic. Through careful observation and records he made the important step away from supernatural based medicine. The Theory of Four Humours is an example. It was developed using the theory of four elements. Greeks believed that everything was made from the four elements: fire, air, water and earth. Elements were then linked to seasons: winter, spring, summer and autumn. Doctors noted how patients' illnesses changed with seasons and linked humours to them: phlegm, yellow bile, blood and black bile. This created a method of diagnosis. For example, water to winter and the humour of phlegm. Galen developed the theory further. The Theory of Four Humours led to the treatment of bleeding which was very popular. The theory lasted over 1000 years. But more importantly the process of observation and record keeping has continued to this day.

8.2 Public health in the Middle Ages

Towns did little to improve public health

- At a local level: most people believed it was not their role to ensure good hygiene for others.
- At a national level: the King's role was to protect people from invasion not prevent disease.

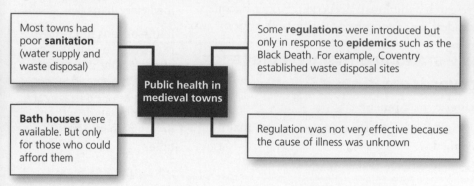

Most towns had poor **sanitation** (water supply and waste disposal)

Bath houses were available. But only for those who could afford them

Public health in medieval towns

Some **regulations** were introduced but only in response to **epidemics** such as the Black Death. For example, Coventry established waste disposal sites

Regulation was not very effective because the cause of illness was unknown

Monasteries had superior public health systems to towns

- Monks were literate (they could read) so they were more informed about **public health** than most people.
- Monks regarded a fresh water supply as a priority when designing monasteries.
- However, the link between germs and illness was unknown which limited their efforts.

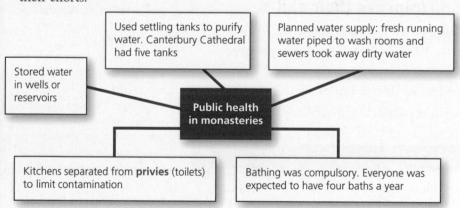

Used settling tanks to purify water. Canterbury Cathedral had five tanks

Planned water supply: fresh running water piped to wash rooms and sewers took away dirty water

Stored water in wells or reservoirs

Public health in monasteries

Kitchens separated from **privies** (toilets) to limit contamination

Bathing was compulsory. Everyone was expected to have four baths a year

Supernatural ideas dominated explanations of the causes of the Black Death

- People believed every aspect of their lives was controlled by God. This led them to believe God must have sent the Black Death as a punishment for sinful acts.
- Others explained it by **astrology** (study of the movement and position of planets). The alignment of the Sun and the planets Saturn, Jupiter and Mars was identified as a cause.
- Minority groups were blamed for the Black Death. For example, Jews were accused of poisoning water supplies.
- Some people blamed bad smells because they believed in **miasma theory** (that bad smells caused illness). This was based on observation and logic but it was mistaken.

Quick quizzes at **www.hoddereducation.co.uk/myrevisionnotes**

Methods of prevention and **treatment for the Black Death** were mainly **based on superstition**

The most popular explanation was sin, so:	Other remedies included:
The King and bishops ordered churches to organise special services and processions asking for God's forgiveness	People had noticed a link between disease and bad smells. This resulted in orders to clean streets of dirt and waste
Ordinary people prayed to God for forgiveness	Bleeding was used to treat victims as recommended by Hippocrates to balance the humours
Flagellants tried to avoid catching the Black Death by travelling from Flanders to London whipping themselves to show that they had repented their sins	Natural potions were advised as forms of prevention and treatment. Smelling posies of flowers were used to avoid bad smells

● All methods had limited success because the cause of the Black Death was unknown and methods were not based on scientific knowledge.

Test yourself

1 Give two examples of the Church's influence on people's responses to the Black Death.

2 Name an ancient treatment used to treat the Black Death.

TIP

When evaluating a source always read the provenance. It will include important information about who wrote it and when.

Consider usefulness

Question 1 in your exam will ask you to assess the usefulness (utility) of a source for a given purpose. For example:

How useful is Source A to a historian studying the Black Death? (8 marks)

You will need to consider both content and provenance. Draw lines to link the inferences below to specific details in the source or provenance.

SOURCE A *Franciscan monks treating victims of the plague, c1474.*

A People believed God sent the Black Death as a punishment.

B The Church was important and influenced lives, especially death.

C Natural explanations for the Black Death were limited.

D Praying for forgiveness was important.

8.3 Impact of the Renaissance on medicine in Britain

The **development of new ideas** during the Renaissance led to some **medical progress**

Development	Impact
The **Reformation** challenged the religious *status quo*	... led individuals to question important aspects of their life such as the role of God and science
Invention of the **microscope**	... helped scientists and doctors to make and explain discoveries
Creation of Caxton's **printing press**	... allowed ideas to spread quickly across Britain and Europe
English people had become **wealthier** since the Black Death and spent more on education	... improved literacy rates increased the number of people accessing new scientific ideas

- However, it took a long time for these new scientific ideas to affect everyday treatments.

> **Key point**
>
> During the Renaissance, knowledge of the human body advanced through the work of key individuals and scientific advancements. However, progress was limited as the cause of disease remained unknown.

Vesalius greatly improved understanding of **human anatomy**

- Vesalius (1514–64) dissected humans rather than animals. This gave him accurate knowledge of human anatomy and allowed him to prove that Galen was wrong in a number of ways.
- Vesalius worked with skilled artists to ensure that his findings on human anatomy were accurately documented and easy for others to learn from.
- In 1543, Vesalius published anatomical drawings in his book *De Humani Corporis Fabrica* (*On the fabric of the human body*).
- His book proved the value of human dissection and the need to question the work of the **ancients**.
- Vesalius' work had limited impact on treatments. Doctors still did not know about the cause of illness or learn new effective treatments.

Paré used scientific method to improve treatments and **surgery**

- Paré (1510–90) was a French army surgeon for twenty years. By experimenting on wounded soldiers he discovered better ways to prevent bleeding.
- Hot oil had long been used for sealing wounds. On one occasion, Paré ran out of oil so instead he used his own mixture of egg yolk, turpentine and oil of roses, an old Roman technique. It worked.
- To prevent bleeding after an amputation, Paré used **ligatures** to tie wounds instead of **cauterising** them with a hot iron. His method had a higher success rate.
- He spread these ideas through his 1575 book *Les Oeuvres* (*Works*).
- Paré's work became famous among British doctors and surgeons who studied in Europe where his ideas were popular.
- However, Paré's impact on British medicine was limited. Only the rich could afford to pay for medical care and only trained doctors knew about it.
- Paré's work was not accepted by everyone in Britain. New ideas were often met with scepticism.

> **TIP**
>
> The key to success in 'Health and the people' is an overview knowledge of the role of factors and being able to explain how they caused continuity and change. Paré is a good example of the factor of 'war' improving medicine. Throughout your revision use the table on pages 184–85 to record, memorise and analyse good examples for your essays.
>
> The chart will also help you compare periods (the focus for question 3).

Quick quizzes at **www.hoddereducation.co.uk/myrevisionnotes**

Harvey discovered the circulation of blood which challenged previously accepted ideas

- Harvey (1578–1657) worked as a doctor in England and held important posts including being doctor to King James I and King Charles I. He was in a strong position to influence medical ideas in Britain.

- Harvey discovered and proved that veins in the body had valves and that blood was pumped round the body by the heart beating constantly.

- Harvey's theory challenged Galen who taught that the liver produced blood. Harvey proved that the liver did not produce blood. This discovery questioned the value of the popular treatment of bleeding.

- Harvey published his work in *On the Motion of the Heart*, 1628. Afterwards, some of his patients refused to be treated by him, as they no longer trusted him.

- Harvey's work was rejected by conservatives who supported Galen. They refused to accept the use of experiments in medicine.

- Some people rejected Harvey's work because they were unable to see capillaries. It was another 60 years before they could.

 ### Develop the explanation

The statements below describe Vesalius', Paré's or Harvey's work. On a separate piece of paper, for each one, add one or two more sentences to turn it from a description into an explanation of how they influenced medicine in Britain. The first one has been done for you.

Description	Explanation
• Paré's ideas and work were taught in European universities	This influenced medicine in Britain because many British doctors trained in Europe and as a result were taught about Pare's ideas and work. When they returned to Britain they used them in their own work
• Vesalius, Paré and Harvey recorded their findings and published them	
• Vesalius used skilled artists to record his work on anatomy	
• Harvey was personal doctor to two kings	

 ### Role of factors

Use the information on these two pages to add examples to your chart on pages 184–85. You should be able to add examples for War, Role of individuals, Science and technology and Communication. For example:

Communication	The invention of the printing press allowed new ideas to be shared quickly and accurately

 ### Practice question

Compare surgery in the Renaissance with surgery in the Middle Ages. In what ways were they similar? Explain your answer with reference to both times. (8 marks)

 ### Test yourself

1 Give two examples of inventions that helped advance British medicine.

2 Provide two reasons why Harvey's work was not accepted in Britain.

8.4 Dealing with disease

Treatments evolved in the Renaissance but were limited by a lack of knowledge about germs

- Improved travel and communication advanced medicine in Britain. New herbs and ideas were introduced that improved treatments.
- Individuals such as Lady Grace Mildmay quickly incorporated new herbs and remedies into their treatments.
- New ideas focused on specific parts of medicine. Robert Burton studied mental illness and Jane Sharp argued for women-led midwifery.
- The working classes often bought their treatments from **quacks**, people who falsely claimed that they held a medical qualification. Quacks travelled around Britain making profits from false treatments.
- A few quacks gained knowledge of treatments through experience.
- Most people continued to be treated by female family members or local wise women. Both groups used herbal remedies and traditional treatments.

> **Key point**
>
> In the Renaissance, treatments started to improve for the wealthy through improved scientific knowledge and limited training for doctors. However, all advancements were limited by a lack of knowledge about germs.

The Great Plague of 1665: prevention and treatments combined traditional and new ideas

Traditional ideas and methods	Combination of traditional and new	New ideas and methods
Prayer: commonly used to ask God for forgiveness for sinful behaviour Miasma theory: 'bad air' was blamed. Streets were cleaned and posies carried	**Plague doctors** were hired by towns: • they wore special clothing that covered all parts of their body to prevent them from catching the disease • they also carried amulets showing people still believed in supernatural causes	Scientific approach: it was observed that death rates were higher in poorer, dirtier places **Watchmen**: prevented people entering and leaving infected houses to try to stop the infection spreading

The numbers of hospitals increased. Some treated patients as well as caring for them

- Most hospitals were funded by rich people through donations, legacies or private subscriptions. The Church's role in funding reduced.
- In 1741, Thomas Coram raised money to open the Foundling Hospital in London. It supported and educated vulnerable children until the age of fifteen. Demand was greater than the places available.
- Some aspects of hospital provision continued from the Middle Ages. For example, nurses continued to be untrained and unskilled.
- Hospitals continued to provide care for the most vulnerable.

The establishment of Royal Colleges improved the training and status of surgeons and doctors

- **1600**: Royal College for Physicians established.
- **1700**: half of all practising physicians had served an apprenticeship.
- **1800**: Royal College of Surgeons established. It examined all surgeons practising within seven miles of London.
- **1811**: compulsory for all surgeons to attend a one-year course in anatomy before they qualified as a surgeon.
- **1813**: surgeons had to work for at least one year in a hospital to qualify.

 Test yourself

1 Identify one similarity and one difference in hospitals between the Middle Ages and the Renaissance.

2 When was the Royal College for Physicians established?

3 When did training of surgeons become compulsory?

Quick quizzes at **www.hoddereducation.co.uk/myrevisionnotes**

John Hunter was a skilled British surgeon who encouraged investigation and experimentation

● Hunter trained many British surgeons after 1768.

● Like Vesalius, Hunter encouraged human dissection to advance the understanding of anatomy.

● He told surgeons to trust the body's natural wound-healing process.

● Hunter taught the importance of observation and experiment.

● Edward Jenner followed these principles when he discovered **vaccination**.

 Compare events

Question 3 of your exam will ask you to compare events or developments from different periods.

The table below shows responses to the Black Death. Complete the second column to explain how responses to the Great Plague were similar or different. Use one colour for similar, another colour for different.

Responses to the Black Death, 1348	Responses to the Great Plague, 1665
People asked God's forgiveness by praying and lighting candles in church	Similar. People continued to pray for God's forgiveness
Some responses were based on observation. For example: they cleaned the streets of dirt and waste; Henry VI banned the kiss of obedience	
Bleeding was used. It was based on the Hippocratic idea of balancing the humours	
Natural potions were also advised for sufferers such as smelling posies of flowers. However, they were not based on scientific knowledge	
The cause was unknown meaning all methods of treatment and prevention were limited	

 Practice question

How useful is Source B to a historian studying the Great Plague of 1665 in Britain? Explain your answer using Source B and your contextual knowledge.

(8 marks)

SOURCE B *An illustration from 1656 showing an Italian plague doctor. The beak of the mask is filled with herbs. The stick is for beating away sick people.*

TIP

Remember that all sources are useful for something. It all depends on what you are using them for. Never dismiss a source as useless because it is one-sided or incomplete. It will be still be very useful for finding out about the attitudes of the person who made it.

8.5A Prevention of disease

In the 1700s, **inoculation** was widely used to prevent smallpox

- Smallpox was greatly feared. It caused death, blindness and scarring. There were frequent epidemics.
- **Inoculation** involved giving a low dose of smallpox to make a person immune to the disease.
- In 1721, Lady Montagu introduced it to England. It became popular.

Jenner introduced the **first vaccination** against smallpox

- Edward Jenner injected James Phipps with pus from cowpox sores. It gave James Phipps immunity against smallpox. This became known as vaccination.
- Jenner was unable to explain why vaccination worked. But it worked so well that the government eventually made it compulsory.

Vaccination faced **opposition**, especially from doctors

- Inoculation doctors opposed it because it threatened their business.
- Many people thought it was wrong to inject cowpox into humans.
- Some saw smallpox as a punishment from God and believed prevention interfered with God's will.
- The Anti-Compulsory Vaccination League was set up in 1866. It argued that it was the right of parents to decide if their child was vaccinated.

> **Key point**
>
> During the 1800s, medical knowledge significantly advanced following major breakthroughs by individuals. These included the discovery of germs and the ability to identify specific bacteria.

1798: Jenner published his findings

1802: government gave Jenner £10,000 to open a vaccination clinic in London

1840: vaccination made free for all infants

1853: vaccination of children was made compulsory

1871: parents fined if their child was not vaccinated

1887: parents given the right to decide if their child was vaccinated

8.5B Germ Theory and its impact

In 1861 **Pasteur's Germ Theory** showed the link between germs and disease

- Louis Pasteur's work was a major breakthrough in **microbiology** (the branch of science that deals with microorganisms).
- Using Jenner's work on vaccination, Pasteur experimented and developed new vaccinations (including vaccines for chicken cholera and rabies).
- Inspired by Pasteur, Joseph Lister successfully used **antiseptics** to reduce infection during and after surgery.

Koch helped identify **specific bacteria** which cause disease

- Robert Koch found a way to stain bacteria, making them easier to identify under a microscope. It allowed him to link specific germs to specific disease.
- Koch identified the causes of Britain's major killers, including **diphtheria** and **typhoid**. Fewer people died.
- His technique allowed other scientists to do their own microbe hunting.

Ehrlich created the first **chemical treatment**, changing the way disease was treated

- Paul Ehrlich used scientific experiments to identify and treat disease.
- In 1910, he created Salvarsan 606. This chemical killed germs causing syphilis (a common sexually transmitted disease in Britain at the time).
- Salvarsan 606 only targeted the specific germ that caused syphilis. This was a major breakthrough in treatments.

Diagnosis was improved by new technology

Invention	Importance
Stethoscope invented in Paris in 1816 and became common from 1850	Enabled doctors to hear the internal workings of the body and assess a patient's health more precisely
X-ray machine invented in 1895	Allowed surgeons to see bones and assess patients' illnesses more accurately
Thermometers	Gave doctors accurate records of patients' temperatures

Test yourself

1 Identify three ways health and medicine improved during the Renaissance.

2 Name two British individuals involved in medical improvements.

3 List three key stages (with dates) in the story of vaccination.

Consider significance

Question 2 will ask you about the significance of an event you have studied. For example:

Explain the significance of the Germ Theory in the development of medicine. (8 marks)

Explain the significance of vaccination in the development of treatment. (8 marks)

Because significance can seem quite a vague idea it is easy to get sucked into including irrelevant details. All you really have to do with a significance question is explain one way the event was significant at the time; and one way it has been significant for people looking back from a later period.

Copy and complete this grid to help you plan your answer to each of these exam style questions.

Event or development	At the time	In later periods
Germ Theory		
Vaccination		

Include general points and specific examples from your own knowledge. Remember to incorporate evidence from different eras.

Practice question

Study Source C. How useful is Source C to a historian studying Edward Jenner's vaccination? Explain your answer using Source C and your contextual knowledge. (8 marks)

SOURCE C *A cartoon by Isaac Cruickshank, 1808, showing inoculators being driven away by Jenner's vaccinators.*

8.6 A revolution in surgery

Simpson developed effective anaesthetics in 1847 solving the problem of pain

- James Simpson was Professor of Midwifery at Edinburgh University.
- He used ether as an **anaesthetic** (pain relief) but wanted to discover a more effective method.
- In 1847, Simpson discovered **chloroform** was an effective anaesthetic after experimenting with friends.
- Simpson quickly used chloroform during childbirth and other operations.
- Simpson wrote articles encouraging other surgeons to use it. He argued that chloroform allowed surgeons to do longer or more complex operations.
- Chloroform was not accepted by everyone until Queen Victoria used it during childbirth in 1853. She later 'blessed' the drug.
- Some surgeons stopped using chloroform by 1870 because it did not reduce **mortality** (death) rates. Longer operations led to increased blood loss and deeper infections. It was also hard for an accurate dose to be given.

> **Key point**
>
> By the late 1800s the chances of a patient surviving surgery greatly increased as solutions were discovered for two major problems: pain and infection. However, the third problem, bleeding, remained unsolved.

In 1867 Lister developed antiseptic surgery

1867: after reading about the Germ Theory, Joseph Lister experimented with carbolic acid spray to reduce infection during surgery. Mortality rates (deaths) fell from 46 per cent (in 1867) to 15 per cent (by 1870)	**1870:** Lister started to sterilise his operating room and patients' wounds with carbolic acid	**1871:** Lister invented a machine to automatically spray his operating room with carbolic acid	**1877:** Lister started to train British surgeons in London	**1880:** Lister started to use sterilised catgut for internal stitches

- Lister's methods were not accepted by everyone because:
  - carbolic spray slowed operations
  - it made operating conditions unpleasant
  - some surgeons were not careful so did not have the same success as Lister.

Individuals pioneered new techniques in surgery increasing survival rates

Person and date	Invention/change	Significance
Charles Chamberland, 1881	Steam steriliser for medical instruments	Removed the need for carbolic acid and increased surgery survival rates. Few surgeons used it due to the time it took and cost
Gustav Neuber, 1886	**Aseptic surgery:** this is when all possible germs are removed from the operating theatre	Built on Lister's ideas and aided by Koch's discovery of the bacterium which caused septicaemia. Reduced mortality rates. In 1886 he set the standards for others to follow
Berkeley Moyniham, 1890s	First in Britain to wear surgical gloves and to change into sterile white garments for surgery	Took a long time for other surgeons to copy him

 Test yourself

1 List two reasons why chloroform did not reduce mortality rates.
2 Give three reasons why surgeons opposed antiseptics.
3 Name the British surgeon who changed his clothes before operating.

Develop the detail

Each of the following statements is vague and lacks detail. Add details to show that you understand the general point made about advancements in surgery. One example has been done for you.

Statement	Development
Chloroform was an effective drug but it was not quickly accepted	Chloroform was an effective anaesthetic and Simpson soon used it to assist with childbirth and other operations. However, it was not quickly accepted as it did not always reduce mortality rates. Also surgeons were always conservative about new ideas
Lister's discovery of carbolic spray reduced his mortality rates	
Many surgeons disliked using carbolic spray	
Lister's work contributed to the development of aseptic surgery	

 Compare periods

The table below shows features of opposition to new ideas in the Renaissance. Complete the second column to explain how opposition to new surgical ideas 1845–70 was similar or different.

Challenge: challenge yourself and add a third column (on a separate sheet) with the heading 'Opposition to new ideas in the twentieth century'.

Opposition to new surgical ideas in the Renaissance	Opposition to new surgical ideas 1845–70
Refusal to accept the use of experiment	
Rejected by conservatives who supported traditional ideas and texts, especially the works of Galen	
Harvey's ideas were dismissed as physicians and surgeons were unable to see capillaries. It took another 60 years for the invention of a microscope powerful enough to achieve this	
New medical ideas took a long time to be accepted. People did not like change	

Practice question

Explain the significance of Lister in the development of surgery.

(8 marks)

8.7 Improvements in public health

In the 1800s, **industrial towns grew rapidly** leading to significant **public health problems**

- **Overcrowding** was a common problem. A large family might live in one small room and share toilets and water pumps with many families.
- Infectious diseases such as typhus and typhoid spread quickly.
- There were few safety rules in the workplace. Many people worked in dangerous environments and became ill. For example, chimney boys suffered from scrotal cancer from soot particles and coal miners from pneumoconiosis from breathing in coal dust.
- There was no regulation of food or hygiene. Milk might be watered down and re-coloured using chalk powder.

Snow proved that cholera was caused by infected water

- Britain faced many deadly cholera epidemics between 1831 and 1866.
- Cholera causes watery diarrhoea and sickness leading to rapid dehydration and death. It was greatly feared.
- People did not know what caused **cholera**. The common explanation was miasma (bad air).
- John Snow thought differently. In 1849 he wrote a book arguing it was caused by infected water.
- During the 1854 epidemic, John Snow proved the link between cholera and dirty water.
  - He did house-to-house interviews and mapped the location of each cholera case.
  - He worked out which water pump the infected houses used. He removed the handle of that water pump. The outbreak ended.
  - Further exploration found that the lining of the nearby cesspit had cracked. Its contents had leaked into the drinking water.
- Snow's discovery was made before Pasteur published his Germ Theory.

Individuals played a significant role in public health reform in the 1800s

Individual	Public health reform
William Farr	Introduced compulsory registration of births, marriages and deaths in 1837. This meant the authorities were more aware of health problems
Thomas Southwood Smith	Studied diseases caused by poverty. His work was used by Edwin Chadwick as evidence for the need to improve public health
Edwin Chadwick, Secretary to the Poor Law Commissioners	Researched living conditions and health of the poor in towns. Published his findings in *Report on the Sanitary Conditions of the Labouring Population*. He linked poverty to poor living standards and ill health

> **Key point**
>
> In the late 1800s, public health improved following greater understanding of the causes of illness and a scientific approach to research. However, the struggle to improve conditions for the working classes continued into the twentieth century.

> **TIP**
>
> Writing frame for significance questions:
> - paragraph 1: significance at the time
> - paragraph 2: significance in a later period
> - paragraph 3: conclusion about whether significance has increased or decreased over time and why this has happened.

Government **attitudes changed** and *laissez-faire* was replaced by legislation

- In the early nineteenth century the government followed a policy of *laissez-faire* (the government should not interfere in people's lives).
- Attitudes were gradually changed by a combination of the growing evidence of health problems in industrial cities, cholera epidemics, the Great Stink of 1858 and the pioneering work of individuals.
- Public health laws were introduced in the second half of the century:

Date	Act	Results
1848	Public Health Act	Voluntary. Allowed councils to raise money to improve conditions in their town. However, very few opted to use this power
1864	Factory Act	Unhealthy conditions in factories became illegal
1866	Sanitary Act	Local authorities became responsible for sewers, water and street cleaning
1875	Food and Drug Act	Regulated food and medicine
1875	Public Health Act	Compulsory. It forced local councils to provide clean water and appoint medical officers of health and sanitary inspectors

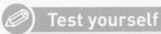 Test yourself

1 Give three reasons why towns had poor public health in early 1800s.

2 What was the key difference between the 1848 and 1875 Public Health Acts?

Part 3: A revolution in medicine

 Key events

Complete the four blank boxes to show your knowledge about John Snow's work and its impact.

In 1849 John Snow published a book arguing that cholera was spread by dirty water rather than through the air					Careful scientific investigation had helped to find the cause of cholera, before Pasteur's Germ Theory was published

You're the examiner

Explain the significance of Edwin Chadwick's work in improving public health. (8 marks)

Edwin Chadwick's work in the nineteenth century meant that the government took action in industrial cities to improve public health conditions. He was appointed Secretary to the Poor Law Commission in 1834. He researched living conditions and health of the poor in towns. Using the data he recorded, he made a link between poor living conditions, disease and life expectancy. This was used to write the influential 1842 'Report on the Sanitary Conditions of the Labouring Population'. His work contributed to the British government changing their attitude towards public health. In 1848, the Public Health Act was passed. It gave councils who wanted to take action the right to make changes. It also contributed to the establishment of the general Board of Health.

Read the sample answer. Use this simple mark scheme to judge what level this answer has reached.

- Level 1: knowing one or two relevant points on the topic.
- Level 2: clearly explaining significance in one period.
- Level 3: clearly explaining significance at the time and in a later period.
- Level 4: two points of significance explained, plus a clear conclusion answering the question.

Annotate the extract and write a comment justifying the level.

8.8 Modern treatment of disease and surgical advancements

REVISED

Penicillin was a great step forward in treatment

- **1880s:** Joseph Lister used **penicillin** to treat an infected wound. He did not continue to use it or leave any records of his work with it.
- **1928:** Alexander Fleming rediscovered the properties of penicillin. He published his findings but took no further action.
- **1937:** Florey and Chain researched penicillin after reading Fleming's article.
- **1940:** they proved penicillin's potential by experiments on mice.
- **1941:** penicillin first tested on a human being. It was a success.
- **1942:** due to Second World War, the US and British governments funded the production of penicillin. By 1944 penicillin was available to treat all wounded Allied soldiers on D-Day.
- **Today:** penicillin is a common form of treatment saving many lives. However, some germs are becoming resistant to antibiotics.

> **Key point**
>
> Medicine in the twentieth and twenty-first centuries greatly benefited from developments in science and technology as well as financial investment from private pharmaceutical firms.

The pharmaceutical industry developed quickly after 1945

- Pharmaceuticals have become an important and wealthy industry.
- A range of life-saving drugs has been developed by private companies.
- Regulation of drug companies has ensured drugs are fully tested following mistakes such as thalidomide which had harmful side-effects.

Alternative treatments have become popular but scientific medicine largely rejects them

- Alternative medicines are treatments outside of mainstream practice.

Example 1: homeopathy	Example 2: acupuncture
Homeopathy uses substances very diluted with water to stimulate the body's natural healing power	**Acupuncture** involves stimulating nerves using needles. It is widely used around the world
It is not recognised by **NICE**, which states that it should not be used for the treatment of any health problems	NICE only recommends it for chronic tension-type headaches and migraines

- Interest in alternative medicine has grown following concerns about modern medicine and the negative side-effects of drugs.
- There is a fierce debate about the benefits of alternative medicines. The British Medical Association has referred to homeopathy as 'witchcraft'.

War led to improvements in surgery in the twentieth century

First World War	Second World War
Harold Giles developed new techniques for treating facial injuries	Cataract surgery developed. Sir Harold Ridley discovered that Perspex splinters were not rejected by the eye
Mobile X-ray machines and blood transfusions saved lives	
1921: British Red Cross created the first blood banks	
1938: British government established the Army Blood Supply Depot. This system still exists	Sir Archibald McIndoe improved treatment for burn injuries

Science and technology are improving modern surgery

- Imaging technology such as MRI scans allows surgeons to see inside the body.
- In 1961 the first heart pacemaker was fitted to a patient.
- **Keyhole surgery** (through a small incision) and laser techniques are making operations quicker and reducing healing times.

 Role of factors

Record examples of each of the following factors helping progress in the twentieth and twenty-first centuries.

Challenge: challenge yourself by adding a fourth column (on a separate sheet) titled 'Government'.

War	Science and technology	Role of the individual
Second World War led government to invest in the production of penicillin. Now a common life saver		

 Test yourself

1   Name two individuals (and their role) in turning penicillin into a life-saving drug.
2   Define alternative medicine and give two examples.

TIP

Candidates find it hard to give time to planning in an actual exam which is why it is so important to practise before the exam so that it becomes instinctive.

 Essay plan

Question 4 of your exam will be a factor-based essay. For example:

Has war been the main factor in the development of surgery in Britain since the Middle Ages? Explain your answer with reference to war and other factors. (16 marks + SPaG 4 marks)

The secret of writing an essay is to have a good plan. Here is a plan.

Paragraph	Purpose/points to include	Comment
Introduction	State your argument: whether you think this was the 'main' factor	This sets your essay off on a positive track and gives you an argument to hold on to throughout your answer
Paragraph 1	Evidence of the named factor at work	Support everything you say with precise knowledge. Use examples from more than one period
Paragraph 2	Reasons why the named factor has had limited impact	This is an opportunity to show your developed understanding of the named factor. For example explain how that factor did not apply at all times
Paragraphs 3 and 4	Consider the role of one (or two) more factors	Choose other factors that had influence and write one paragraph on each. Link them clearly to the development stated in the question. Compare each to the main factor
Conclusion	Restate your judgement. Is the named factor more important than those in paragraphs 3 and 4? Include one strong argument as to why	This should be easy to write if you have kept your focus through the rest of the essay. Remember SPaG: there are 4 marks for spelling, punctuation and grammar so use your final minutes to check your work and correct it if necessary

Use this plan to answer the question above:

- Step 1: note evidence and examples for paragraphs 1 and 2.
- Step 2: choose what factor(s) to focus on for paragraphs 3 and 4 and note evidence and examples.
- Step 3: in the exam you write your full essay, but for this task just practise writing your conclusion.

8.9 Modern public health

Reformers highlighted the poor health of working-class people in Britain

- **1889**: Charles Booth found that 35 per cent of Londoners lived in poverty.
- **1899**: many Boer War volunteers were found unfit to fight due to bad diet and illness.
- **1901**: Seebohm Rowntree discovered over half of York's working-class people lived in poverty.
- **1913**: Maud Pember's *Round About a Pound a Week* highlighted how hard it was to survive on the average labourer's wage of £1 per week.

> **Key point**
>
> During the twentieth century, there was greater government involvement in improving public health. During the twenty-first century, government policies and spending have become major political issues as costs increase.

The Liberal government introduced social reforms to benefit the working class

Year	Act	Effect
1906	Education (Provision of Meals) Act	Free school meals
1908	Old Age Pensions Act	People over 70 receive 5 shillings (25p) a week; 7 shillings and 6 pence (37.5p) for a married couple
1909	Housing and Town Planning Act	Illegal to build back-to-back housing
1909	Labour Exchanges Act	Help unemployed people find work
1911	National Insurance Act	Introduced contribution scheme for sick and unemployment pay

The Beveridge Report led to further welfare reform and the National Health Service

- The **Beveridge Report** (1942) set out proposals for **welfare** changes after the Second World War.
- The **National Health Service (NHS)** was a central feature. It aimed to provide free healthcare 'from cradle to grave'.
- The NHS was created in 1948. Health providers were brought together to provide a free service at the point of delivery.
- The British Medical Association reported that only ten per cent of doctors supported the creation of the NHS.
- Improved welfare system included a comprehensive system of benefits paid through taxation and workers' contributions.
- The NHS and welfare reforms transformed the health of ordinary people.

Government tackled other public health issues in cities

- In response to bad air pollution in 1952, two Clean Air Acts in 1956 and 1968 encouraged people to use gas and electricity rather than coal.
- During the 1960s, the government ordered slums to be cleared. Councils built modern homes with central heating and bathrooms. These were often in tower blocks.
- Government established new towns, such as Milton Keynes, to help solve the problem of overcrowding in major cities.

Pressures on the NHS and welfare system have increased because of Britain's ageing population

- Government spending reviews have led to shortages and even removal of some drugs and treatments.
- The government has also focused on prevention through:
  - education about healthy eating (for example, 'five a day')
  - compulsory vaccination against diseases such as polio
  - screening for common cancers (such as breast screening).

Test yourself

1 Give two reasons why concern about public health increased at the start of the twentieth century.

2 List three examples of government public health measures since 1900.

Compare periods

Question 3 will ask you to compare periods. For example:

Compare government action in public health in the early twentieth century with its role in the mid-1800s. In what ways were they similar? Explain your answer with reference to both times. (8 marks)

The table below lists government actions to improve public health in the mid-1800s. Add your own annotations to highlight what was similar or different to this in the twentieth century.

Year	Government actions to improve public health in the nineteenth century
1848	Public Health Act was voluntary allowing councils to improve conditions in their town. However, they had to pay for changes. Very few opted to use it
1853	Compulsory vaccination against smallpox introduced
1858	London started a sewer-building programme
1864	Factory Act made unhealthy conditions in factories illegal
1866	Sanitary Act made local authorities responsible for sewers, water and street cleaning
1875	Food and Drug Act regulated food and medicine
1875	Public Health Act was compulsory. It forced local councils to provide clean water and appoint medical officers of health and sanitary inspectors
1875	Housing Act enabled councils to demolish and replace poor housing

TIP

- For a 'compare' question you will be asked about either similarities or differences. You don't need to write about both. Aim to cover at least two similarities or two differences. Write a paragraph on each.
- Good words to use when writing about similarities are: *likewise, also, both, in the same way, similarly.*
- Good words to use when writing about differences are: *on the other hand, in contrast, whereas.*

Overview

The key to understanding 'Health and the people' is overview knowledge of the role of factors and your ability to explain how they caused continuity and change. This table will help you analyse and memorise good examples for your essays. It will also help you with comparing periods (the focus for question 3).

Aspect or theme	Middle Ages				Renaissance			
	Beliefs about the causes of illness	Treatments	Surgery	Public health measures	Beliefs about the causes of illness	Treatments	Surgery	Public health
War						Battles gave surgeons many bodies to work on Paré introduced ligatures and created a herbal treatment for raw wounds		
Religion	Strong belief God sent illness as a punishment for sinful behaviour Church leaders prevented individuals investigating. Roger Bacon imprisoned for advocating experimentation					Reduced influence on medicine allowing research, observation and dissection		
Chance						Paré: ran out of hot oil and used a new herbal treatment for raw wounds		
Communication						Improved travel brought new herbs to Britain		
Government						Encouraged the use of religious treatments during the Great Plague		
Science and technology						Printing press allowed surgeons to share their ideas		
Role of individuals	Galen dominated medical texts and training. He supported the design theory							

Quick quizzes at www.hoddereducation.co.uk/myrevisionnotes

Basic: place a cross in each box if the factor influenced the aspect.

Developing: colour each box to show if the factor caused **continuity** or change.

Expert: add a specific example of the influence of the factor on each aspect. Some examples have been started for you.

Industrial Britain				Twentieth and twenty-first century			
Beliefs about the causes of illness	Treatments	Surgery	Public health	Beliefs about the causes of illness	Treatments	Surgery	Public health
							Boer War highlighted poor health of British population
							Increased regulation Establishment of the NHS and welfare system in 1948
		Invention of the steam steriliser					
		Simpson discovered chloroform, an effective anaesthetic Lister produced the first antiseptic					The reports of Charles Booth, Seebohm Rowntree and Maud Pember in the early twentieth century

Model answers

Here are model answers for each question type on the thematic study. The annotations highlight what makes each one a good answer.

Question 1: Usefulness of a source

Study Source B on page 173.

How useful is Source B to a historian studying the Great Plague of 1665? Explain your answer using Source B and your contextual knowledge. (8 marks)

Source B shows the plague doctor's protective outfit as designed by Charles de Lorme in 1619. It is useful because it shows that people were unaware of the causes of the plague, but had many theories that combined natural and supernatural ideas. The nose cone full of sweet-smelling herbs relates to the belief in the miasma theory. People thought that 'bad air' was the cause. The link between dirt and disease was being made, but a lack of understanding and limited technology meant the link could not be scientifically explained. In contrast to natural ideas the plague doctor can also be seen wearing an amulet, jewellery worn to ward off evil spirits, in the sleeve of the coat. Supernatural beliefs also influenced methods of treatment and prevention of the Great Plague as people searched for cures. Yet the source is limited as it fails to inform historians about the more organised and local regulations enforced to reduce deaths. For instance the actions of the Mayor of London to prevent those infected leaving their houses. Overall Source B is useful for a historian studying the actions of plague doctors in treating the disease during a period when new scientific approaches to medicine and public health were emerging but had limited effect.

- The answer gives specific details from the source
- The details in the source are then clearly explained
- Here specific contextual knowledge is used to explain how far the source is useful for understanding the issue in the question
- The answer finishes with a clear judgement about how useful the source is

Question 2 – Explain significance

Explain the significance of Galen in the development of medicine. (8 marks)

Galen's work was significant during the Middle Ages because it was supported by the Church and used to train physicians in universities across Europe. Consequently, his ideas greatly influenced practice and training of the most qualified and their apprentices. Furthermore, the Roman Catholic Church dominated life and only texts it approved were taught. Galen's work was accepted by the Church because it upheld the position of God as the creator. His dominant position and support from the Church made it extremely hard to question or oppose. Those who did, for example Roger Bacon, were sentenced to prison terms. This made Galen very significant in the short and medium term.

A long-term significant contribution Galen made to the development of medicine was highlighting the importance of clinical observation. He advocated the need to carefully watch and monitor a patient's symptoms to enable the correct treatment to be given. This idea, taken from Hippocrates, influenced the work of many individuals who brought later advancements to medicine in Britain. Clinical observation is a fundamental part of diagnosis today.

- This answer opens by directly addressing the question. This shows the examiner that you have understood, but will also help you to focus your answer as you write
- The answer begins by identifying the short-term significance and giving evidence which supports this
- In a separate paragraph, the long-term significance is considered and supported with precise evidence

While clinical observation is a vital part of modern-day medicine, much of Galen's work greatly limited the development of medicine until it was challenged during the Renaissance. For example, the flow of blood in the heart. However, the discovery that aspects of Galen's work were inaccurate showed that human dissection was important and it is vital that ideas are questioned.

> Here the answer links the evidence back to the question by explaining why this was significant

Question 3: Compare events

Compare public health in the Middle Ages with public health in early nineteenth-century industrial towns. In what ways were they similar? Explain your answer with reference to both times. **(8 marks)**

Public health in the medieval period and early nineteenth century were similar for the poorest town dwellers. Late medieval period towns were dirty places where animals roamed freely and excrement covered the streets. Sanitation was poor and in many places did not exist. A lack of knowledge about germs and a strong belief in supernatural causes limited advances in public health. Similarly, newly established industrial towns of the nineteenth century also suffered from dirt. Human and animal waste was discarded in the streets and rivers. While supernatural beliefs were less influential, germs were unknown until 1861. The miasma theory dominated and waste was removed because of its smell. The miasma theory had also existed during the Middle Ages. During the Black Death, individuals had carried posies to prevent the disease. A lack of knowledge hindered progress in both eras.

> Each paragraph opens by giving one reason why these events are similar

> Specific knowledge is then given about one of these events which is relevant to the point made in the opening sentence

In both eras conditions were poor due to a lack of central regulation or control. Most people believed it was not their responsibility to ensure good hygiene. In the Middle Ages the King's role was protecting his people from invasion and leading an army in battle. It was not preventing disease. Similarly, in the early nineteenth century the government did not believe it was part of its role to interfere with people's lives. It followed the policy of laissez-faire. There were some local exceptions but their efforts were limited. For example, in the Middle Ages both London and Coventry introduced local measures. Coventry identified waste disposal areas. In the nineteenth century, local actions were taken to try and prevent cholera in Manchester.

> Examples are then given from the second event which are also relevant to the point in the opening sentence

Poor public health had consequences for society in both eras. In the medieval period epidemics were common, the Black Death came to Britain in 1348 and the plague revisited many times. In the early nineteenth century, contagious diseases also spread quickly, including cholera. Both epidemics forced authorities to take action. However, their actions were limited by a lack of knowledge about the cause of disease.

Question 4: Factor-based essay

Has war been the main factor in the development of surgery in Britain since the Renaissance? Explain your answer with reference to war and other factors. **(16 marks + SPaG 4 marks)**

War has been one of the main factors in the development of surgery in Britain since the Renaissance. It advanced surgery in many ways, including the creation of new methods and technology. However, the work of key individuals cannot be underestimated.

> The answer opens by directly addressing the factor which is given in the question

During the Renaissance, war provided surgeons with many patients. This gave them opportunities to try different methods and improve core skills, including amputations. Paré was a war surgeon who developed improved methods during warfare. He used a herbal-based treatment for raw wounds, moving away from the common method of applying hot oil to cauterise them. He also used ligatures to tie-off wounds instead of cauterisation. Both of these led to improved success rates. Yet his impact was limited as not everyone accepted his ideas.

> The argument in the paragraph is then supported by a range of detailed, specific knowledge

> Here the paragraph links the evidence to the issue in the question

War played a major role in the twentieth century following the two world wars. As surgeons were faced with new wounds and demands new treatments and technologies were advanced. During the First World War, Harold Giles developed new techniques to treat facial injuries and burns. Mobile X-ray machines and blood transfusions were introduced, enabling injuries that frequently led to death to be treated. The British Red Cross created the first voluntary blood banks in 1921. In 1938, the British government established the Army Blood Supply Depot in Bristol. This system still exists. The Second World War led to developments in cataract surgery after it was discovered by Sir Harold Ridley that Perspex splinters were not rejected by the eye. Recent wars have advanced improvements in prostheses. All examples involving war highlight its importance and how it has progressed the major need at the time. Yet, war alone has not progressed surgery. Instead, it has enabled some significant barriers to be broken.

More recently, advancements in technology, not war, have driven surgery. Improved machines have enabled less-invasive surgery such as keyhole and laser techniques. Imaging technology has also become a central part of surgery. CT and MRI scans allow surgeons to see inside the body without opening it.

> Later paragraphs open with another factor which is relevant to the issue in the question

Individuals have also played an important role in advancing surgery, especially in the late 1800s. Following Pasteur's Germ Theory in 1861, advances in surgery followed. Joseph Lister used Pasteur's work to develop his own observations. This led to him creating the first antiseptic in 1867. In the short term it reduced Lister's death rates by 35 per cent. In the long term it was a major factor in the development of aseptic surgery. Another key individual in the development of surgery was James Simpson. His discovery of chloroform as an effective anaesthetic allowed surgeons to attempt longer and more complex operations. Modern anaesthesia and aseptic methods are a significant part of surgery. They allow it to be safe and effective. To a lesser extent the work of John Hunter also needs to be noted. He ensured human anatomy was studied and trained many British surgeons from 1768. Without individuals making new discoveries and experimenting, surgery would still be very risky. It was individuals who removed the major causes of death in surgery, infection, pain and blood loss.

To conclude, war and technology have been major factors in the development of modern British surgery, especially in the twentieth century following the First and Second World Wars. However, it must be noted that the fundamental basics of modern surgery were due to the work of key individuals, Simpson and Lister.

> The answer closes with a final judgement which carefully weighs up the role of the given factor against other factors

Acupuncture A form of alternative medicine that involves stimulating sensory nerves under the skin and in the muscles of the body using needles

Amputation Surgical removal of part of the body

Anaesthetic Pain relief

Anatomy The science of understanding the structure of the body

Ancients A collective term for doctors such as Hippocrates and Galen who worked in ancient Greek and Roman empires

Antiseptic Method to prevent infection

Aseptic surgery When all possible germs are removed from the operating theatre

Astrology The study of the movement and position of planets

Bath house A place where people paid for a bath to get clean

Beveridge Report Set out proposals for welfare changes after the Second World War

Bleeding Opening a vein or applying leeches to draw blood

Cauterising Medical practice or technique of burning a part of a body to remove or close off a part of it

Chloroform Type of anaesthetic

Cholera Watery diarrhoea and sickness leading to rapid dehydration and death

Clinical observation Examining and observing a patient and keeping careful records

Design theory The belief that God designed humans

Diphtheria Infectious disease spread through bacteria

Dissection Cutting up and examination of a body

Doctrine of Signatures States that herbs that resemble various parts of the body can be used by herbalists to treat ailments of those parts of the body. The doctrine dates from Galen's time

Epidemic Widespread outbreak of disease

Flagellants People who whipped themselves to show that they had repented their sins

Homeopathy A form of alternative medicine based on the use of substances diluted with water

Infection Formation of disease

Inoculation Involves a person being given low dose of smallpox making them immune to a serious outbreak

Keyhole surgery Surgery through small incision

Laissez-faire Belief that the government should not interfere in people's lives

Ligature A cord used to tie something very tightly, for example in order to stop bleeding

Miasma theory Belief that bad smells caused illness

Microbiology Branch of science that deals with microorganisms

Mortality Death

National Health Service (NHS) Taxpayer-funded state healthcare for UK citizens

NICE The National Institute for Health and Care Excellence which approves new drugs or treatments for use in Britain

Overcrowding Too many people in a space

Penicillin Life-saving antibiotic

Physician Doctor

Plague doctor A doctor who treated victims of the plague

Privies Toilets

Public health Helping people keep healthy by protecting them from disease and promoting health to prolong life

Quack A person who falsely claims they hold a medical qualification

Regulation Rules made by authorities

Sanitation Methods to ensure hygiene and prevent disease, for example sewers

Theory of Four Humours A theory advocated by Hippocrates on the working of the human body. It stated that the body was made up of four humours that needed to be balanced for good health. The four humours were blood, phlegm, black bile and yellow bile. Each humour was linked to an element and in turn a season

Typhoid Infectious disease spread through bacteria

Urine charts Used by doctors to identify the colour of a patient's urine when diagnosing illness

Vaccination Injection into the body of killed or weakened organisms to give the body resistance against disease

Watchman Prevented people entering and leaving infected houses during the Great Plague

Welfare Statutory procedure or social effort designed to promote the basic physical and material well-being of people in need

Zodiac charts A diagram used to explain how star formations influenced each part of the body

Chapter 9 Power and the people: c1170 to the present day

9.1 Magna Carta: the relationship between a feudal king and the people

REVISED

Medieval kings depended on their barons to run the country

- Medieval society was built on the **feudal system**.
- The King ruled the country but granted land to nobles. In return, the nobles provided loyalty and service.
- The nobles maintained law and order in their areas and raised an army for the King when needed.
- The King could call a **Great Council** of the nobles and bishops to ask for advice but did not have to act on what they suggested.

> **Key point**
>
> Magna Carta was an agreement between the King and the barons. John simply ignored it but the document became a powerful symbol for later movements where, if leaders misused power, they could be challenged.

King John did not live up to the barons' expectations of a medieval king

- The King was expected to be a strong leader, an excellent warrior and to consult with his barons.
- King John's father had been a successful king. King John's brother, Richard I, was seen as one of the best kings ever. So the barons had high expectations of John.

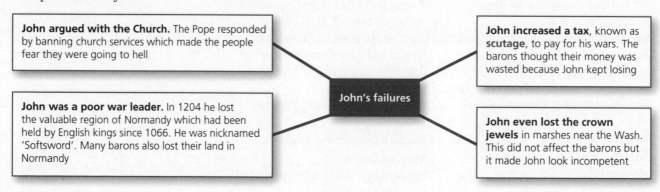

John argued with the Church. The Pope responded by banning church services which made the people fear they were going to hell

John was a poor war leader. In 1204 he lost the valuable region of Normandy which had been held by English kings since 1066. He was nicknamed 'Softsword'. Many barons also lost their land in Normandy

John's failures

John increased a tax, known as **scutage**, to pay for his wars. The barons thought their money was wasted because John kept losing

John even lost the crown jewels in marshes near the Wash. This did not affect the barons but it made John look incompetent

Magna Carta was the barons' way to limit John's power

- The barons were tired of John's poor kingship and formed an army to fight him. John had no army of his own so he had to negotiate. He met the barons on 15 June 1215 at Runnymede.
- The barons presented demands for John to sign. John agreed to:
  - stop unfair taxation
  - ensure a baron's heir **inherited** his land
  - let the Church make its own appointments
  - prevent arrest without trial
  - protect merchants
  - create a group of 25 barons to monitor the king.
- The barons' main concerns were taxation and unfair arrest. The barons included merchants and the Church to get more support against John.
- It was called Magna Carta (Latin for Great Charter).

> **TIP**
>
> All the key terms in **purple** are defined in the glossary at the end of each chapter.
>
> Make sure that you can spell the key terms, know what they mean and aim to use them in your written work.

At the time Magna Carta was a failure. It became more significant as the centuries passed

Significance at the time	Significance in later periods
It did not solve the problem. John only agreed to avoid a **civil war**. John soon went back on his word. Civil war restarted. It only ended when John died in 1216	**As more people became free it applied to more people**. As Magna Carta applied to more people, its significance increased
It had limited scope. Magna Carta was about the relationship between the barons and the King. The barons were not interested in the rights of ordinary people such as peasants. It only applied to **freemen**. **Peasants** and **villeins** were not free.	**It established some core principles**: that the king had responsibilities to the people and would be held to account by the barons if he did not live up to those responsibilities
However, the barons must have thought the Magna Carta significant because it was reissued in later years. The new king, nine-year-old Henry, agreed to it	**It became a symbol** of people power. When later protest movements tried to challenge a strong authority, they used Magna Carta as their reference point
	It came to be seen as the first step in a long process towards **democracy** (ordinary people having a say in how they are governed)

 ## Key events

Complete the flow chart to summarise the story of Magna Carta.

The barons raise an army					Magna Carta reissued by Henry III

 ## Eliminate irrelevance

Question 2 in your exam will focus on significance. For example:

Explain the significance of Magna Carta in the relationship between the monarch and their subjects. (8 marks)

Read the paragraph below. Cross out aspects of the answer that you think are irrelevant. Justify your deletions in the margin.

John became king after his much more popular brother Richard died. John's kingship angered the barons. By forcing John to sign Magna Carta at Runnymede they were stating what powers the King had. The 25 Barons would monitor John's behaviour and intervene when they thought it was necessary. Magna Carta was not significant at the time because it did not apply to all people. It only applied to freemen. Peasants worked in the fields and depended on their lord for survival and were not free. It was also limited because John had no intention of keeping to it. In the long term, however, Magna Carta provided a symbol for other protests such as the American Declaration of Independence and the Chartist movement, so copies have been kept safe down the centuries.

 ## Test yourself

1 List three reasons why the barons were unhappy with John.
2 List three promises made in Magna Carta.
3 List three reasons Magna Carta has become more significant over time.

TIP

In this study you will often find that events become more significant in later periods than they were at the time. So you need to think big to answer significance questions. Magna Carta was a failure at the time but proved powerful in later centuries.

9.2 Simon de Montfort and the origins of Parliament

REVISED

Henry III repeated the mistakes made by King John

- Henry became king aged nine. A Council of Barons helped him rule.
- When he was old enough to rule, he ruled in a very **arbitrary** (unpredictable) way.
- He lived an **extravagant lifestyle** and was always short of money.
- He lost two major wars in France and only listened to a few advisers.
- The barons felt that history was repeating itself. They decided to take action as they had against his father.

Simon de Montfort had a complicated relationship with Henry

- Simon de Montfort had lost land (in war) which he wanted back.
- Simon was **pious** (religious) and was known to keep to his promises.
- Simon married the King's sister and fought wars on Henry's behalf.
- Henry put Simon on trial several times for some of his actions, but **acquitted** him (let him off) each time.

The Provisions of Oxford did not please everyone and led to civil war

- Simon led the barons in calling a Great Council in 1258 where they forced the king to agree to the following:

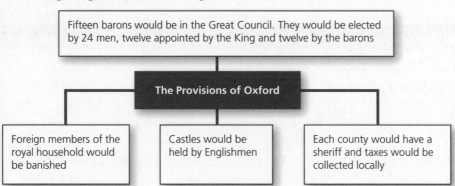

- The Provisions of Oxford gave the barons more power over decision-making than the King. It made the King **accountable**.
- However, the barons were divided. Because Henry could see they were divided he refused to sign the Provisions.
- The barons asked Simon de Montfort to lead an army against the King. Simon won the Battle of Lewes and captured the King and his son.

De Montfort called the first Parliament but he was then brutally killed

- With the King in prison, de Montfort was effectively in charge:
  - he formed a council of nine people; mostly his friends and family
  - he reissued Magna Carta and the Provisions of Oxford.
- Many barons thought he was too powerful and turned against him.
- To increase his support, Simon asked merchants and knights from every county to attend the meeting of the Great Council.

Key point

Simon de Montfort established the first Parliament and for the first time invited commoners to attend.

TIP

Because significance can seem a vague idea, it is easy to get sucked into including irrelevant details. All you really have to do with a significance question is to explain one way the event was significant at the time, and one way it has been significant for people looking back from a later period.

- This was the first time that **commoners** were consulted on national matters. This is regarded as England's first Parliament.
- However, de Montfort did this without consulting the other barons. The barons were furious with him. They thought he was acting like a king. They switched support to Henry III.
- At the Battle of Evesham, the King's forces crushed de Montfort's men. Simon was hacked to death on the battlefield.

Test yourself

1 What were the Provisions of Oxford?
2 What was new about de Montfort's Great Council?
3 Why did the barons turn against de Montfort?

De Montfort is **significant** because of his impact on the **development of Parliament**

Commoners to be consulted	De Montfort's Parliament did not represent ordinary people but it was the first to include representatives from the whole country and include commoners (knights, gentry and merchants, not just nobles)
Parliament to approve taxes	It established the principle that a king called Parliament to raise taxation. When Henry's son Edward became king he knew he could not demand money from the barons so he called the Model Parliament to request it instead
Symbol of democracy	Like Magna Carta, de Montfort's Parliament became a symbol of democratic principles that were more fully realised hundreds of years later
Martyr for freedom	De Montfort himself believed he had a duty to rebel against unfair kingship. The way he died means he has been regarded as a **martyr** for freedom

Compare events

Question 3 in your exam will ask you to identify similarities or differences between events. Practise for this by comparing the first two topics you have studied.

	Conflict between John and the barons	Conflict between Henry III and the barons	Similarities or differences
Causes			
Key features			
Consequences			

Eliminate irrelevance

Here is another chance to practise a significance question.

Explain the significance of Simon de Montfort in creating a system of democracy in England. (8 marks)

Cross out aspects of the answer below that are irrelevant (that have nothing to do with significance!). Justify your deletions in the margin.

Simon de Montfort was a key figure in the development of England as a democracy. He was a very pious man who wore a hairshirt under his clothes. He was a key figure in the Provisions of Oxford which gave more power to the barons over the King. The Provisions also banned foreign advisers, gave Englishmen their castles back and meant taxes were collected locally. These Provisions meant that the monarch could not rule without the agreement of the Great Council. This is significant in creating a system of democracy in England because it established accountability between the monarch and the people. Simon de Montfort was hacked to death and became a martyr. These ideas were further developed over the centuries but started with the actions of Simon de Montfort.

9.3 The Peasants' Revolt: medieval revolt and royal authority

The **Black Death** killed one-third of the people in England

- The Black Death was carried to England by trading vessels. It arrived in England in 1348.
- Infected people developed a fever, then thick black **buboes** (boils) appeared in the armpits and groin. The victims would then experience excruciating pain before dying.
- There was no cure and people did not know the cause. Many believed it was God's punishment for people being wicked.
- The devastating plague killed one-third of the population.
- It killed people from all aspects of medieval society but it had greatest impact on the peasants who made up the majority of the population.

The **feudal system couldn't cope** with the **population decrease**

- The surviving peasants could choose who they worked for and for what price. This angered the lords as they could no longer exert as much control over the peasants.
- Some lords became worried that their crops would fail and their income would plummet.
- King Edward III passed the **Statute of Labourers** to try and control the peasants, telling them they had to work for their pre-Black Death wages.
- Because of the decreased population, the government's revenue from taxes fell.
- To raise funds for a war with France, King Richard II introduced a **poll tax**. Everyone in England had to pay the same: 1 shilling and 4 pence (about 5.5p). This was over two week's wages for a labourer.

> **Key point**
>
> In the fourteenth century, the Black Death helped end the feudal structure of English society, giving peasants more power and freedom. The peasants revolted against an unfair tax but the revolt was suppressed.

 Test yourself

1 What was the Statute of Labourers?

2 Why was the poll tax introduced?

3 List two consequences of the Peasants' Revolt.

A **protest** against the poll tax led to a **serious rebellion**

Dates in 1381	Events
30 May	Villagers in Kent and Essex refused to pay their taxes and threatened the tax collector, John Bampton
2 June	The Chief Justice attempted to collect the money but was also threatened. The locals beheaded his clerks
7 June	The rebels freed a radical priest, John Ball, from prison. John Ball and Wat Tyler headed towards London with an increasingly large crowd
7 June	The crowd attacked symbols of the rich. They burned records, attacked clerks and killed the **Archbishop of Canterbury**
13 June	When the crowd reached London the city gates were opened by supporters and they continued burning down symbols of authority and wealth
14 June	Richard II met Tyler and the rebels at Smithfield. Tyler asked that all villeins are made freemen. The King agreed but the rebels went on another killing spree
15 June	The King met with Tyler again. Tyler was now more confident and asked for changes to the system of law and for Church land to be given to the people. Before the King responded, one of the King's supporters killed Tyler. To prevent a riot the King told the crowd he would grant their requests

The revolt was the **first uprising** against royal power involving **commoners**

● Although this is called the Peasants' Revolt, it was not only villeins who were involved. Some were the leading men from their villages such as constables or reeves. Some were freemen. But the significant thing is they were commoners not nobles.

● As with the other protests, its significance has changed over time.

Significance at the time	Longer term significance
It was the first time commoners (rather than nobles) had rebelled against royal power. This scared the King and the nobles In the short term, the rebellion failed. Richard went back on his promise. The leaders of the revolt were hanged	However, the rebels succeeded in important ways: ● peasants were never taxed so heavily again ● peasants' wages continued to rise ● more peasants became freemen and were able to buy their own land

 ## Spot the mistakes

Explain the significance of the Peasants' Revolt to changing the political structure of England. (8 marks)

Below is a sample answer to the question. Cross out any incorrect information and annotate the paragraph with the correct information.

The significance of the Peasant's Revolt was how it changed England. The population had decreased by half as a result of the Black Death. This severely affected the peasant population and in turn the nobles. They could no longer demand that the peasants work for low wages. The nobles convinced the King to introduce the Statute of Labourers to try and force the peasants to accept their old wages. Leaders like Wat Tyler convinced the peasants that they did not have to accept their old role. For the first time ever, the peasants directly stood up to the King.

 ## Role of factors

Question 4 of your exam will ask you to explain the role of factors in causing an event. There were lots of factors that helped cause the Peasants' Revolt. Connect each of the factors in the left column with an explanation in the right-hand column. Then write an explanation of your own for another factor, for example individuals or the economy.

Factor	Explanation
War	The radical priest John Ball claimed that all people were created equal and that peasants should 'throw off their bondage'. His preaching inspired some of the rebels
Chance	The poll tax was introduced because the government needed money to pay for conflicts with France
Government	The Black Death was a chance event which killed many peasants yet gave greater opportunity to those who survived it
Ideas	The King was preoccupied with gaining more territory in France rather than dealing with issues in England.

> **TIP**
>
> Question 4 will require you to cover the whole course from medieval to the present day so you will not be practising those questions until the modern case studies. However, you should be working on this throughout your revision by filling out the chapter overview chart on pages 208–9.

9.4 The Pilgrimage of Grace: challenges to Henry VIII's controversial kingship

REVISED

Henry broke the power of the Catholic Church in England

- Henry was a **devout** Catholic but he resented the power the Church had in England and wanted some of its wealth.
- He was angered when the Pope refused him a divorce.
- Henry responded by making himself head of the new Church of England and stopped paying taxes to the Pope.
- To further limit the power of the Church, Henry closed down (dissolved) the monasteries and sold off monastery land to the gentry.
- This **dissolution** made Henry very rich.

> **Key point**
>
> Henry VIII broke with the Catholic Church which upset many people in England. Their protest failed when the King executed their leader.

The religious changes were very unpopular because they destroyed the social fabric of England

Social problems: the Church and monasteries were the centre of people's social lives. The King had taken this away

Economic problems: even though closing the monasteries made Henry rich, he still increased taxes

Problems caused by religious change

Political problems: many prominent nobles lost influence after the change of religion and Henry's divorce while other families gained

Religious problems: the Church of England was different to Catholicism and many people did not like the changes to church services

The Pilgrimage of Grace was a popular protest against these changes

- In 1536, an uprising broke out against the changes to the Church in Lincolnshire and Yorkshire, led by a lawyer named Robert Aske.
- The protesters called it the **Pilgrimage** of Grace to demonstrate their peaceful intentions.
- They demanded that England return to Catholicism and that Henry fire his corrupt ministers.
- The 8000 pilgrims captured towns in the north.
- The King sent the Catholic Duke of Norfolk to negotiate with the rebels hoping that they would listen to someone who shared some of their sympathies.
- Norfolk assured the pilgrims that the King would listen. Aske was invited to spend Christmas with the King at Windsor. The pilgrims went home.

The leaders of the pilgrimage were dealt with ruthlessly to prevent further uprisings

- In January 1537, the rebels attacked castles in the north. As a warning to others, Norfolk hanged 74 rebels.
- Aske was called back to London and immediately arrested and executed. Henry had brutally ended the Pilgrimage of Grace.
- No more religious rebellions took place in England during Henry's reign. Henry had total control of the country and ended the power of the Catholic Church in England.
- Protestants became more confident in introducing Protestant ideas, leading to more changes in church services.

 Test yourself

1 Where did the Pilgrimage of Grace begin?

2 Why did the pilgrims call their protest a pilgrimage?

3 What happened to Robert Aske?

Compare events

Here is a typical question 3.

Compare the Peasants' Revolt with the Pilgrimage of Grace. What are the similarities? (8 marks)

This tests your detailed knowledge of both events. But it is up to you to decide what aspects to compare. Copy and complete this chart to compare the two events. Once your chart is complete:

● in one colour highlight the similarities between the two and

● in another colour highlight the differences.

Then use your chart to write a full answer to the practice question.

Aspect	Pilgrimage of Grace	Peasants' Revolt
Cause	Henry VIII's religious changes had angered the pilgrims	
Actions of the people	Inspired by the speeches of the lawyer Robert Aske, the pilgrims made their way to London in a peaceful march	
Actions of the King	The King sent the Duke of Norfolk to speak with the pilgrims He asked Aske to spend Christmas with him. At the earliest opportunity he went back on his promise and executed Aske	
Consequences	No more rebellions Henry had full control of the Church and the country	

TIP

● For a 'compare' question you will be asked about either similarities or differences. You don't need to write about both. Aim to cover at least two similarities or two differences. Write a paragraph on each.

● Good words to use when writing about similarities are: *likewise, also, both, in the same way, similarly.*

● Good words to use when writing about differences are: *on the other hand, in contrast, whereas.*

 Consider usefulness

Question 1 in your exam will ask you to assess the usefulness (utility) of the source for a given purpose. For example:

How useful is Source A to a historian studying religious change in England? (8 marks)

SOURCE A
'The Pope Suppressed by King Henry VIII', a woodcut by an unknown artist made in 1534. It is a satirical comment on Henry's action. It was later used in Puritan anti-Catholic propaganda in the 1570s.

You will need to think about:

● provenance: who made the source, when, and why?

● content: what it says about the topic. Does this agree with what you know?

Listed below are points that you might make. Draw lines between the source and the notes. On a separate sheet, complete these annotations.

A Archbishop Cranmer passing a copy of the Bible to Henry. This suggests that …

B Pope sprawled under Henry's foot. This suggests that …

C People looking distressed. These are probably …

D Used as anti-Catholic propaganda. This suggests that …

9.5 The English Revolution

The English Revolution was **caused** by a **breakdown in the relationship between Charles and Parliament**

Religion	Money	Power
Puritans dominated Parliament. They did not like the Catholic changes to churches made by Archbishop Laud	Ever since Simon de Montfort, the King had called Parliament to approve taxes. Yet Charles ruled without Parliament for eleven years (**Personal Rule**) and raised taxes without Parliament's permission	Charles believed he was appointed by God (**Divine Right of Kings**). He preferred the advice of his favourite ministers to consulting with Parliament

- In 1640, Charles finally recalled Parliament to approve new taxes to fund his disastrous war in Scotland.
- Many MPs did not trust Charles, so insisted Parliament control the army.
- They drew up The **Grand Remonstrance** of complaints and demands.
- Charles tried to arrest the leading MPs. They had already fled. Charles left London and prepared to fight Parliament.

In the Civil War **the New Model Army** emerged as the **most powerful force** in England

- The Royalists did well to start with but Oliver Cromwell created the **New Model Army** which was better equipped and trained than the Royalists. Parliament won the Civil War.
- Its soldiers were very religious and believed that God was on their side.
- Many members of the army had radical ideas such as that all men should have the vote.

The trial and **execution of Charles I** was the key moment of the English Revolution

- MPs were divided over how to treat the King. The army ejected 300 MPs leaving only a **Rump** who put the King on trial.
- The King was found guilty of treason and executed on 30 January 1649.
- Charles was not the first king to be killed by his subjects. The difference this time was that he was not replaced with another king. Instead England became a republic, known as the Commonwealth.
- From 1649 to 1660, England tried three ways to rule without a king: rule by Parliament, rule by Cromwell, and rule by the army.
- None worked, so after Cromwell died, Parliament restored the monarchy. However, the relationship was different:
  - Charles I's son became king but only because Parliament asked him.
  - Parliament met more regularly and was not as influenced by the abilities and temperament of each king.

Practice question

Explain the significance of the execution of Charles I.   (8 marks)

Key point

In 1649, King Charles I was executed on the order of Parliament. For eleven years England was ruled without a King. When this did not work, the monarchy was restored but the relationship between Crown and Parliament was changed forever.

 Test yourself

1 What was the Personal Rule?
2 What was the Rump Parliament?
3 What was the Commonwealth?

 Role of factors

On pages 208–9 record examples of each of the following factors affecting the English Revolution:

- war
- religion
- government
- ideas
- individuals.

For each factor write some sentences to explain how it affected the English Revolution. For example:

Many MPs were Puritans. They did not like the religious changes made by Archbishop William Laud. This made them distrust the king and his advisers.

Quick quizzes at **www.hoddereducation.co.uk/myrevisionnotes**

9.6 The American Revolution

The American Revolution began as a **dispute over taxation** and **ended with American independence**

- The thirteen British colonies in America had a population of 25 million.
- Many had gone there to escape persecution in Europe or gain greater freedom, so searching for freedom was an ingrained attitude.
- They were taxed by Britain but did not send MPs to Parliament. The colonists demanded 'No taxation without representation'.
- The British government would not budge and a series of protests led the colonists to declare themselves independent from Britain in 1776.
- Their Declaration of Independence said that 'All men are created equal'.
- Britain sent a large army to reassert control but could not keep up the fight over such a long distance and surrendered in 1783.
- The colonies became the United States of America. It had its own **constitution**, Congress (Parliament) and President.

The American Revolution **scared rulers** in Europe but **inspired radicals** in Britain and Europe

- To start with, the British were most worried about the economic impact. However, trade with North America soon picked up. In fact, the British Empire grew as Britain took over Australia, New Zealand and India.
- The war defeat exposed incompetent leadership in Britain. Even moderate politicians in Britain were ready to criticise their government.
- The longer term significance was about ideas:

This was the first time a **colony** had rejected rule by a European power. In later centuries other colonies followed its example	The idea that ordinary people have fundamental 'rights' spread to France where the government was violently overthrown in the French Revolution	British leaders feared a similar revolution in England. For the next 50 years political radicals were dealt with harshly

Key point

Colonists in North America protested against being taxed by Britain without being represented in Parliament. The protest led to a war of independence which ended with Britain losing control.

Test yourself

1 What was the slogan of the American colonists?
2 Why did the American Revolution worry politicians in Britain?

 Compare events

Make a list of similarities and differences between the English and American Revolutions. Think about

- causes
- events
- role of individuals
- consequences
- ideas.

 Practice question

Explain the significance of the British defeat against the thirteen American colonies. (8 marks)

 Practice question

How useful is Source B for explaining the causes of the American Revolution?   (8 marks)

SOURCE B *Extract from Thomas Paine's* Common Sense, *which urged the American colonists to rebel against British control. Published in America in 1776.*

This new world hath been the asylum for the persecuted lovers of civil and religious liberty from every part of Europe. Hither have they fled, not from the tender embraces of the mother, but from the cruelty of the monster; and it is so far true of England, that the same tyranny which drove the first emigrants from home, pursues their descendants still.

Part 2: Challenging royal authority

9.7 The fight for the franchise in the early nineteenth century

In the early nineteenth century the British electoral system was corrupt and out of date

- **Rotten boroughs** (for example, Old Sarum) sent an MP to Parliament though no one lived there, while the city of Birmingham had no MP.
- Only people who owned property had the franchise, that is, they could vote.
- Factory owners were not represented in Parliament.
- There was no **secret ballot**. Voters could be intimidated or bribed.

> **Key point**
>
> In the nineteenth century, the Great Reform Act gave the vote to many middle-class people but the Chartists failed to win the right to vote for working-class people.

The government tried to prevent reform meetings

- After the Napoleonic Wars, the government made poverty worse by increasing taxes on corn which made bread more expensive.
- Working people could see that MPs were not acting in their interests.
- A meeting at St Peter's Fields in Manchester in 1819 attracted 60,000 to hear a radical speaker, Henry Hunt, call for the reform of Parliament.
- It was peaceful but it scared the authorities who sent militia (soldiers) into the crowd. Eleven people were killed including women and children.
- This was called the **Peterloo Massacre** (a mocking reference to the heroic Battle of Waterloo).
- The government then introduced the **Six Acts**. These banned meetings of more than 50 people. Asking for reform became an act of treason.

The Great Reform Act of 1832 gave the vote to more middle-class people

- In 1830, Thomas Attwood organised a petition calling for reform. It was signed by 8000 people. This peaceful method of protest was copied throughout the country.
- Britain's new King was keener on reform than his father, George III.
- The Whig government introduced a Reform Act. When it was blocked by the House of Lords, the King helped forced it through.
- The Act redistributed MPs, so that industrial towns were represented. It gave merchants and factory owners the vote. But you still had to own property to vote.

The Chartists failed to win the vote for working-class people

- The Chartists were formed in 1836 to demand more reform (see panel).
- To achieve this, some Chartists favoured peaceful methods such as petitions. Others favoured strike action or violence.
- The Chartists presented their Great Petition to Parliament in 1848. They claimed it had 5 million signatures but in fact had less than 2 million.
- In 1848, there were revolutions in Europe. Authorities were worried by the Chartists. They dealt harshly with violent protest (for example, Newport).
- The Chartist movement faded away without having achieved its aims. Former Chartists put their energy into other reform movements.

Chartist demands
Votes for all men
Equal-sized constituencies
Voting in secret
Wages for MPs
No property qualification for voters
Annual elections

 Develop the detail

Add some relevant and specific detail to these general statements.

A   Voting was corrupt.

B   Industrial towns had no MPs.

C   The Great Reform Act gave more people the vote.

D   Working people were disappointed with the Reform Act.

E   The Chartists failed.

 Test yourself

1   What was a rotten borough?

2   What was the Peterloo Massacre?

3   Who could vote after the Great Reform Act?

9.8 Organised protest in the nineteenth century

The Corn Laws were repealed due to popular protest and famine

- To control the price of wheat, the government introduced **Corn Laws**. This made bread expensive which helped the landowners but hurt the poor.
- The **Anti-Corn Law League** used pamphlets and meetings to protest. It was the best-organised protest group ever. Richard Cobden and John Bright became MPs and won the support of the Prime Minister.
- Bad harvests led to **famine** in 1845. This allowed Peel, the Prime Minister, to convince Parliament to repeal the Corn Laws in 1846.
- This was the first time that the government acted in the interests of the poor over the landowning gentry.

> **Key point**
>
> Campaigners were successful because they were led by middle classes and focused on specific issues and social reform rather than electoral or political change.

Slavery was abolished in 1833 due to abolitionists, the economy and slave resistance

Protests by abolitionists in the UK	Slave rebellions	Economic changes
The Anti-Slavery Society was led by William Wilberforce. It challenged slavery by holding meetings, producing pamphlets, signing petitions and speaking in Parliament. Many abolitionists were motivated by their religious beliefs	Rebellions such as in St Dominique in 1804, threatened the lives of plantation owners who wanted to appease the slaves	The price of sugar fell dramatically due to overproduction and it became too expensive to keep slaves

Factory working conditions were improved by individuals and government

- Britain had become economically powerful thanks to its textile industry. However, working conditions in the factories were terrible.
- Individual industrialists improved conditions in their own factories:

Individuals	Actions
Robert Owen	Introduced the eight-hour day and opened a school for his child workers
Titus Salt	Built a whole town, Saltaire, next to his mill for workers. It included bathhouses, a hospital and a church
George Cadbury	Created a model town called Bourneville. He had pensions, workers' committees and a workers' welfare scheme

- The old idea of *laissez-faire* (that governments should not interfere) was being challenged in many different ways.
- Lord Shaftesbury campaigned in Parliament which passed a Factory Act (1833) limiting the hours children could work and the Mines Act (1842) banning women and children from working in mines underground.
- Workers themselves did not always support the Acts as they limited the income of families.

 Develop the explanation

The statements below describe factors that helped each movement on this page. Add sentences to each to explain how and why each factor helped.

A The Anti-Corn Law League succeeded because of good communication.

B The Anti-Slavery Society was helped by economic change.

C Individuals improved conditions for factory workers.

Practice question

Compare the Chartists with the Anti-Corn Law League. In what ways are they different? (8 marks)

9.9 Workers' movements in the nineteenth century and workers' rights in the twentieth century

Work changed because of the Industrial Revolution

- Before industrialisation, work was based on crafts which took years to learn. As machines took over many craft jobs work became less skilled.
- Workers were more vulnerable to economic depressions.
- Industrialisation also separated employers and workers. Rather than feeling they shared a common interest, there was 'class' division.
- Attitudes to workers were changing too. The French Revolution (1789) spread fear in England of workers rising up against the rich.

Workers used different methods to help themselves and improve their living conditions

Friendly societies	Trade societies	Violence
Every member contributed each week then drew out money if they hit hard times	Specialist craftsmen organised themselves into trade societies to control quality and maintain prices	Some weavers destroyed machines that they feared had taken their jobs. They were called **Luddites**

- In the 1830s, Robert Owen organised the **Grand National Consolidated Trades Union (GNCTU)** with half a million members from different trade societies to protect each other's interests.
- This union failed but it worried the government. Some employers forced their workers to sign a pledge not to be a member of a union.

The Tolpuddle Martyrs were punished harshly when they formed a farm workers' union

- In 1834, farm workers in Tolpuddle, Dorset formed a union when their employer tried to cut their wages.
- The leaders were arrested, not for being part of a trade union, but for getting their members to sign a secret oath of loyalty (which was illegal).
- The government was worried about trade unions and set a harsh example. The leaders were sent to Australia for seven years' hard labour.
- This punishment was out of proportion. 200,000 people attended a protest meeting in London and the government reversed the decision.
- In the long term, the treatment of the Martyrs helped the union movement.

The new unions succeeded when the workers acted together and had public support

- From the 1850s, the union movement flourished, helped by education becoming compulsory (1880) and working men getting the vote (1884).
- Unions for skilled workers were known as **New Model Unions**. Unions for unskilled workers were known as **New Unions**.
- The match girls ran the first successful strikes by unskilled workers in 1888.
- In 1889, London dockworkers went on strike for better pay and conditions. They were more militant. They picketed to keep out replacement labourers.
- The strike had public support and the dockworkers got a pay increase.
- Workers created their own political party (the Labour Party) in 1893.

> **Key point**
>
> Through the nineteenth century, trade unions were created to allow workers in particular trades to protect their interests. Some succeeded. Many failed. In the twentieth century, trade union power increased remarkably which led to major restrictions on union activity by the end of the century.

 Test yourself

1 What was a Friendly society?

2 What were the Tolpuddle Martyrs accused of?

3 What is a picket?

In 1926 the unions organised a **General Strike** but it failed and **harmed the union movement**

- During the First World War the government ran British coalmines. It increased wages and improved conditions as coal was in demand.
- After the war, the mines were given back to the mine owners. Demand for coal dropped. Imported coal was cheaper and prices fell. Mine owners reduced miners' wages and increased their working hours.
- The **TUC** called a General Strike of all workers to support the miners. On 4 May 1926, miners, railway workers and dockers went on strike, supported by many other workers.
- The government had prepared for the strike. The army did some workers' jobs and the government used radio and newspapers to turn public opinion against the strikers. The strike ended after nine days.
- Union membership fell dramatically. Public support for strikes fell. The Labour Party was weakened due to its association with unions.

Unions lost membership and influence following the miners' strike of 1985

- Union membership rose again after the Second World War.
- **Nationalisation** of many industries meant many workers were employed by the government. They found it easy to press the government for better pay and conditions. Workers' pay rose and rights were improved, including more security against redundancy and better training.
- The 1970s and 1980s saw frequent large-scale strikes. Government usually gave in to strikers' demands.
- Margaret Thatcher's government introduced laws to reduce union power in 1980 and 1982:

Ban flying pickets	Restrict the closed shop	Money for secret ballots	Fined unions for losses
Ban **flying pickets** to stop workers from one industry picketing in another dispute	A **closed shop** was a factory where you had to be a union member to work there. The government compensated workers who lost their job because of a closed shop	Moderate union members would not be intimidated by a 'show of hands' vote	Caused by unlawful strikes or unlawful secondary picketing

- The turning point came with the miners' strike of 1985.
- The government had stockpiled coal to keep the power stations running. The miners were not united and many pits kept working. The government sent police to prevent striking miners picketing working pits.
- The striking miners returned to work after one year. The union movement has not been as strong since.

 ## Explain significance

Copy and complete this table to analyse the significance of each event or development.

Event	At the time	In later periods
Tolpuddle Martyrs, 1834		
Dockers' strike, 1889	*Better pay for dockers*	
General Strike, 1926		
Miners' strike, 1985		

9.10 Women's rights

In 1900 women did not have the same rights as men

- Victorians thought a woman's place was in the home, raising children.
- Working-class women usually had to do paid work, but they were paid less than men and were still expected to raise children, cook and clean.
- The law favoured men. Men could file for divorce, own property and most could vote. Women could do none of these things.
- From the 1850s some women campaigned against these inequalities.
- Many felt that the most fundamental right of all which would help achieve the other aims would be to have the right to vote (**suffrage**).

> **Key point**
>
> Women's groups used both peaceful and violent methods to campaign for the right to vote but it was their contribution to the war effort in the First World War that finally helped them succeed.

The suffragists used peaceful methods to win the vote

- There were many regional groups campaigning for women's suffrage.
- In 1897, these united as the **National Union of Women's Suffrage Societies (NUWSS)**, led by Millicent Fawcett and known as **suffragists**.
- They used peaceful methods such as marches, meetings and petitions.
- They gained the support of many MPs who campaigned for women to get the vote. However, they were always defeated and some felt that progress was too slow.

The suffragettes took violent action in their campaign

- In 1903, Emmeline Pankhurst broke away from the NUWSS and formed the Women's Social and Political Union (WSPU), known as **suffragettes**.
- The suffragettes favoured direct action. They smashed windows, heckled at meetings, chained themselves to railings, set fire to postboxes and poured acid on golf courses.
- In 1913, Emily Wilding Davison threw herself in front of the King's horse at the Derby horse race and died from her injuries.
- They used these tactics to draw attention to their campaign. The suffragettes made 'Votes for Women' a national issue but many thought they were too extreme which lost support for women's suffrage.

The First World War changed the role of women and as a result they were given the vote

- During the First World War, millions of men went to fight in the army which left a big gap in the workforce.
- The suffragettes suspended their campaign and both the NUWSS and WSPU encouraged women to support the war effort.
- Hundreds of thousands of women were recruited to work in government **munitions** factories, producing weapons. They also did other traditionally male jobs such as bus driving.
- Women showed how well they could do 'men's jobs'.
- The war changed attitudes. In 1918, the Representation of the People's Act gave women over 30 (who owned property) the right to vote. In 1928 this was extended to all women over 21.

> **Compare events**
>
> Create a table comparing the Chartists, the NUWSS and the WSPU. Create rows for
>
> - leadership
> - membership
> - aims
> - tactics.
>
> Then write a paragraph about either:
>
> - differences between the Chartists and the NUWSS or
> - similarities between the NUWSS and the WSPU

> **TIP**
>
> Remember that all sources are useful for something. It all depends on what you are using them for. Never dismiss a source as useless because it is one-sided or biased. It will be still be very useful for finding out about the attitudes of the person who wrote it.

Through the twentieth century the **struggle for equal rights** for women continued with **partial success**

- Getting the vote did not give women equal employment rights. Women were still paid less than men and faced obstacles in their careers. For example, they were expected to leave work if they became pregnant or when married.

- The Second World War had a similar impact to the first, only more so. More than 7 million women joined the workforce.

- It gave women opportunities and it changed attitudes to women's rights. This was reflected in various reforms in the years after the war:

Test yourself

1 Who was given the vote in 1918?

2 What does NUWSS stand for?

3 List three examples of suffragette direct action.

Abortion Act, 1967	Divorce Act, 1969	Equal Pay Act, 1970	Contraception	Employment Protection Act, 1975
Gave women access to abortion if they faced an unwanted pregnancy	Gave women the right to seek a divorce	Made it illegal to pay women less than men for the same work	Became available on the National Health Service (NHS) from 1974	Made it illegal to sack a woman because she was pregnant

- Britain got its first female Prime Minister in 1979. In 2017, 32 per cent of MPs were women.

- However, women still earn 30 per cent less than men on average.

Consider usefulness

How useful is Source C in explaining attitudes to women's suffrage in the early twentieth century? (8 marks)

SOURCE C *'A suffragette's home', a poster published in 1912 by the National League for Opposing Women's Suffrage. This poster was produced to encourage people to join the organisation.*

Make notes in a grid like this to plan your answer.

Provenance	Content
Who made it, when and why?	What does it say about the attitudes of anti-suffrage campaigners?
	From your knowledge of these events, is this accurate?
How does this affect its usefulness?	How does this affect its usefulness?

9.11 The rights of ethnic minorities

After the Second World War Britain became a much more multi-cultural society

- The government needed many workers to rebuild the war-ravaged country and to run essential services such as public transport and the NHS.
- The British Nationality Act 1948 allowed anyone from the **Commonwealth** to come to Britain and gain full British citizenship.
- Employers such as London Transport held job fairs in the Caribbean to recruit workers. The government offered interest-free loans so that people could afford to travel to Britain.
- Britain has always had an ethnically diverse population but this immigration from Commonwealth nations significantly increased the Black and Asian population of Britain.

> **Key point**
>
> People from the Caribbean and India were invited to England to help rebuild the country after the Second World War but they experienced prejudice and discrimination. Their struggle for equal rights continues through to the present.

Many immigrants faced discrimination

- Immigrants lived where the rents were affordable often in the most run-down areas of Britain's cities, which were usually working-class areas.
- There was discrimination in housing. Many landlords refused to let their properties to immigrants and put out signs saying 'No blacks'.
- More skilled immigrants, such as doctors or nurses, got well-paid jobs in the NHS but other new immigrants had low-paid, insecure jobs.

In 1958 racial discrimination turned to violence. Immigration became a controversial political issue

- In 1958, there was serious racial violence in Notting Hill. Some black homes and shops were attacked and firebombed by white gangs.
- In response to the violence, Claudia Jones, a Trinidad-born journalist, organised a carnival which later became the Notting Hill Carnival.
- In May 1959, Kelso Cochrane, a young Antiguan man, was murdered by a white gang. His funeral became a mass anti-racism demonstration.
- In 1968, Enoch Powell, a leading Conservative politician, gave his 'Rivers of Blood' speech predicting civil war if immigration was not stopped.
- The National Front was formed. It called for an end to immigration and stirred up racial hatred in some inner-city areas.
- The government introduced two Commonwealth Immigration Acts in 1962 and 1968 to limit black and Asian immigration.

At the same time laws were passed to protect the rights of minorities and improve race relations

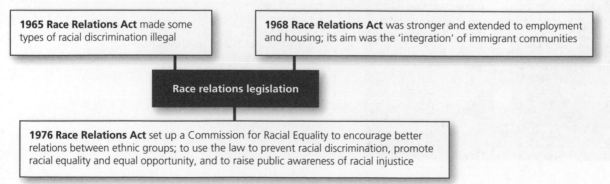

1965 Race Relations Act made some types of racial discrimination illegal

1968 Race Relations Act was stronger and extended to employment and housing; its aim was the 'integration' of immigrant communities

Race relations legislation

1976 Race Relations Act set up a Commission for Racial Equality to encourage better relations between ethnic groups; to use the law to prevent racial discrimination, promote racial equality and equal opportunity, and to raise public awareness of racial injustice

Quick quizzes at **www.hoddereducation.co.uk/myrevisionnotes**

The **Brixton Riots in 1981** turned the spotlight on policing in black communities

- Brixton, south London, had a large Afro-Caribbean population.
- The early 1980s was a time of economic depression. Unemployment was high (55 per cent among young people) and there was a lot of crime.
- Relationships between the police and young black people were strained.
- In April 1981, a police 'stop and search' incident turned into serious rioting. There were battles between black youths and police with arson and looting.
- The Scarman Report investigated the causes of the riots and blamed police tactics for causing the riots. It also identified a racist culture within the police.
- Others blamed economic factors including unemployment and poverty.

> **TIP**
>
> Candidates find it hard to give time to planning in an actual exam which is why it is so important to practise it before the exam so that it becomes instinctive.

 ## Test yourself

1 Who was Kelso Cochrane?
2 What body was created by the 1976 Race Relations Act?
3 What was 'stop and search'?

 ## Essay plan

Has war and violence been the main reason that rulers have granted rights to minorities since medieval times? Explain your answer with reference to war and violence and other factors. (16 marks + SPaG 4 marks)

The secret or writing an essay is in the planning. Here is a plan.

Paragraph	Purpose/points to include	Comment
Introduction	State your argument. whether you think this was the 'main' factor	This sets your essay off on a positive track and gives you an argument to hold on to throughout your answer
Paragraph 1	Evidence of the named factor at work	Make sure you support everything you say with detailed and precise knowledge Make sure you are using examples from more than one period
Paragraph 2	Reasons why the named factor has had limited impact	This is an opportunity to show your developed understanding of the named factor. For example explain how that factor did not apply at all times
Paragraphs 3 and 4	Consider the role of one (or two) more factors	Choose other factors that had influence and write one paragraph on each. Link them clearly to the development in the question. Write a paragraph on each. Compare each to the named factor
Conclusion	Restate your judgement. Is the named factor the main one, that is more important than those in paragraphs 3 and 4? Include one strong argument as to why	Here you need to sum up your answer and offer a balanced judgement. This should be easy to write if you have kept your focus through the rest of the essay. *Overall I think that _____ is the main reason that rulers have granted minorities their rights. This is because … It is more important than _____ and _____ because* Remember SPaG: there are 4 marks for spelling, punctuation and grammar so use your final minutes to check your work and correct it if necessary

Overview

This table will help you deal with two aspects of your thematic study:

- To record factors which affected each of the case studies. Your 16-mark essay question will be based on these factors.
- To compare events which is the basis for question 3.

Fill out the boxes that have been highlighted for each case study and then draw lines with annotations between topics that are similar or different.

	Middle Ages			Early Modern		
	Magna Carta	Simon de Montfort	Peasants' Revolt	The Pilgrimage of Grace	The English Revolution	The American Revolution
War	The barons went to war with the king to make him sign Magna Carta					
Religion						
Government					Parliament fought against Charles I for control of the country	
Communication						
The economy						
Ideas (equality, democracy, representation)						
The role of individuals						

Nineteenth century			Twentieth century		
The extension of the franchise	Protest	Workers' movements	Workers' rights	Equality of women	Minority rights
				The suffragists used lots of forms of communication to campaign for the vote	
	William Wilberforce led the opposition to slavery in Parliament				

Exam focus: Power and the people: c1170 to the present day

Question 1: Usefulness of a source

Study Source A on page 197.

How useful is Source A to a historian studying religious change in England? (8 marks)

The source is useful because it comes from a period when Henry had made religious change in England and was used when Henry's daughter Elizabeth was Queen. In the source, Henry is shown sitting on his throne and at his feet lies the Pope. The inscription P. Clem and the Papal cross are both used to make it clear that it is the Pope that Henry is standing on. This is a reference to Henry becoming Head of the Church of England through the Act of Supremacy in 1534. This is useful because this was a complete change to the structure of the Church in England. Under Catholicism, the Pope was the Head of the Church but now Henry VIII was now in control of all matters of faith in England.

> The answer gives specific details from the source

> The details in the source are then clearly explained

> Here specific contextual knowledge is used to explain how far the source is useful for understanding the issue in the question

This source may have been produced to demonstrate how controversial this change was and as we do not know who produced the source a historian cannot look further into the background of the artist. The monks on the right of the picture look distressed which could be a reference to the King, not the Pope, being Head of the Church. However, this is not made clear and they could just be shown reacting to the Pope's situation.

Overall, this source is useful for studying the change in who was Head of the Church in England but it does not cover the wider changes that happened in England.

> The answer finishes with a clear judgement about how useful the source is

Question 2: Explain significance

Explain the significance of Magna Carta on the relationship between the monarch and their subjects. (8 marks)

The Magna Carta had a small significance when it was signed by King John but it has become significant as the first step in the transition of power from the monarch to the people.

> This answer opens by directly addressing the question. This shows the examiner that you have understood, but will also help you to focus your answer as you write

John had repeatedly refused to listen to the barons over taxation and they had threatened to fight him if he didn't listen to their demands. The 63 promises of Magna Carta clearly defined the King's power over his subjects and established certain rights for freemen. This was not as significant as it seemed because most people in England were not freemen. Magna Carta really only applied to the barons, the church and merchants. They received significant protection and would therefore see it as very important. King John also ignored the provisions of Magna Carta almost immediately which shows that he did not believe it was a particularly meaningful document.

> The answer begins by identifying the short-term significance and giving evidence which supports this

As time passed however, the significance of Magna Carta grew. Magna Carta was reissued several times during the thirteenth century which shows that the barons believed that the King needed to be reminded of these constraints on his power. As the centuries passed, more people fought for the same protections that Magna Carta guaranteed, such as the Chartists. Magna Carta's significance is also felt in other countries. The USA based its constitution on Magna Carta and has even created a monument to the Magna Carta in Runneymede. These factors demonstrate that people have felt that the Magna Carta has become significant because it was the first time that a King had his power formally limited and allowed further changes to this power to happen.

> In a separate paragraph, the long-term significance is considered and supported with precise evidence

> Here the answer links the evidence back to the question by explaining why this was significance

Question 3: Compare events

Compare the reasons for strikes in the nineteenth century with reasons for strikes in the twentieth century. In what ways are they different? (8 marks)

Strikes in the nineteenth century and the twentieth century happened for different reasons.

The main focus of strike action was different. Strikes in the nineteenth century were to combat the horrific working conditions that workers had to experience. The match girls, for example, went on strike because many women developed cancer of the jaw due to working with harmful phosphorus. In contrast, the strikes of the twentieth century were to protect the jobs of people that worked in declining industries. The General Strike of 1926 was a response to the decline in the coal industry and the threat of pit closures. This issue repeatedly surfaced during the twentieth century, showing it was a consistent reason for strike action.

The leadership that instigated the strikes was also different. Strike action in the nineteenth century was on a small scale and led by a few individuals that had to get the support of all of their fellow workers. Annie Bessant organised the match girls' strike almost single-handedly and only six men organised the Tolpuddle strike. In contrast, the strikes of the twentieth century were instigated by national unions. The Trades Union Congress instigated the General Strike of 1926. This large organisation was able to make the General Strike a national event, rather than the small-scale, single-profession strikes of the nineteenth century.

> Each paragraph opens by giving one reason why these events are different

> Specific knowledge is then given about one of these events which is relevant to the point made in the opening sentence

> Examples are then given from the second event which are also relevant to the point in the opening sentence

Question 4: Factor based essay

Has war and violence been the main cause of giving people their rights since the medieval period? Explain your answer with reference to the economy and other factors. (16 marks + 4 SPaG)

War and violence have been a major factor in giving people their rights since the medieval period, but it is not the only factor. Other factors such as protest, government and the economy have given people their rights.

War is the most direct challenge to authority within society. Throughout British history, since the medieval period, war has caused huge changes in society. The most dramatic change was the Civil War. The Parliamentarians overthrew the power of the King and ended the belief in a divine right of kings to rule as they pleased. This changed society as it gave more power to Parliament and made the King more accountable to the people. The threat of war caused King John to sign

> The answer opens by directly addressing the factor which is given in the question

> The argument in the paragraph is then supported by a range of detailed, specific knowledge

the Magna Carta, soldiers returning from the Battle of Waterloo pushed for reform in the nineteenth century and soldiers fighting in the First World War and women that worked in the factories were rewarded with the vote. It took war or the threat of war for people to get their rights because there was no desire to make these changes to society before the war began. It took the extreme impact of war to cause such dramatic change in society, it wasn't just a law that was changed, it was every aspect of the way that people lived their lives.

The power of protest increases the call for change in society. Throughout British history, groups of individuals have sought to change society. The trades union movement of the nineteenth and twentieth centuries showed how the actions of groups such as the match girls, dockworkers and the miners could change the conditions in which they worked. The suffragettes fought for the vote, William Wilberforce led the campaign to end slavery and the Anti-Corn Law League repealed the Corn Laws. There are just as many instances, however, where protest was not able to achieve the change in society that they wanted, for example the ultimate failure of the Chartist movement. Protest could give people their rights but it would usually be focused on an aspect of society, rather than whole-scale change.

The government is ultimately responsible for instigating the changes that have happened in British society. The King's actions have caused enormous changes to society, most notably Henry VIII's decision to break with Rome and become Supreme Head of the Church. However, kings have not been able to do as they wished, John was forced to sign Magna Carta, for example. It is the government that has consistently been the political force of change in society. The government has changed society by increasing the franchise. The Glorious Revolution of 1688 meant that the King was restricted in his power. The Reform Acts of the 1800s increased the franchise to men and the 1911 Parliament Act made the House of Commons more important than the House of Lords. All of these laws changed society because they made the country more democratic. These changes have progressed throughout British history and have been a slow movement towards greater representations, not the dramatic impact that war has.

Overall, I mostly agree with this statement. War has been the most important factor in giving people their rights in Britain since the medieval period. Eras have been defined by the changes that have happened in war. People have been given rights in other circumstances, through economic change, individuals and through the government but the key instigator of the biggest acquisition of rights has been through the consequences of war.

> Here the paragraph links the evidence to the issue in the question

> Later paragraphs open with another factor which is relevant to the issue in the question. Another one that could have been included would be the economy

> The answer closes with a final judgement which carefully weighs up the role of the given factor against other factors

Glossary: Power and the people: c1170 to the present day

Accountable Being responsible for something and having to justify what you do to someone else

Acquitted To free someone of a crime with a verdict of not guilty

Anti-Corn Law League A successful political movement, formed in 1839, whose aim was to repeal the Corn Laws

Arbitrary Making unpredictable and unfair decisions

Archbishop of Canterbury The highest position of the Church in England

Buboes Boils

Civil war War between different groups in one country

Closed shop A factory where you had to be a union member to work there

Colony A country under the full or partial political control of another country that is occupied by settlers from that country

Commoners Anyone in medieval England without land or a title

Commonwealth An independent state or community, usually democratic, without a king

Constitution The formal legal framework for how a country will be governed

Corn Laws A series of laws aimed to keep the price of grain high by imposing taxes on imported grain from other countries

Democracy Ordinary people having a say in how they are governed

Devout Someone with deep religious faith

Dissolution Formally ending an organisation

Divine Right of Kings The belief that medieval kings were chosen by God and therefore could not be challenged by the people

Extravagant lifestyle Spending a large amount of money on luxury items

Famine Starvation due to crop failure

Feudal system The system of land ownership in England where land was given out in return for loyalty

Flying pickets Workers from one industry picketing in another dispute

Freemen Peasants who lived in towns and cities who did not work for a specific lord

Grand National Consolidated Trades Union (GNCTU) An unsuccessful attempt in 1834 to form a national organisation of trade unions

Grand Remonstrance A list of complaints that Parliament had with King Charles I, leading to the Civil War

Great Council A meeting of the King and his most important landowners and churchmen

Inherit When land is passed from a lord to his son when he dies

Laissez-faire A belief that it is up to each individual, not the government, to put right the wrongs of society

Luddite A generic term given to weavers and textile workers in the nineteenth century who destroyed the machinery that replaced their jobs

Martyr When someone dies for what they believe in

Munitions Military weapons, ammunition, equipment and supplies for war

National Union of Women's Suffrage Societies (NUWSS) The non-violent political organisation that aimed to gain the vote for women

Nationalisation When a government takes over the running of an industry

New Model Army The professional army developed by Oliver Cromwell in the English Civil War

New Model Unions Unions that developed in the 1850s focused around a specific skill or trade

New Unions Unions that favoured organised strike action to argue for better pay and conditions

Peasant A poor labourer or farm worker who paid rent to his or her landlord as part of the feudal system

Personal Rule The eleven-year period when Charles I ruled without consulting Parliament

Peterloo Massacre A mocking reference to the heroic Battle of Waterloo

Pilgrimage A religious journey

Pious Putting religious beliefs before other things

Poll tax A tax that every adult has to pay, regardless of their income

Puritans Protestants who believed that religion should be as simple as possible, without decoration or celebration

Rotten boroughs A seat in Parliament with just a few voters, which could easily be bought or bribed

Rump The name for the Parliament that tried Charles I for treason after the other MPs had been expelled

Scutage Tax paid to the king instead of fighting for him

Secret ballot When a voter's choice is kept a secret during an election, preventing intimidation, blackmail and buying of votes

Six Acts Laws passed after the Peterloo Massacre to prevent large-scale public demonstrations

Statute of Labourers The law created by Edward III that said peasants had to be paid wages that were the same level as they had been before the Black Death

Suffrage To have the right to vote

Suffragettes The militant political organisation that aimed to give women the vote

Suffragists The nickname given to the NUWSS

TUC Trades Union Congress

Villein A peasant tied to the manor, unable to move away, who had to work for his lord in return for land

How the British Depth Study will be examined

Overview of the British Depth Study

A study of a short period (just 35 years) which allows you to understand the complexities of the period and draw links between events.

In this book we cover:
- Norman England, c1066–c1100
- Elizabethan England, c1568–1603.

The British Depth Study focuses on the people, events and issues that shaped Britain's development in that short period.
- You will need to understand
  - how **causes link together**
  - the extent and nature of **change** over time.
- You will need to evaluate **interpretations** of the period.
- You will use your knowledge of the period to help you to understand a **particular historic site** such as a castle, or a stately home or a battle site.

There are a number of key skills you will need for the British Depth Study

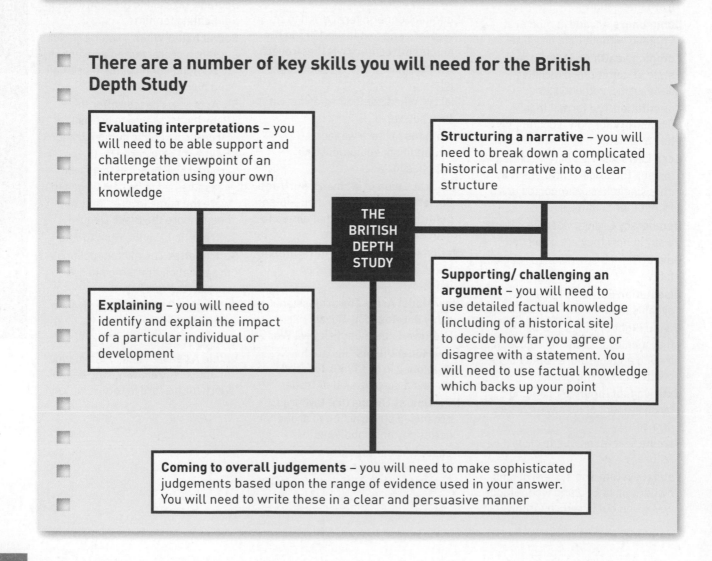

Evaluating interpretations – you will need to be able support and challenge the viewpoint of an interpretation using your own knowledge

Structuring a narrative – you will need to break down a complicated historical narrative into a clear structure

THE BRITISH DEPTH STUDY

Explaining – you will need to identify and explain the impact of a particular individual or development

Supporting/ challenging an argument – you will need to use detailed factual knowledge (including of a historical site) to decide how far you agree or disagree with a statement. You will need to use factual knowledge which backs up your point

Coming to overall judgements – you will need to make sophisticated judgements based upon the range of evidence used in your answer. You will need to write these in a clear and persuasive manner

There are four main question types in the British Depth Study exam

This is Section B of Paper 2. It is worth 40 marks in total. You will be asked the following types of question:

1   How convincing (or accurate) is this interpretation?   *(8 marks)*

You will be given a visual or written interpretation. You will have to identify the main arguments in this interpretation and consider how accurate it is based on your own contextual knowledge.

2   Explain the importance of …   *(8 marks)*

This will focus on a key event, person, group or development. You will need to identify and explain the importance or significance of this. You will need to show your understanding of **second-order concepts** such as **causes** or **consequences** or **change** over time.

3   Write an account of …   *(8 marks)*

You will have to write an analytical narrative account of an event in the period you have studied. This will need to be structured clearly and contain a wide range of specific factual knowledge. But it will also need to use second-order concepts such as **cause** or **change**.

4   An essay question linked to a specific site   *(16 marks)*

You will be given a statement about the site in the period studied and asked how far you agree. You will need to form and support your own judgement about the issue in a sustained manner. You will need to refer to your contextual knowledge of the period as a whole **as well as** your knowledge of the site you have studied.

Note: the content is not covered in this revision guide as the location changes each year.

How we help you develop your exam skills

- The **revision tasks** help you build understanding and skills step by step. For example:

  Eliminate irrelevance will help you to focus on the question.

  Develop the explanation will help you to make your writing more analytical.

  Spot the interpretation will help you to identify arguments in an interpretation.

  Support or challenge will help you to write balanced essays.

- The **practice questions** give you exam-style questions.

- **Exam focus** at the end of each chapter gives you model answers for each question type.

Plus:

There are **annotated model answers** for every practice question online at **www.hoddereducation.co.uk/myrevisionnotes** or use this QR code to find them instantly.

10.1 The causes of the Norman Conquest

Edward never enjoyed full control of his kingdom due to the **power of the Godwin family**

- Edward was half-brother of King Harthacanute. In 1041, Harthacanute invited Edward to become King, probably because he was ill.
- In 1041, Edward took over as King of England. He needed the support of the powerful Godwin family.
- In 1051, the Godwins rebelled against Edward. Although Edward survived the rebellion, the Godwins kept their powerful positions.
- After the rebellion, Edward named William, the Duke of Normandy, as his **successor** (the person who should take over as King after he died).
- However, the Godwins continued to grow in power. By 1057 they controlled earldoms in every part of England except Mercia.
- In the late 1050s, Harold Godwinson (Earl Godwin's son) was made **sub-regulus** (which meant he could rule in the King's place).

After Edward's death, **Harold Godwinson** became king

- Edward died in January 1066. He had no **heir**.
- Edgar Aetheling was Edward's closest blood relative, but he was only fourteen years old and did not have much support or military experience.
- Harold Godwinson made himself King. He made this official (in a coronation or crowning ceremony) the day after Edward's death.
- Harold was the richest man in England. Harold was a skilful military leader. He also had the support of the **Witan** (the King's council).
- Harold also claimed that, just before he died, Edward had said he wanted Harold to be the next king.

William, Duke of Normandy claimed the throne

- William was a distant cousin of Edward. However, he was **illegitimate** (his father was the Duke of Normandy, but his mother was not the Duke's wife).
- There had been strong trade links between England and Normandy since the 990s. Normandy had also helped England against the Viking threat.
- Edward had grown up in Normandy. When the Godwins rebelled in 1051, William had sent soldiers to help Edward deal with the rebellion.
- In 1064, Harold had travelled to Normandy and sworn an **oath** (a promise) to support William's claim to the throne.
- William was also a powerful warrior who had won many battles.

The third claimant was the Viking **Harald Hardraada**

- Harald Hardraada believed that he had a claim to the English throne because of a promise made to his father.
- By 1066 Hardraada was an experienced ruler. He was a famous warrior.
- He was supported by Tostig Godwinson (one of Harold's brothers).
- Many people in the north of England had Scandinavian (the area where the Vikings came from) roots and so might have supported a Viking King.

> **Key point**
>
> When Edward died in 1066 there was no obvious heir to the throne. There were four people who all had a claim to be the next King of England.

> **TIP**
>
> All the key terms in **purple** are defined in the glossary at the end of each chapter.
>
> Make sure that you can spell the key terms, know what they mean and aim to use them in your written work.

Test yourself

1 Why was there doubt about who should be the next King?

2 What was Harold's main claim to the throne?

3 What was William's main claim to the throne?

4 What was Harald Hardraada's main claim to the throne?

Develop the explanation

Question 2 in your exam will ask you to explain. The mistake people commonly make is they describe events rather than explaining why they happened.

The statements below identify some of the reasons why Edward's position was weak. For each one, add one or two more sentences to turn it from a description into an explanation. The first one has been done for you.

Statement	Developed explanation – why this made Edward's position weak
Edward was invited to take over from Harthacanute	This made his position weak because he was not actually the heir to the throne; he was a descendant of a previous King. This meant that the King of Norway could also lay claim to Edward's position
Edward needed the support of the Godwins when he became King	
The Godwins rebelled against Edward in 1051	
Edward exiled the Godwins but was persuaded to allow them to return by the Witan	
By 1057 the Godwin family controlled every earldom except Mercia	

 Support or challenge?

Below is a series of statements. For each one decide whether it supports or challenges the overall statement 'Harold Godwinson had the best claim to be King of England'. The first one has been done for you.

Statement	Support	Challenge
Harold Godwinson was the richest man in England	X	
Edgar Aetheling was the closest blood relative of Edward		
Harold swore an oath to William in 1064		
Harold had been appointed sub-regulus by Edward		
Edward promised the throne to William in 1051		
Harold Godwinson was a strong military leader		

 Practice question

Explain what was important about Harold's claim to the throne in 1066. (8 marks).

There is advice on answering 'importance' questions on page 215.

TIP

To help make sure you turn your writing from description into explanation use words and phrases like:
- because …
- this meant that …
- this was important because … .

10.2 1066 and the battle for the English Crown

Harold prepared for an invasion by William of Normandy

- The most important soldiers in Harold's army were the **housecarls**. They were full-time professional soldiers in the Saxon army.
- They were joined by **thegns** (knights called up when needed).
- The thegns brought with them ordinary men known as the **fyrd**.
- Harold also called on his subjects to provide a **navy** (a fleet of ships) to defend the south coast from invasion.

William's preparation was more extensive

- William did not have an army. He called on his lords to bring themselves and their knights to fight with him.
- There was some opposition to the invasion, but many were convinced by William's reputation as a warrior and by the **papal banner** which the Pope had given him to show that God was on his side.
- William asked his **vassals** (the lords who had sworn loyalty to him) to give him ships, but also built many. Historians estimate he may have had around 600–700 ships in total.
- William had around 7000 men including **cavalry** (soldiers who fought on horseback) and archers, and up to 3000 horses.
- The Normans also arranged materials for building castles before they landed in England. For example, they prepared all the timbers to the correct sizes and all the bolts needed to fit them together.

First, Harold had to fight the Vikings in the north of England

- Through the summer Harold's army waited. Keeping an army fed was extremely expensive. Many of his men needed to return to gather the harvest. They were sent home. Most of the fleet was dismissed.
- Soon afterwards, Harald Hardraada joined forces with Tostig Godwinson and landed at Ricall near York. They defeated English earls Edwin and Morcar on 20 September 1066 at the Battle of Fulford. The Vikings captured York.
- Harold regathered his army and marched north incredibly quickly (200 miles in less than a week).
- On 25 September, part of Hardraada's army was on its way to collect **tribute** (payments) and hostages from local leaders. As it was a hot day they had left their mail shirts behind.
- Harold's army surprised them at Stamford Bridge. He won a stunning victory. Hardraada and Tostig were killed. The Vikings returned with 25 out of 300 ships and promised not to attack again.

While Harold was still in the north, William landed at Pevensey and immediately secured his position

- Pevensey had an old Roman fort and a large bay so was a perfect landing spot. The Normans quickly built a castle and others rode twelve miles to Hastings and built a castle there.

> **Key point**
>
> Harold had to fight two major battles in 1066. Although he defeated the Vikings with a surprise attack, he was defeated and killed in a close battle with William at Hastings.

- Harold quickly marched to London (200 miles in four to five days). He probably left his foot soldiers in the north and gathered a new army in London.

- Rather than wait in London, Harold set off to fight William. Possibly he hoped to surprise William's army (like he had the Vikings) but he also wanted to stop the Normans terrorising the local population.

- William knew Harold was coming and expected a surprise attack. His army rode out to meet Harold's on the morning of 14 October.

Harold's men had the high ground and some strategic advantages but were defeated

- Harold's men formed up on Senlac ridge (a hill near Hastings). Their **flanks** (the sides of the army) were protected by woodland and the ground was damp and difficult.

- The Saxons formed a **shield wall** on foot. This was a strong defensive position – Harold only needed to stop the Normans from taking the hill and clearing the road to London.

- William attacked the shield wall with archers and then with his foot soldiers. The hill made it difficult for the cavalry to charge at any great speed so the English shield wall stayed firm.

- At some point, the shield wall fell apart as some Saxons chased a group of Normans who were retreating (or pretending to!).

- William appeared to target Harold and at some point Harold was killed (perhaps by an arrow, perhaps hacked to death).

- After this, the Normans continued to chase the remaining English ferociously but the battle was really over – William had won.

 Test yourself

1 How did Harold and William prepare for battle in 1066?

2 Why did Harold win the Battle of Stamford Bridge?

3 Why did William win the Battle of Hastings?

 Key events

Question 3 of your exam will ask you to write an account. The first step is to get events in order.

In the flow chart below summarise the events which led to William's victory at Hastings.

William prepared an invasion force early in 1066. Harold gathered an army to defend the south coast of England					

 Improve the paragraph

Explain the importance of Harold's victory at Stamford Bridge. (8 marks)

Below is a sample paragraph answering the question above. It is missing a key feature. Work out what is missing and rewrite the answer to improve it.

Harold's victory was very important because he defeated the invaders. He took them by surprise and they didn't have all of their equipment. Although the fighting took all day Harold's army eventually won and he killed the King of Norway and his supporters. This was so important because it ended the threat to the North of England. It also showed that Harold was a powerful King which was important because he had only just become King. It also allowed Harold to focus his attention on the south of England which could be attacked.

10.3 Establishing Norman control of England

After the Battle of Hastings, William still had to fight to make himself King of England

- Many English lords wanted Edgar Aetheling to be next King rather than William.
- William marched through Kent attacking towns and forcing them to surrender. In each place, he built a castle and left a **garrison** (a group of his soldiers) to defend the area.
- English barons started to change their minds as they saw the destruction caused by William. They also doubted Edgar's ability to rule because of his age.
- In December, Edgar and some English lords met William at Berkhamsted and submitted to him.
- On Christmas Day, 1066, William was crowned king by the **Archbishop** of York, Ealdred.

> **Key point**
>
> Although William tried to gain the support of English lords, he faced serious rebellions from 1067. He used force to stop these rebellions and by 1071 was securely in control of England.

William tried to keep the support of English lords but began to face rebellions

- To keep English support William:
  - continued to use English for **royal writs** (instructions from the King)
  - allowed Stigand to remain Archbishop of Canterbury
  - allowed English lords who pledged loyalty to him to keep their land (even Edgar Aetheling was given land)
  - encouraged English lords to marry Normans.
- Opposition increased because of high taxes and the harsh rule of his supporters Odo and Fitz Osbern (who William left in charge when he returned to Normandy).
- In 1067, there was a rebellion in the north of England against the Norman Lord Copsig and a rebellion in Kent.
- The Normans also lost many men trying to capture the Welsh borders.

In 1068 the rebellions became more serious and organised

- The city of Exeter refused to swear loyalty to William. It was an area with a lot of Godwin support. William **besieged** the city for eighteen days before it gave in.
- In Mercia there was a rebellion led by Edwin and Morcar.
- Later in the year there were further rebellions in the south-west as Harold Godwinson's sons made two failed attempts to sail back from Ireland and attack England.

In 1069 William dealt harshly with rebellion in the north of England

- In 1069, there was an even more serious rebellion in the north of England. It started as a revolt against William's new earl, Lord Cumin.
- This led to a full rebellion supported by Edgar Aetheling. King Swein of Denmark also brought soldiers in a fleet of 240 ships.
- The rebels attacked York. William defeated them quickly and built a second castle in York. He put William Fitz Osbern in charge. He paid the Danes to go away (although they didn't!).
- To deter future rebels he slaughtered people throughout the region. He burnt their homes, animals and crops so the land was unusable. This is known as the 'Harrying of the North'.

Quick quizzes at www.hoddereducation.co.uk/myrevisionnotes

By 1071 the last English rebellion was over and William was in control of England

- The last major rebellion was in 1070 when some Danes allied with people from the marshy fenlands in East Anglia and took control of Ely.
- They were joined by a famous Saxon warrior called Hereward the Wake and Earl Morcar.
- William defeated them. Morcar was imprisoned for the rest of his life.
- English resistance was over.
- William did face one more rebellion in 1075 (the Earls' Revolt) but you can tell how thoroughly he had dealt with the English rebels from the fact that this time the rebels were not English but Norman. It was badly planned and ended before it had really started.

William built castles to prevent rebellion

- Throughout this period, hundreds of castles were built all over the country at strategic sites or in vulnerable areas, such the border with Wales.
- These were usually a **motte and bailey** design: a large mound of earth (the motte) with a wooden tower on top.
- They were built quickly. English workers were forced to build them.
- The castles housed Norman cavalry and their horses so that they could easily defend the local area.

 Test yourself

1 What was a royal writ?
2 What and when was the Harrying of the North?
3 How long did it take William to take full control of England?

 Practice question

Write an account of resistance to William from 1066 to 1070 to show why this was not successful. (8 marks)

 Topic summary

Summarise the key ideas and vocabulary on these two pages by copying and completing the topic pyramid opposite. This should help your factual recall.

- **One** word that summarises this topic
- **Two** peaceful ways William tried to secure English loyalty
- **Three** reasons why rebellion against William grew
- **Four** examples of rebellions
- **Five** methods of preventing rebellion
- **Six** words to sum up the situation in 1076

Develop the explanation

The statements below describe how William gained control of England. For each one, add one or two more sentences to turn it from a description into an explanation of why this allowed William to gain control of England. Include relevant factual information. One example has been done for you.

He attacked towns in Kent	News of this spread and the Normans' harsh treatment of Romney encouraged the people of Dover and Canterbury to surrender without much resistance
He built motte and bailey castles	
He gave land to loyal English lords	
He paid money to the Danes	
He burned land and cattle across the north of England	

10.4 Norman government and law

Land distribution changed under the Normans. It was the main way William imposed control

- William owned 22 per cent of the land in England himself. (Edward had only owned 12 per cent.)
- William made his most loyal supporters **tenants-in-chief** (barons and bishops). He granted them huge areas of land, but spread around the country.
- The biggest change from Saxon times was that in return for land, military service became a formal **obligation** (something that the lords had to do).
  - ○ Tenants-in-chief had to provide an agreed number of soldiers usually for 40 days per year. This was called *servitium debitum*.
  - ○ To fulfil this duty, many barons either granted land to knights (in return for military service) or paid knights to be part of their own household army.
  - ○ These knights had to swear the **oath of fealty** (loyalty) to their lords.
  - ○ By 1100, the King could call on about 5000 knights.
- William dealt with the Welsh border (called the Welsh **Marches**) by granting the land to his most trusted supporters (Chester, Shrewsbury and Hereford). These **Marcher Lords** had special powers, such as building castles without the King's permission.
- William created a new system of **feudal incidents** to control **inheritance** of land. For example, he could take back land if the owner died without a male heir.

> **Key point**
>
> William increased the power of the King and increased his military strength through feudal agreements with his lords. He also made law and government more consistent and organised.

William kept some features of Anglo-Saxon government

- Saxon England had been efficiently run. William used this system. England was divided into 134 **shires** just like in Saxon times, but the power of the **Shire Reeve** (sheriff) increased.
- William gave the impression of continuity with Saxon government.
  - ○ He issued a **charter** (a written royal order) guaranteeing the people of London the same liberties as under Edward.
  - ○ Royal orders (**writs**) were produced by the **Chancery** (a group of educated officials who served the King). This was the same as in Saxon England. He even continued to use English. However, the Normans issued far more orders.
- After the rebellions of 1067–71 the **Royal Assembly** (the gathering of the King's most important lords) was increasingly dominated by Normans.

> **Test yourself**
>
> 1 How did William ensure he had an army available to deal with rebellions?
>
> 2 List three ways in which the Normans changed the legal system.
>
> 3 Why did William commission the Domesday Survey?

William kept many Saxon features but tried to make the legal system more uniform across the country

Courts and trials	Law enforcement
The Normans introduced the **honourial court** (or Lord's court) where the lord dealt with crimes or property transactions on his land	Most villages had **constables** to arrest people and break up fights, and also **watchmen** to enforce the **curfew** (the time when villagers had to return to their houses)
Shire courts continued to judge crimes such as violence and theft, but they now met more regularly. The most serious crimes could now only be tried in the King's court	After a crime took place, the **hue and cry** meant that everyone shared responsibility to alert people to a crime and help catch the suspect
Trial by ordeal continued (either by cold water or hot iron) but the Normans also introduced trial by combat	In some places freemen joined groups of ten to twelve men in a **tithing**. They promised to stop each other committing crimes

William commissioned the **Domesday Survey** in 1085 to give a full account of land ownership

Reasons	Process	Write up
England was under threat of invasion from the Count of Flanders and the Vikings	The country was divided into seven circuits	The findings were compiled into two accounts, ordered by individual and by location
Also a huge amount of land had changed hands and the Normans wanted to be certain about who owned what	Anglo-Saxon records were studied and then **commissioners** visited each hundred	The findings were presented to William at Salisbury in August 1086
	Some areas were left out such as northern areas which weren't fully under Norman control	At a formal ceremony his main tenants had to swear loyalty to the King
	The findings were presented to a jury at the shire court – a mix of Norman and Saxon landowners. The jury had to check that the account in Domesday was accurate	

 ## Develop the detail

The diagram below summarises changes William made to English government. But each of the statements is vague and lacks details. Make a larger version of your then add details so that you understand the general point made. One example has been done for you.

William passed laws about inheritance
These laws, called feudal incidents, allowed the Normans to gather rent from lands which were left to a son who was not old enough to own it or to take land when there was no one to inherit

William controlled more land than Edward

Changes to English government

The Domesday Survey allowed William to raise more taxes

William's lords were given more power on the Welsh border

New courts were created

 ## Evaluate the interpretation

Question 1 in your exam will give you a written or visual interpretation of Norman England and ask you to say how convincing it is. This is about content not provenance. You check the content of the interpretation against your knowledge.

Here is an interpretation of how the Normans changed government in England. What is convincing (fits with your knowledge)? What is not? The annotations and questions around it will get you started.

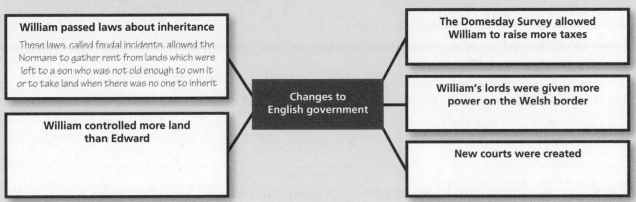

INTERPRETATION A

The impact of the Normans on government was huge. The King became more powerful under the new feudal system which William imported. William introduced new laws to control his kingdom and reformed the justice system. These changes were spread to the ordinary people of towns and villages through the wholesale replacement of English lords by Norman conquerors.

Was the impact 'huge' in every area? Can you think of examples where there was not much change?

Many laws and legal practices were the same as under the Saxons. Can you think of some examples?

Were all lords replaced? Can you think of an example of a Saxon who kept power after the invasion?

What similarities were there between William's feudal system and the Saxon hierarchy?

10.5 Economic and social changes under the Normans

Daily life in villages remained much the same

- Village life occurred on a cycle depending on the seasons. It revolved around farming.
- In February, the fields would be ploughed. In March, seeds would be sown by hand. In April, trees would be pruned.
- June was the harvest and the most important time of year. Crops had to be gathered quickly to prevent damage. Sheep were also often sheared in June.
- Sheep farming remained the main industry.
- However, the amount of cultivated land (land used for crops) was also increasing.

> **Key point**
>
> Life in villages remained mostly the same, although there was a significant drop in the number of free peasants. Economic changes led to more and larger towns.

There were major differences between the life and diet of the poor and rich

Life for the poor	Life for the rich
Usually had a small strip of land to farm	Lived off the rents paid by tenants and the produce grown by tenants on their land
All work done by hand, except when an ox-drawn plough was used	Knights would spend time perfecting their military skills
Bread and pottage (soup) was the main food	Diet was probably worse than that of the poor
Had small gardens to grow vegetables and **common land** to graze animals (land which everyone could use)	Did not eat each much dairy or vegetables as these were seen as food for the poor
Most were peasant farmers, but there were more specialised jobs such as blacksmiths and carpenters	Many had bad teeth, and diseases like scurvy or rickets

There were a number of economic consequences of the Norman Conquest

- The power and wealth of lords increased. One Norman lord called Alan Rufus managed to increase income from his lands in Norfolk by 40 per cent.
- Many previously free peasants (known as **ceorls**) lost their freedom because they could not afford to pay higher rents. In Bourn, Cambridgeshire, over half of the freemen had become villeins (tied to a lord) by 1086. The number of slaves fell by 25 per cent by 1086.
- Trade increased as England was now more connected with Europe. A new wool trade was opened up with cloth markets in Flanders.
- Jewish moneylenders were brought to England to manage finance and fund businesses.
- Some villages, particularly in the north, fell in value. One example is Pickering which fell from £88 to £1 probably because of the Harrying of the North.

In the longer term the Conquest also had a significant impact on towns

- Some large Saxon towns such as Oxford, York and Norwich saw a fall in population. Stafford had 179 houses and 40 per cent of these were empty in 1086.
- However, some new towns developed, mostly around castles (such as Ludlow) or trading links such as rivers or bridges.
- Norman castles or cathedrals were often built in existing towns and most towns got new lords.

- By 1086, there were eighteen towns with a population of over 2000 and 112 smaller towns. However, only five per cent of the population lived in towns.
- It was 50 years after the conquest before Norman market towns really began to grow and thrive.

Life in towns was very different to life in villages

- Town citizens (**burgesses**) had special freedoms such as the right to be tried only in the town court.
- There was a wider range of occupations and trades in towns including bakers, blacksmiths, armourers, **apothecaries** (who provided treatments and remedies) and barbers.
- There were opportunities to join a trade. Young men could become an **apprentice** for seven years, before becoming a **journeyman** and eventually a master craftsman.

 Test yourself

1 List three economic impacts of the Norman Conquest.
2 List three differences between village and town life.
3 List three differences between the life of rich and poor in villages after the Norman Conquest.

 Topic summary

Use the diagram below to summarise the main impacts of the Norman Conquest on town and village life.

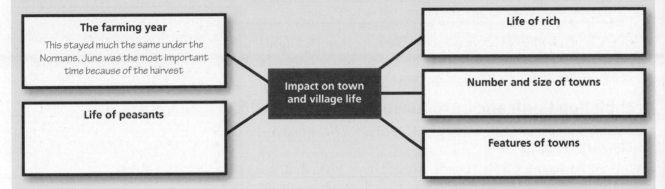

 Support or challenge?

Below are seven statements. For each one decide whether it supports or challenges the overall statement:

'The Norman Conquest significantly changed the life of English villagers and townspeople.'

The first one has been done for you.

Statement	Support	Challenge
The number of towns and cities increased later in the Norman period	X	
Some towns initially reduced in size		
The farming year changed very little		
Rents went up and there were less free peasants		
There were new buildings in many towns		
Trade with Europe increased		
Jewish moneylenders offered loans to help set up businesses		

 Practice question

Explain the significance of the Norman Conquest for life in towns and villages.   (8 marks)

10.6 The effect of the Conquest on the English Church

One of **William's aims** in the Norman Conquest was to **reform the English Church**

- William had been given a Papal banner by Pope Alexander II to show his support for the Norman conquest of England.

- One reason for this was because William had promised to sort out problems in the English Church.

- There were some good leaders in the English Church, such as Bishop Wulfstan. Others did not seem to take their religious duties seriously.

Key point

The Normans made significant changes to the English Church. Relations between the Pope and the English King were difficult for much of the period.

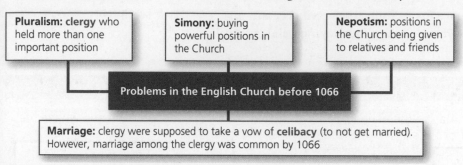

Pluralism: **clergy** who held more than one important position

Simony: buying powerful positions in the Church

Nepotism: positions in the Church being given to relatives and friends

Problems in the English Church before 1066

Marriage: clergy were supposed to take a vow of **celibacy** (to not get married). However, marriage among the clergy was common by 1066

- Some Church leaders were considered corrupt, for example Stigand, the Archbishop of Canterbury, was one of the richest men in England and was **excommunicated** (cut off from the Church).

Archbishop Lanfranc introduced **reforms** from 1070

- Lanfranc was appointed Archbishop of Canterbury (one of two Archbishops in England) in 1070.

- He came into conflict with Thomas, Archbishop of York. Both wanted to show the **primacy** of their position (that it was the most important).

- Eventually, Thomas submitted to Lanfranc, but only after King William and the Pope got involved.

- Lanfranc created **synods** (Church councils) and Church courts.

- Lanfranc wanted the clergy to face trial only in Church courts. William supported this, but it became a big issue under later kings.

- He introduced new positions into the Church hierarchy. These included **archdeacons** (who served bishops) and **deans**. He also officially ended marriage amongst the clergy.

- The role of the **parish** (local) church also increased. The number of parish churches doubled from 1070 to 1170.

The Normans drastically changed **church buildings**

- By the early 1100s, the Normans had knocked down almost every Anglo-Saxon cathedral except for Westminster Abbey. This was spared because it had been built by King Edward in a similar style to Norman cathedrals.

- Cathedrals were moved to larger towns and cities.

- The Normans wanted cathedrals and churches in a **Romanesque** style with thick walls, rounded arches and sturdy pillars.

- Norman churches were built out of stone.

- These churches were a display of Norman power and a sign that God favoured the Normans.

- The first Norman cathedrals, such as Canterbury, were similar size to those in Normandy. Later cathedrals, like Durham, were much bigger.

William I had a good relationship with the **Pope**

- Many popes in this period wanted to reform the Church across Europe. They wanted it to follow religious rules more strictly and follow the instructions of the Pope.
- William had originally had a good relationship with the Pope. He had helped Lanfranc get rid of **simony** in the English Church.
- However, William came into conflict with Gregory VII who became Pope in 1073. William refused to swear loyalty to Gregory.

Serious conflict emerged under William Rufus

- The Archbishop of Canterbury, Anselm, openly criticised William Rufus for not being religious enough.
- William put the Bishop of Durham, William of St Calais, on trial in 1088 because he did not provide troops to stop a rebellion. Rufus refused to let St Calais be tried by a Church court.
- Simony reappeared. Ranulf Flambard paid £1000 to be made Bishop of Durham.
- There was a row over whether the Archbishop should swear loyalty to the Pope or the King. This was resolved at the **Council of Rockingham**.
- Henry II (who became King in 1100) had a similar dispute over **lay investiture** (the King giving new bishops the symbols of their position).
- The Concordat of London in 1107 agreed that bishops would be given their investiture by the Pope, but would swear homage to the King.

 Test yourself

1 List three problems of the English Church before 1066.

2 List three reforms by Lanfranc.

3 List three changes Normans made to church buildings.

 Key events

Below is a flow chart summarising the main events in the story of how the Normans took over control of the Church. The first box is done for you. Use the information on this spread to complete the others.

William was supported by the Pope in his invasion of England						

 Improve the paragraphs

Write an account of the relationship between English kings and the Pope to show why there was tension between the two. (8 marks)

Below is a sample answer to the question above. It is missing specific details and events. Work out what could be included to improve the answer and rewrite it.

There were some problems between the King and the Pope. When William was King there weren't many problems because he actually had the Pope's support. However at the end of his reign they did disagree a bit.

Under William Rufus the problems were much worse. He wasn't very religious and he didn't really respect the power of the Church. He also allowed some problems to come back in to the Church which William had got rid of.

Henry's relationship was better although he did have one big disagreement about the power of the King and the Pope. This was eventually solved, however, and his relationship was definitely more positive than the relationship with the Pope under William Rufus.

10.7 Monasticism and language

The Normans **wanted English monasteries** to be **stricter** like the new monasteries in Normandy

- **Monasteries** had existed since Roman times. They were religious houses where monks or nuns lived and worked.

- Most monasteries in England belonged to the **Benedictine** order.

- Monks and nuns took three vows:
  - ○ **poverty** (giving up all of their possessions)
  - ○ **chastity** (promising not to marry and remain celibate)
  - ○ **obedience** (to follow the instructions of the abbot/abbess or prior/prioress).

- Most monasteries were supported by a rich **patron** who paid for their building but expected some control (and often monetary rewards) in return.

- Viking raids, poverty and the power of local lords had led to a decline in **monasticism** (the number of people who were monks or nuns) before the Conquest.

- The Normans wanted to:
  - ○ Reduce the power of the local lords over the monastery. They often decided who became abbot and took money made by the monastery.
  - ○ Ensure that monks and nuns followed traditional rules such as **fasting** (not eating).

Lanfranc introduced **monastic reforms** from 1077

- Lanfranc had been a monk himself and he was keen to reform English monasteries.

- In 1077, he introduced new **constitution** at Canterbury. This laid out strict rules for monks' daily lives and for the creation of saints.

- He also reformed the **liturgy** (the words used at religious services).

- Although some monasteries were already following these strict rules, this made others more like the monasteries in Europe.

- There was some resistance to these changes. In 1083, Thurstan, the Abbot of Glastonbury, sent knights to force his monks to accept a new chant. Three people were killed and eighteen injured.

- The Normans also gradually replaced English Church leaders. Although abbots were replaced less quickly than bishops, by 1086 there were only three Anglo–Saxon abbots remaining.

The reforms **dramatically increased monasticism**

- Between 1066 and 1135, the number of monks and nuns had increased from 1000 to 5000.

- The number of religious houses grew from 60 to 250.

- Many monasteries became **Cluniac** monasteries. These were less independent than earlier monasteries and had to follow the rules of Cluny Abbey in France.

- The first Cluniac monastery was Lewes Abbey, which was founded in 1077. By 1135 there were 24 Cluniac monasteries in England.

Monasteries had a significant impact on **education**

- There had been schools (such as King's School in Canterbury) before the Conquest. These were attached to cathedrals and monasteries.

Key point

The Normans reformed monasteries and revived monasticism in England. The Normans also developed school and university education.

 Test yourself

1 What were the problems of English monasteries before 1066?

2 What changes did Lanfranc introduce to the monasteries?

3 What is a Cluniac monastery?

4 How did education and language change under the Normans?

Quick quizzes at **www.hoddereducation.co.uk/myrevisionnotes**

- Many more Church schools were formed under the Normans. Church schools focused on teaching Latin, music, law and mathematics as well as the text of the Bible.

- The first university in England, at Oxford, was running by 1096. It was the only university in England until Cambridge was founded in 1209.

- **Secular** (non-religious) education did not begin until 1382 when Winchester College was founded.

The use of **language** also transformed under the Normans

- Latin was the language used by government and the Church. It was also used by merchants across Europe.

- English was no longer used in official documents. One Anglo-Saxon chronicle continued (written in English) but this ended in 1154.

- In everyday life, people continued to speak English. However, people were increasingly taught Norman-French and this became the main language for the upper and middle classes.

- This developed into **Anglo-Norman** (a mix of English and Norman-French). This was the main language of the upper classes and was used in law courts, schools and universities.

- Today, around a quarter of modern English words are based on French.

 Develop the detail

The diagram below summarises the main changes the Normans made to the monasteries of England. Use the information on this spread to add further detail to each point.

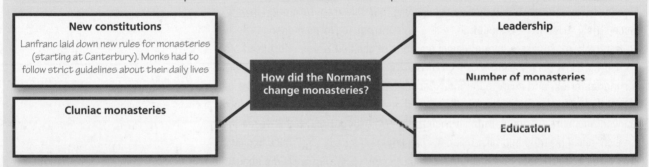

New constitutions

Lanfranc laid down new rules for monasteries (starting at Canterbury). Monks had to follow strict guidelines about their daily lives

Cluniac monasteries

How did the Normans change monasteries?

Leadership

Number of monasteries

Education

 Spot the interpretation

Interpretation B is commenting on the impact of the Normans on monasteries. Highlight where the interpretation makes the following points:

A The Normans built new monasteries

B These were under the control of French monks

C The traditions of English monasteries were not respected

D Norman monasteries were in some ways an improvement

INTERPRETATION B *Adapted from an article by Hugh Lawrence in* History Today, *1986.*

English monasticism after the Conquest was transformed by the aggressive building of new monasteries occupied by monks from France. This was deeply disturbing for English monks, who had to accept new Norman superiors. Tension was heightened by the lack of respect shown for English customs. But the Normans breathed fresh intellectual life into the English monasteries through new learning from the continent along with different customs.

 Practice question

Read Interpretation B. How convincing is this interpretation of the impact of the Normans on English monasteries? (8 marks)

Here are model answers for each of question type on the British depth study. The annotations highlight what makes it a good answer.

Question 1: Evaluate content of interpretation

Study Interpretation B on page 229.

How convincing is Interpretation B about the Norman impact on monasteries?   **(8 marks)**

Overall, this interpretation gives an effective summary of changes to monasticism, but it overstates the speed at which these changes happened. The 'aggressive' pace of monastery building was a key feature of the impact of the Normans (the number of religious houses grew from 60 to over 250) and there was also a dramatic revival of monasticism, with the number of monks and nuns growing from 1000 pre-Conquest to over 4000 by 1135. Increasingly these monasteries were grand buildings attached to the great Norman cathedrals. The Saxon source material also supports the assertion that Saxon customs were not respected. We hear, for example, of Saxon tombs being demolished at St Albans and Canterbury and even of isolated incidents of violent resistance at St Augustine's Abbey.

However, the interpretation implies too heavily that this transformation began immediately after the Conquest. In reality, in contrast to Norman changes to the government for example, monasticism was one of the last areas addressed by the Normans. It was not until 1077 that Lanfranc introduced new constitutions for monasteries, and even then initially only at Canterbury. The replacement of monastic leadership was also much slower than the replacements of feudal lords or even members of the church hierarchy. By 1075, 13 out of 21 abbots were still English (while bishops had been almost completely replaced). By 1086, however, only three English abbots remained and thus the interpretation's claims about the extent of the change are far more applicable to the late 1070s and early 1080s than the period immediately after the Conquest.

> Picks specific details in the interpretation and clearly explains them

> Clearly states an answer to the question

> Uses specific contextual knowledge to challenge or support the interpretation

Question 2: Explain importance

Explain what was important about Harold Godwinson's position before 1066 in the succession crisis following the death of Edward the Confessor.   (8 marks)

The most important thing about Harold's claim to the English throne in 1066 was his support from the English lords. Harold's family were the most powerful in England. They controlled every earldom except Mercia. They were also the richest – richer than the King himself. The Witan largely supported the Godwins. There were no set rules for who took over when a King died in England, so it was often the contender with most support from the Witan who would succeed. Edward relied on the support of the Godwins when he took over in 1042. Due to the support from English lords, Harold could proclaim himself King immediately after Edward's death.

> Directly addresses the question. This helps you to focus your answer

> Uses relevant, precise and detailed knowledge to support the point

Harold also had the right experience to qualify him as the next King of England. In the 1050s he had been Edward's sub-regulus. This meant that he could act on the King's behalf and meant that he had been trusted by Edward. Harold also had military experience which was crucial for an English king who might have to fight Viking invasion. Harold had won a great victory against Gruffyd, the King of North Wales, which had led to Gruffyd's men turning on their King and killing him.

> Another reason is considered and supported with precise and detailed knowledge

> Links the evidence back to the question by explaining why this was significant

His support and experience made his claim much stronger than that of Edgar. Even though Edgar was a close relative of Edward, he lacked military experience. It also meant that he had the support of the English lords in fighting the other claimants, William and Harald Hardrada.

Question 3: Write an account

Write an account of resistance to William from 1066 to 1070 to show this was not successful.   (8 marks)

Through the period 1066 to 1070, resistance to Norman rule was widespread but ineffective in the face of the well-organised and ruthless Normans.

> Opens with a statement which is directly relevant to the question

Early opposition to William was disorganised and quickly dissolved. After the Battle of Hastings William terrorised the town of Romney which crushed potential resistance in Kent. William's deadly march around the south of England led Edgar and a number of key Saxon lords to submit to him at Berkhamstead.

> Uses precise knowledge. Relevant, detailed knowledge shows your grasp of the topic

William faced a number of rebellions across England in 1067–68. The cause was hatred of Norman castle building, taxation and the rule of Odo and Fitz Osbern. The most dangerous rebellion was in Exeter where they refused to swear loyalty to William. William sent soldiers and built castles to secure control of each area. At Exeter he also did a tax deal with the city which dampened support for a rebellion led by the sons of Harold Godwinson in 1069. The common theme through the period is that potentially dangerous rebellions fell apart as William's response frightened the rebels.

> Analyses developments by showing how these actions made rebellion unsuccessful. This is particularly important in a 'write an account' to make your answer analytical

> Clear paragraph starters give clear structure to the answer

William's most ruthless action followed the northern rebellion of 1069. This began as a protest against the new Lord Cumin of Northumbria. Rebels got support from Danish invaders and captured York despite the Norman castle garrison there. William responded ruthlessly. He nearly destroyed York and terrorised the local area in the 'Harrying of the North' in order to make further rebellion impossible. He also paid off the Danish invaders to divide his opponents.

> The answer explicitly links to the issue raised in the question

Question 4: Historic environment essay

This question will mention one development or cause and you have to argue that this was (or was not) the main change or cause. For example:

'The main change the Normans made to churches was the introduction of Romanesque architecture.' How far does a study of Durham Cathedral support this statement?

This requires a balanced essay combining your general knowledge of the impact of the Norman Conquest on England with specific knowledge from the site you have studied. A good answer will consider the point mentioned in the question and at least two others, and reach a judgement which carefully weighs up the stated change or reason against the other changes.

Here is an example of how to write a paragraph combining general knowledge about the Norman Church with specific site knowledge about a Norman cathedral.

The introduction of Romanesque architecture was one of the most visible changes made by the Normans to the English Church. It is also one of the most lasting. Romanesque architecture features large arches and high, stone construction. Widespread building in Romanesque style began quickly after William established control. Canterbury Cathedral (begun in 1070) replaced the old Anglo-Saxon church with a distinctly Romanesque church. As time went on the scale of these projects increased reaching a peak with the magnificent cathedral at Durham which was 143 metres long (equal to St Peter's in Rome). There can be no doubt that the scale of these buildings impressed contemporaries. In the early eleventh century Orderic Vitalis commented on the sheer scale of the Norman church-building programme. Durham also pioneered the use of ribbed vaults to support pointed arches which allowed a wider nave. The awesome size and the magnificent Romanesque features underlined the power, wealth and religious zeal of the Normans at the time and through to the present day.

> Directly addresses the impact mentioned in the question. Later paragraphs would deal with other important changes which occurred such as:
> - changes in Church leadership
> - reform of the monasteries
> - bringing the Church under control of the Pope.

> **General knowledge** of the topic supports the argument of the paragraph

> Detailed, **site-specific knowledge** supports the argument of the paragraph

> Connects the evidence back to the point of the paragraph

Glossary: Norman England, c1066–c1100

Anglo-Norman A mix of the Norman and English languages which became the official language of England

Apothecary Specialist who provided treatments and remedies

Apprentice A form of training in a skilled trade for seven years

Archbishop The most powerful positions in the English Church

Archdeacon A powerful position in the regional Church created by the Normans

Benedictine An order of monasteries which most English monasteries belonged to

Besieged A military tactic which involves surrounding a town or castle and preventing supplies from reaching the people inside

Burgesses Citizens of a town

Cavalry Soldiers on horseback

Celibacy A vow to not get married or have sexual relations

Ceorls Previously free peasants

Chancery A group of educated officials working for the King

Charter A written royal order

Chastity A vow to not get married or have sexual relations

Clergy Members of the Church

Cluniac A strict order of monasteries introduced by the Normans

Commissioners The officials who carried out the Domesday Survey

Common land Land which everyone could use

Constables Individuals in towns and villages with the power to make arrests

Constitution A set of rules for monasteries

Council of Rockingham A council which led to an agreement between William Rufus and the Pope

Curfew The time after which villagers and townspeople had to return to their houses

Dean A new senior position in the English Church created by the Normans

Earl England was divided into earldoms, areas of land ruled by powerful earls. These earls took orders from the King but some were as powerful as the King himself

Excommunicated Being cut off from the Church by the Pope

Fasting Refusing to eat for religious reasons

Feudal incidents Laws about the inheritance of land which enabled the Norman kings to gain more power and money, for example if a tenant died without heirs, the land would be returned to the lord (this would often be the King)

Flank The side of an army

Fyrd The rest of the Saxon army made up of ordinary peasant soldiers

Garrison A group of soldiers

Heir The next in line to the throne

Honourial court A court set up by the Normans to deal with land disputes

Housecarls Full-time, professional soldiers in the Saxon army

Hue and cry The responsibility of everyone in a town or village to try to catch a criminal

Illegitimate A child who is not the product of a formal marriage

Inheritance The passing on of land or money after death

Journeyman A tradesman who had completed an apprenticeship

Lay investiture The practice of kings giving new bishops the symbols of their position

Liturgy The words used at religious services

Marcher Lords Powerful Norman lords who defended the Welsh borders

Marches The Welsh borders

Monastery A religious house where monks or nuns lived and worked. Also known as abbeys, priories or nunneries

Monasticism The religious way of life practised by monks and nuns

Motte and bailey A Norman castle design with a strongly defended mound and surrounding living area

Navy A fleet of warships

Oath A promise

Oath of fealty An oath of loyalty to the King

Obedience A vow to follow the orders of leaders in the monastery

Obligation Something that someone has to do

Papal banner A banner given to William by the Pope to show his support for the invasion of England

Parish The local area of a church

Patron A rich landowner who provided money for someone or something, for example monasteries

Poverty A vow to give up all possessions

Primacy The most powerful position

Romanesque The Norman style of church architecture with large round arches

Royal Assembly A meeting of the King's most powerful lords

Royal Writs Written laws passed by the King

Secular Non-religious

Servitium debitum The number of knights each lord had to provide for the King

Shield wall The Saxon tactic of forming a wall of interlocked shields to defend a position

Shire A large administrative area (England was divided into 134 shires)

Shire Reeve A powerful official in control of one shire

Simony Important positions in the Church being bought by rich individuals

Sub-regulus Someone who could rule in the King's place

Successor The person who should take over as King after he died

Synods Church councils

Tenants-in-chief William's most powerful lords

Thegns Knights who could be called on to fight when needed

Tithing Groups of ten to twelve men who tried to prevent criminal activity in the group

Trial by ordeal Using cold water or hot iron to see whether someone who is accused of a crime is guilty

Tribute A payment to show loyalty

Vassals Lords who have sworn loyalty to the King

Watchmen Individuals who had the power to enforce a curfew

Witan The King's council

Writs Royal orders

11.1 Elizabeth's character and Court life

Elizabeth's **early experiences** shaped her time as Queen. The difficulties she faced **made her stronger**

- Elizabeth's mother, Anne Boleyn, was executed by her father, Henry VIII.
- Elizabeth herself came close to being executed for **treason** on two occasions. She was accused of being involved in plots against her brother Edward and sister Mary.
- Her traumatic experiences helped mould her character. She was self-reliant, determined, yet cautious. She was also very well educated. These qualities helped make her a successful queen.
- Her right to rule (**legitimacy**) was questioned by some. Others questioned her ability to rule because she was a woman in what many thought should be a man's role – ruling England.
- Despite this, she ruled for nearly 45 years from 1558 to 1603 and is widely regarded as a very successful monarch.

The **Queen's Court** was the centre of political life and courtiers competed to get access to Elizabeth

- The Court was not a place but a collection of people. It was made up of the Queen, her advisers and servants together. It existed wherever the Queen was.
- She had about 500 **courtiers** who lived with her and competed for power and influence. In an age when the monarch was so powerful, access to the Queen was crucial to any politician.
- Elizabeth encouraged loyalty by giving loyal courtiers duties at Court (**patronage**).
- To prevent a courtier becoming too powerful, Elizabeth sometimes used a 'divide and rule' tactic (giving competing courtiers equally powerful jobs). This caused rivalry but kept people loyal.
- Life at Court was not all work! There were lavish banquets, masques, plays and tournaments to entertain the Queen and courtiers.

The **Privy Council** included Elizabeth's **most powerful advisers. They met almost every day**

- The **Privy Council** was a group of trusted ministers who helped Elizabeth govern England. The most important ministers are shown in the panels.
- Elizabeth's Privy Council had only nineteen members (much smaller than her sister's, Queen Mary, had been). Elizabeth believed that a small group would be more efficient
- Elizabeth's first Council showed her skill as a politician. It was a clever compromise including some of Mary's men but also her own loyal advisers.
- Over time, the Council became a group of full-time politicians including skilled members of the gentry.
- The most important ministers were:

Key point

Elizabeth's troubled early life prepared her well for the task of ruling England. As Queen she was at the heart of the whole political system. She had to be a strong ruler and choose and use her advisers carefully.

William Cecil (Lord Burghley) – Elizabeth's chief minister

- Member of the gentry and former MP. Secretary of State – the most powerful minister. All correspondence passed through him
- Intelligent and hard working
- Loyal but knew how to manage the Queen
- Moderate and cautious. A stabiliser

Robert Dudley (Earl of Leicester) – Elizabeth's favourite

- A member of the nobility
- 'Master of the Horse' – responsible for the Queen's safety
- Committed **Puritan**
- Often disagreed with Cecil about religion and foreign affairs
- Ambitious and a radical. Liked stirring things up

Sir Francis Walsingham – Elizabeth's spy master

- A member of the gentry and an MP
- Keen Puritan
- Secretary of State for foreign affairs. Also in charge of Elizabeth's 'secret service' controlling spies and informers
- Often clashed with Cecil

The Queen used **progresses** and **portraits** as **propaganda** to maintain her image

- A **progress** was when the Queen and her Court went to stay with powerful nobles.
- It was very expensive to entertain the Queen and her Court but rich nobles liked it because it gave them access to the Queen. Some built big houses just so they could attract the Queen to stay with them.
- The progress was also a **propaganda** opportunity for the Queen. It allowed her to impress her leading nobles with her power. They in turn laid on sumptuous banquets and masques to impress her.
- Another way to show your loyalty to the Queen was to have a portrait of her. Many courtiers commissioned one for their house or as miniature to carry with them.
- The Queen's image was strictly controlled. There were approved portraits which artists had to copy.

 Spot the mistakes

For all your answers you need accurate and precise knowledge. This paragraph has five factual errors. Find them and correct them.

> The Privy Council were trusted ministers who helped Elizabeth govern England. They were all members of the gentry. Walsingham handled her correspondence. William Cecil controlled Elizabeth's spy network. Dudley was her most powerful minister and personal favourite who liked to stir things up. One thing her Privy Councillors all agreed about was religion.

 Develop the explanation

Question 2 in your exam will ask you to explain importance. The mistake people commonly make is to describe features rather than explaining their importance.

The statements below describe some features of Elizabethan politics. For each one, add one or two more sentences to turn it from a description into an explanation of its importance. The first one has been done for you.

Description	Explain why it was important in Elizabethan politics
Elizabeth was surrounded by 500 courtiers	Individuals competed with each other to influence the Queen. This allowed Elizabeth to control them by 'divide and rule' tactics
The Queen travelled around the country on progress	
Elizabeth's chief minister was William Cecil	
Elizabeth used patronage	
Portraits of the Queen were controlled	
As a young woman Elizabeth faced many dangers	

 Test yourself

1 When did Elizabeth become Queen?
2 How long did she rule?
3 List three important features of Elizabeth's Court which begin with the letter P.
4 What was William Cecil's job?

 Practice question

Explain what was important about the Privy Council in Elizabethan England. **(8 marks)**

TIP

To help make sure you turn your writing from description into explanation use phrases like:
- this meant that …
- this was important because …
- this allowed Elizabeth to … .

11.2 Elizabeth and Parliament

Elizabeth had a **difficult relationship** with Parliament

- The Queen had the power to call, dissolve, and **prorogue** (postpone) **Parliament**.

- Elizabeth saw Parliament as a 'necessary evil' (necessary because she had to get its permission to raise money, evil because she thought some MPs were troublesome). It met only thirteen times in 44 years.

- Parliament's role was to pass laws and approve **subsidies** (grants of money to the Queen). They only twice refused her money. She usually got what she asked for.

- Over time, the MPs (Members of Parliament) grew in confidence and tried to influence her decisions.

Elizabeth controlled MPs through various tactics including **flattery and bullying**

- She reminded MPs of her **prerogative** (that she had the final say) on religion, whether to get married, who should be her heir, going to war and the treatment of Mary, Queen of Scots.

- In 1576, Peter Wentworth demanded that MPs should be able to talk freely in the House of Commons on all subjects including religion. Elizabeth was outraged. Wentworth was imprisoned.

- Her leading Councillors were also MPs. They planned Parliamentary business in advance in order to control it.

- In 1601 she granted **concessions** to MPs on the issue of **monopolies**. She did this to appease Parliament in order to raise taxes to fund activities in Ireland.

Elizabeth's **early reign** was dominated by the 'marriage question'

- Elizabeth was an unmarried woman in a male-dominated world. Both MPs and her councillors expected Elizabeth to marry because:

  ○ They questioned a woman's ability to rule England alone.

  ○ They wanted her to use her marriage to make a good **alliance** with a foreign power.

  ○ They wanted her to produce an heir to rule after her.

- There were many **suitors** (possible husbands) from England and abroad. The main ones were:

From England: Robert Dudley, the Earl of Leicester	From Spain: King Philip of Spain	From France: Francis Duke of Alencon and Anjou
Dudley was the Queen's favourite adviser. They had been close friends since childhood and he wanted to marry her. His wife died in 1560 and so marriage might then have been possible	Philip had been married to Elizabeth's sister Mary. Spain was the most powerful country in Europe so marriage to Philip might have been useful	Her last serious suitor, Francis, was younger brother to the King of France. Marriage might have been good for England's relationships with Catholic France
However, his wife died in suspicious circumstances – possibly murdered – so it would have been scandalous for the Queen to marry him	However, Elizabeth rejected him because he was a Catholic and she had completely different religious beliefs	However, after the massacre of French Protestants in 1572, there was strong anti-French feeling in England and negotiations were called off

Key point

Parliament tried to influence Elizabeth and she used various tactics to keep control. The last years of her reign were difficult and one of her top ministers rebelled.

TIP

All the key terms in **purple** are defined in the glossary at the end of each chapter.

Make sure that you can spell the key terms, know what they mean and aim to use them in your written work.

- We don't know if Elizabeth was truly interested in her foreign suitors but she strung them along and made them think marriage was possible in order to keep good relationships with those countries.
- Elizabeth never married. Instead she used her single status to her advantage. Propaganda portrayed her as 'Gloriana – The Virgin Queen' who was married to her people and country.

The 1590s were a very difficult decade for Elizabeth

- A series of bad harvests led to food shortages, rising prices and increased poverty.
- England was fighting an expensive war with Spain.
- All Elizabeth's closest advisers died: Dudley in 1588, Walsingham in 1590 and Cecil in 1598.
- A power struggle followed with the two most powerful people being Dudley's stepson, the Earl of Essex, and Cecil's son Robert.
- Elizabeth had no children and refused to name a successor until she was on her death bed. This created political insecurity.

In 1601 the Earl of Essex failed in his attempt to seize power

- Essex was an unpredictable person but Elizabeth gave him an important mission – to defeat a rebellion in Ireland. Instead of crushing it, Essex made a truce.
- Elizabeth was furious that he had done this without her permission. Elizabeth banned him from Court and removed his 'sweet wine' monopoly which ruined him financially.
- Essex mounted a poorly thought-out rebellion. With other disgruntled courtiers, he marched to London to take Elizabeth prisoner.
- He underestimated support for Elizabeth. His route was blocked. He was soon arrested and executed for treason in February 1601.
- The failed rebellion showed that despite Elizabeth's problems, loyalty to the Queen remained firm.

Test yourself

1. How often did Parliament meet in Elizabeth's reign?
2. What was Parliament's role?
3. List four issues which were part of the Queen's prerogative.
4. Why did Elizabeth reject each of her three main suitors?

Support or challenge?

Below are five knowledge statements. Decide whether each supports or challenges this overall interpretation of Elizabeth's power:

'Despite being queen, Elizabeth's actual power was quite limited throughout her reign.'

Add at least one more statement of your own that supports or challenges this view.

Statement	Support	Challenge
Elizabeth called Parliament when she wanted to		X
Elizabeth chose and dismissed her Privy Councillors		
Elizabeth had to ask Parliament's permission to raise taxes		
Elizabeth was a woman in a man's world		
Elizabeth controlled Parliament through flattery and bullying		

11.3 The Elizabethan 'Golden Age'

Elizabethan England was **influenced** by new **Renaissance ideas** from Europe

- **Humanist** scholars stressed the power of the human mind.
- Science flourished. Scholars observed the planets and the workings of the human body. More rational explanations were put forward.
- The printing presses meant such ideas could spread more quickly.
- New schools were set up offering a broader curriculum. English people became better educated.

The **gentry** were becoming **richer** and **more powerful**

- In previous centuries the **nobility** (large landowners) had been the most powerful people in England.
- The gentry were a step below them. They owned land but did not have titles (Lord *this* or Earl of *that*). They helped the monarch keep control in their local area but did not usually have national influence.
- The Tudors deliberately overlooked old nobility. They feared they were too powerful. Instead, they promoted talented members of the gentry.
- Under Elizabeth, the influence of the gentry grew further. Many also grew richer from trade, exploration, rising population and rising prices.

The **'Great Rebuilding'** saw magnificent new houses like Hardwick Hall built **by the gentry**

- The wealthy gentry wanted to show off their wealth and status.
- They built grand and impressive new houses (as at Hardwick Hall) or renovated their existing ones (as at Little Moreton Hall).
- **Renaissance** ideas (particularly the use of symmetry) influenced design.
- They had fashionable features such as intricate chimneys, oak panelling, plasterwork ceilings and a lot of glass which was very expensive.
- Some houses were built on old monastery land bought by the gentry.

Elizabeth's advisers used culture as **propaganda**

- Portraits of Elizabeth were used for propaganda. They showed a young and commanding Queen. They were full of symbols. For example, in the Rainbow Portrait painted when Elizabeth was old:
  - she is shown as a much younger woman
  - her dress has angel's wings and she is holding a rainbow in her hand symbolising her god-like status.
- The government licensed printing presses to control what was published. The bestseller was *Foxe's Book of Martyrs*. It supported the idea that Elizabeth had rescued England from Catholic threats.

Theatre was **transformed** partly thanks to the greatest English playwright, **Shakespeare**

- Travelling players had been popular in England since medieval times. Wandering bands of actors performed in market squares or inns.
- The government feared these wandering actors were a threat to law and order, so from 1572 actors had to be licensed. This led to actors forming companies to perform in purpose-built theatres.

Key point

Elizabeth's reign is often seen as a 'Golden Age' of cultural achievement, when new ideas flourished. The gentry built grand new homes and spent their money on impressive new clothes, art and theatre going.

- The first, called simply 'The Theatre', opened in 1576. Others followed including 'The Globe' in 1599 where Shakespeare made his name.
- Theatre became very popular. Prices varied so everyone could afford to go. The rich sat in the tiered galleries which had roofs. In the centre was an unroofed pit where the poor (the groundlings) stood.
- Themes reflected Elizabethan interests, for example, romance, magic and history.
- The Queen never went to a theatre. Actors performed for her at Court.

London theatres faced local opposition from London authorities and from Puritans

London authorities	Puritans
London's theatres were outside the city walls – particularly on the Bankside area of the Thames which was an area well-known for bear-baiting, drinking and prostitution	Puritans were extreme Protestants. Puritanism was strong in London
	They associated theatres with paganism (non-Christian religion)
There was concern that theatres encouraged crime and the spread of plague and that plays took apprentices away from their work	Theatres also reminded Puritans of Catholic miracle plays
The authorities wrote to the Privy Council asking for closure of theatres	Puritans thought theatres and plays encouraged sinful behaviour, particularly sex outside of marriage

Test yourself

1 What was humanism?
2 List three reasons for the Great Rebuilding.
3 When did the first theatre open in London and what was it called?
4 Which religious group opposed the theatre and why?

Write an account

Question 3 in your exam asks you to write an account. For example:

Write an account of the reasons for opposition to the theatre in Elizabethan England. (8 marks)

What the examiners look for is

- relevant, detailed and accurate knowledge
- well organised into an orderly account which answers the question.

The question will always have a focus on causation or change. So 'write an account' is not 'everything you know about ...'. It should be carefully structured so that every paragraph connects to the focus of the question.

Here is a good paragraph taken from a longer answer. Connect these comments to the highlighted parts of the answer.

When Elizabeth became Queen there were no purpose-built theatres in England. Groups of actors toured around performing in market squares and inn yards. The government were suspicious of them. It was not a respectable profession and actors were considered to be lowly troublemakers rather like beggars and a threat to law and order. There had been a rebellion in the north in 1569 and a plot to murder Elizabeth was uncovered in 1571 so the government continued to be worried.

A Focus on second-order concept of change, continuity, cause or consequence

B Links back to the focus of the question

C Relevant and detailed knowledge

D Accurate use of subject specific key terms

Practice question

Explain why the gentry class grew in importance in Elizabeth's reign. (8 marks)

11.4 Poverty: attitudes and responses

Poor people faced major problems in Elizabethan England – particularly in the 1590s

- Half the people in Elizabethan England were **labouring poor**. They did not own land or have a trade or a business.

- The labouring poor worked for wages. They did not grow their own food so spent 80 per cent of their income on food and drink.

- If they were unemployed or faced disease or disability they could not earn money to buy food.

- During Elizabeth's reign, these people faced real problems for a range of connected reasons summed up in the diagram below. Added to all these there were regular outbreaks of plague.

- North-west England was the poorest part of the country but poverty affected all areas and eventually became a national crisis.

> **Key point**
>
> During Elizabeth's reign there was a poverty crisis. The Elizabethan government had to get involved. In 1601, the Elizabethan Poor Law was passed. This provided help for the poor and was a turning point in attitudes.

Population growth: the population of England rose by 43 per cent from 1550 to 1600. There were fewer jobs to go round and increased demand for food in turn increased food prices

Inflation: food prices rose more than wages due to rising population and bad harvests. Inflation was made even worse by monopolies and rack-renting

War: injured soldiers could not work. War also disrupted trade which added to inflation

Bad harvests led to food shortages. This pushed up prices, especially in the 1590s. Some faced the threat of famine

Causes of poverty in Elizabethan England

Enclosure: good farming land had been fenced off for sheep grazing (to provide wool for the cloth industry – which was England's main industry). Sheep farming employed fewer labourers than crop growing so some labourers lost their jobs and lost common land on which they used to graze animals or grow crops to feed their families

Rents: landowners increased rents paid by the poor. This was known as rack-renting

Closure of monasteries: monasteries had previously helped the poor when they hit hard times but they had all been closed by Henry VIII

The problem of 'sturdy beggars' particularly scared the authorities

- The Elizabethans classified the poor into two groups:

Impotent or deserving poor	Idle or undeserving poor
They were too young, old, ill or disabled to help themselves. They should be helped	They were also referred to as 'sturdy beggars' or **vagrants**. They were considered dishonest. They could help themselves if they wanted to. They should be punished

- Many of the poor headed for nearby towns to look for work or to beg. Large groups of unemployed people roaming the country scared the authorities.

- To start with they were more worried about keeping law and order than they were about helping the poor. Many did not think it was the government's job to sort out such problems.

- Vagrants were seen as a threat to social order and were also blamed for spreading plague.

Quick quizzes at **www.hoddereducation.co.uk/myrevisionnotes**

The problem became **a national crisis** leading to important legislation, the **Elizabethan Poor Law**

- To start with, Elizabeth was reluctant to accept that poverty was a national problem for her government.
- Local measures were taken in Norwich where money was collected (known as **alms**) and numbers of poor people recorded in a census. Work was provided for the unemployed in a **workhouse**.
- Gradually, the government became more and more involved, passing laws to reduce the problem.
- In 1601, these were brought together as the Elizabethan Poor Law:
  - ○ Justices of the Peace had to appoint four Overseers of the Poor in each parish.
  - ○ Almshouses were provided for the old or sick to work in.
  - ○ Beggars had to be returned to their place of birth or put into the House of Correction. This was a prison for those who refused to work.
  - ○ A poor rate was charged to pay for these measures.

 Evaluate the interpretation

How convincing is Interpretation A about the lives of the poor in Elizabethan England? Explain your answer using Interpretation A and your contextual knowledge. (8 marks)

Sometimes interpretation questions ask you to focus on provenance (authorship). This one is different. It is all about using your knowledge of the period to say how convincing it is.

Look at Interpretation A. Opposite it are some inferences you can draw from it.

- Link each inference to a specific detail in the interpretation.
- For each inference, add a specific piece of your own knowledge that supports or challenges this interpretation of the life of the poor in Elizabethan times.
- Use your notes to write your answer.

> **Interpretation A** *From* Family Life in Shakespeare's Time, *an online resource for American schools by Joseph Papp and Elizabeth Kirkland, 2003.*
>
> If you woke up one morning and suddenly found yourself in a sixteenth-century family, you might be surprised at how familiar everything seemed. Although you would be getting off a lumpy straw mattress and planting your feet on a floor covered with rushes instead of rugs, when you went downstairs you would find a very modern-looking nuclear family – mother, father, and a few sisters and brothers – sitting on stools around the breakfast table drinking their morning beer (that might be different!) and eating their bread and butter before getting on with the day's work.

A The family live in a two-storey house

B They are well fed

C They are much like a modern family

D Life was pleasant

 Test yourself

1 List five reasons why poverty increased during Elizabeth's reign.
2 List two reasons why wandering beggars were feared by the Elizabethan authorities.
3 Name a law (with date) that the Elizabethans passed to deal with the problem of poverty.

 Practice question

Explain what was important about the problems of poverty in Elizabethan England.
(8 marks)

11.5 English sailors: Hawkins, Drake and Raleigh

Elizabethan **privateers and traders** challenged **Spanish power** in the New World

- Before Elizabeth's reign, Spain and Portugal dominated European exploration. This made them rich and gave them large empires in North, South and Central America (called the 'New World').

- Elizabeth and her government wanted England to join in this exploration and expand English trade.

- Catholic Spain was very hostile to England and would not grant the English sailors a licence to trade with its colonies.

- The English response was **privateering**. Privateers were licensed by the government to attack Spanish ships which were carrying precious cargos back to Europe.

- Privateers were really pirates but they were funded by rich Elizabethans including Elizabeth herself who took a share of their profits.

> **Key point**
>
> The achievements of the Elizabethan 'Sea Dogs' were celebrated and made England richer. But England made enemies and mistakes along the way.

Drake became the **most celebrated** English explorer and the first to **sail round the world**

- In the 1560s, John Hawkins made three voyages to the Caribbean, trading slaves that he had captured in west Africa. On his last trip he was attacked by the Spanish.

- Francis Drake was John Hawkins' cousin. He accompanied Hawkins on his final voyage. He was driven by patriotism and an anti-Catholic desire to seek revenge for the attack on Hawkins.

- Drake attacked Spanish treasure ships travelling from Mexico and Peru. He also attacked the Spanish port of Nombre del Dios in Panama.

- Drake then became the first Englishman to **circumnavigate** (sail right around) the globe in 1577–80.

- He attacked Spanish ships on his way and returned with treasure worth £200 million in today's money. He was knighted by the Queen on the deck of his flagship, *The Golden Hind*.

- Drake became vice-admiral of the navy and later played a key role in the defeat of the Spanish Armada.

- John Hawkins designed improved ships for the navy based on his experience of fighting the Spanish.

Raleigh failed in his attempts to set up the **first English colonies** in America

- Spain and Portugal had successful colonies in the New World. Elizabethans wanted something similar.

- It was hoped an American colony would provide wine, oil, sugar and **flax**. It was also thought that poor people from England could go to live there and so help reduce poverty problems in England.

- Sir Walter Raleigh was one of Elizabeth's favourite courtiers. She granted him a **patent** (a licence) to set up a **colony** in America.

- He claimed an area of north America and named it Virginia to honour Elizabeth, the 'Virgin Queen'. He never visited North America himself.

- Both his attempts to found a colony failed. In 1585, the first settlers faced so many problems that they left after a year; the second group disappeared without trace.

- In 1595, Raleigh led another unsuccessful expedition to search for a supposed 'city of gold' named El Dorado in South America. He hoped to achieve fame and fortune. He failed again.
- People learned from Raleigh's mistakes. Just four years after Elizabeth died the first successful English colony was established at Jamestown.

English traders set up important **new trading links** with the **Far East**

- It was not all about America. English explorers also joined in the search for new routes to China and the Far East.
- England's trade was over-reliant on the cloth industry and on Antwerp. This was disrupted by war with Spain and Elizabeth's government wanted to find new trading partners and markets.
- New companies were set up such as the East India Company in 1601 bringing silk, spices, cotton and tea from the Far East.

 Test yourself

1 Why did Elizabethan explorers undertake voyages of discovery?
2 Name three explorers and what they were famed for.
3 What collective name was given to these Elizabethan adventurers?
4 What was the name of the first successfully established English colony?

 Develop the explanation

Question 2 in your exam will ask you to explain importance. For example:

Explain what was important about exploration in Elizabeth's reign. (8 marks)

The statements below identify some features of Elizabethan exploration. For each one, write some notes to explain its importance. The first one has been done for you.

Feature	Explanation – why this was important in Elizabethan England
Hawkins' early voyages	Hawkins began the slave trade operating between West Africa and the West Indies. His cousin, Francis Drake went with him on his last voyage. They were attacked by Spaniards. This fired up Drake to seek revenge and encouraged Hawkins to design improved ships which helped defeat the Spanish Armada
Privateering	
Drake's round the world voyage	
Raleigh's North American colonies	

 Practice question

How convincing is Interpretation B about the motives for Raleigh's colonisation plans?
Explain your answer using Interpretation B and your contextual knowledge. (8 marks)

INTERPRETATION B *From* Elizabeth: The Forgotten Years *by John Guy, 2016.*
... in July 1584 Raleigh began building a team of experts skilled in ... astronomy, geometry, cartography and arithmetic. He was intent on merging his plans for colonization and conquest in the New World with a daringly global solution to the problem of King Philip and the Netherlands.

11.6 Religion: plots, threats and government responses

Elizabeth's religious settlement is known as the 'Middle Way' because it was a compromise

- Under Edward and Mary, England had seesawed between Protestant and Catholic ways.

- Elizabeth was a Protestant. She rejected Catholic beliefs such as **transubstantiation**.

- But she was not a religious **radical** like a Puritan. She still liked church decoration, music and ceremonies.

- Elizabeth passed two important laws in May 1559 to establish what her Church should be like:

> **Key point**
>
> In Elizabethan England, religion was a major issue and Catholics were seen as a threat. Some plotted against Elizabeth which led to further repression. However, most people accepted Elizabeth's 'Middle Way' in the end.

Act of Supremacy	Act of Uniformity
Re-established that the Church of England was independent – not ruled by the Pope in Rome Made Elizabeth Supreme Governor of this independent Church of England	Attendance at Anglican services made compulsory Bible and services should be in English Clergy could marry Catholic practices such as pilgrimages and saints days banned Altars replaced with Communion tables But as a compromise to Catholics, candles, clothes and colourful robes (**vestments**) were allowed

Some Puritans opposed the Middle Way

- Some senior people at Court were Puritans who wanted to get rid of all Catholic features.

- Some MPs spoke in favour of Puritan ideas in Parliament. Elizabeth forbade them to debate religion. Peter Wentworth was imprisoned for challenging her right to decide on religious issues.

- Even the Archbishop of Canterbury, Edmund Grindal, lost his job because he refused to close down Puritan meetings called **prophesyings**. Elizabeth thought these meetings encouraged people away from the religious doctrine she had settled.

- John Stubbs wrote a Puritan pamphlet criticising Elizabeth's religious settlement. He had his right hand cut off as punishment.

The Middle Way also faced Catholic opposition. Leading Catholics plotted against Elizabeth

- Some Catholics refused to attend Anglican services. They were known as **recusants**. They were fined.

- Some Catholics went further and plotted against Elizabeth.

- This threat increased in 1568 when Mary, Queen of Scots came to England. She was kept in prison by Elizabeth but became the focus of Catholic plots.

- Catholics in England got support from Europe. For example, in 1568 a **seminary** was set up in the Netherlands to train **missionary** priests to come to England to keep Catholicism alive.

The **Northern Earls** rebelled in **1569**

- **Causes**: The Catholic Earls of Northumberland and Westmoreland were unhappy with the religious settlement. They planned to free Mary, marry her to the Duke of Norfolk who would overthrow Elizabeth, and return the country to Catholicism.
- **Events**: 5000 rebels heard an illegal Catholic mass at Durham Cathedral then captured Barnard Castle and Hartlepool. They hoped for help from Catholic leaders in Europe. This never came. When Elizabeth's army moved north, the rebels retreated.
- **Consequences**: Elizabeth reorganised the Council of the North (which had failed to crush the rebellion). She confiscated rebel lands. Northumberland was executed along with 500 rebels.

After the rebellion **fear** of Catholic plots and **repression** of Catholics increased

- In 1570, the Pope **excommunicated** Elizabeth. His **Papal Bull** ordered Catholics to disobey the Queen's laws. This encouraged other rebels. All recusants were seen as potential plotters.

Test yourself

1 What two laws established Elizabeth's religious settlement?
2 What was a recusant?
3 Why did the Northern Earls rebel?
4 What was the Papal Bull of 1570?

1571	From 1580	1581	1585	1603
The Treason Act made distributing the Papal Bull or denying the Queen's supremacy punishable by death To prevent Catholics going on missionary activity, any land left unoccupied for six months could be confiscated	Jesuit missionaries posed a new threat. They travelled secretly around the county, hiding in 'safe houses' owned by wealthy Catholics. They conducted Catholic services to keep Catholic beliefs alive in England	Recusancy fines were raised from 12 pence to £20. Few people were rich enough to pay	A law stated that if you were **ordained** (made into a Catholic priest) that was treason. All existing priests had to leave the country within 40 days	By the end of the reign there were still Catholic sympathisers, but only two per cent were actual recusants

Improve the paragraphs

These paragraphs attempt to answer the question:

Write an account of the ways in which the Northern Rebellion affected England. (8 marks)

It has some good points but it also includes some unsubstantiated points and does not connect back to the question. Highlight the weaknesses and then rewrite it to improve it.

> The Northern Rebellion was the first rebellion faced by Elizabeth. It was triggered by Mary, Queen of Scots. It was led by some earls. They were unhappy with Elizabeth but also wanted power.
>
> Thousands marched to Durham and illegally heard mass. Then they marched to Hartlepool for Spanish help. When they heard Elizabeth's army was marching north the rebels fled to Scotland. They were rounded up and killed.
>
> The rebellion showed how weak Elizabeth was in northern England and it made her change things. It also increased anti-Catholic suspicion.

Practice question

What was important about the problem of recusancy in Elizabethan England?   (8 marks)

11.7 Mary, Queen of Scots: threat, plots, execution and impact

Mary's **arrival in England** posed a big **problem** for Elizabeth

- Mary was Elizabeth's cousin. Some saw her as the rightful heir to the throne of England.
- She was a Catholic who had been married briefly to the King of France. When he died she returned to Scotland and married Lord Darnley.
- They had a son, James (who would later become James VI of Scotland and James I of England).
- Darnley was a violent drunk. He was murdered. Mary then married the Earl of Bothwell who was chief suspect in Darnley's murder.
- Gossip was that Mary was involved in the crime. She was forced to **abdicate** (give up her throne) in favour of her son.
- In May 1568, Mary fled to Cumberland in the hope that her cousin Elizabeth would help her.
- Elizabeth feared Mary would become the focus of Catholic plots. She never met Mary but kept her under house arrest in isolated locations.

> **Key point**
>
> Mary was a constant threat to Elizabeth. Elizabeth continually refused to execute Mary despite her involvement in plots and pressure from key advisers. Discovery of her involvement in the Babington Plot finally led to her trial and execution in 1587.

Mary became the **focus for Catholic plots** but they all failed

- The first major plot led to the Northern Rebellion of 1569 (described on page 245).
- The Pope then excommunicated Elizabeth, which encouraged Catholics to rebel against her because if she did not have the Pope's blessing she could not be the rightful ruler.
- Two more plots soon followed although they never got as far as being actual rebellions:

The Ridolfi Plot, 1571	The Throckmorton Plot, 1583
Ridolfi was an Italian banker living in London. He plotted that Elizabeth would be killed. Mary would marry the Duke of Norfolk and become Queen	This plot had Spanish and Papal backing. Mary would be Queen. The rebellion would be supported by French soldiers and Jesuit priests as well as English Catholics
Ridolfi calculated that half the English nobles were Catholic and could raise 40,000 supporters and he expected 6000 Spanish troops to come to support the rebellion	Once again Elizabeth's spies uncovered the plot. Throckmorton was tortured and confessed
Elizabeth's spies uncovered the plot before anything happened. Norfolk was executed in 1572 but, despite pleas from Parliament and the Privy Council, Mary was spared	The Spanish ambassador was expelled. No more Spanish ambassadors were allowed in England under Elizabeth
	Once again lack of evidence meant Mary remained untouchable

- Following this, a **Bond of Association** was established that anyone associated with a plot against Elizabeth could not benefit from her death in any way.

The Babington Plot finally led to Mary's execution. Mary became a martyr

- Mary had been the focus of the Catholic plots but there had been not enough evidence of her involvement for a conviction. Spymaster Walsingham was determined to find hard evidence. The Babington Plot gave him the opportunity to prove Mary was involved.

- In 1585, Mary was a 'prisoner' at Chartley Hall. She was losing hope and became resentful. She corresponded in code with the French ambassador and Anthony Babington, a recusant. They hatched a plot (just like the other plots) to kill Elizabeth and put Mary on the throne helped by a Spanish invasion force.

- Mary's letters were intercepted by a double agent and decoded. Walsingham found out about the plot but let them carry on their correspondence.

- Once Walsingham had proof of Mary's guilt, she was put on trial. She was executed in February 1587.

- Elizabeth was wracked with guilt over this **regicide** (killing of a monarch). She had signed Mary's death warrant but claimed that had only been a precaution so the Council had acted without her consent in executing her.

- The execution made Mary a **martyr** (someone who dies for their religious beliefs). Despite this, English Catholics mostly remained loyal to Elizabeth. However, Catholics abroad were shocked. Mary's execution led King Philip of Spain to declare war and launch the Armada invasion force in 1588.

 ## Topic summary

Complete the diagram below in your own words or phrases to sum up this topic.

- **One** phrase to sum up the topic

- **Two** words to describe Mary

- **Three** plots to make Mary queen

- **Four** words to sum up why Mary's presence in England was a problem for Elizabeth

- **Five** words describing how Elizabeth managed the tricky situation

- **Six** words describing Mary's execution and its consequences

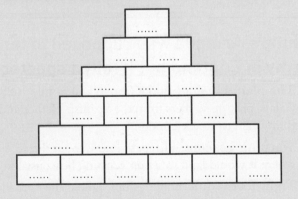

Use your completed pyramid to tackle the practice question.

 ## Practice question

Write an account of the impact of Mary, Queen of Scots on England after 1568. (8 marks)

 ## Test yourself

1 Why did Mary come to England?
2 List three plots linked to Mary (with dates)
3 How did the Babington Plot help Walsingham?
4 Why did Elizabeth feel guilty over Mary's death?

11.8 Conflict with Spain and the defeat of the Spanish Armada

The execution of Mary, Queen of Scots led **Philip of Spain** to launch his **Catholic crusade** against Elizabeth

- Philip II was the most powerful man in the world. He had been married to Queen Mary (Elizabeth's sister).

- He hoped to marry Elizabeth to control England, but Elizabeth turned him down because she did not want to marry and because he was a Catholic.

- Over the coming years Elizabeth's actions antagonised Philip. The execution of Mary, Queen of Scots was the final straw.

Key point

After years of hostility, Philip launched his 'Enterprise of England'. Against the odds, England triumphed. This boosted national pride and Elizabeth used this propaganda opportunity to enhance her reputation.

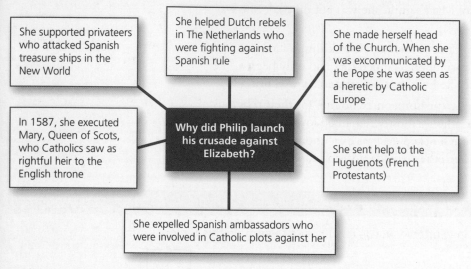

She supported privateers who attacked Spanish treasure ships in the New World

She helped Dutch rebels in The Netherlands who were fighting against Spanish rule

She made herself head of the Church. When she was excommunicated by the Pope she was seen as a heretic by Catholic Europe

In 1587, she executed Mary, Queen of Scots, who Catholics saw as rightful heir to the English throne

Why did Philip launch his crusade against Elizabeth?

She sent help to the Huguenots (French Protestants)

She expelled Spanish ambassadors who were involved in Catholic plots against her

Philip's Armada was supposed to land a **Spanish army** in England but it **failed spectacularly**

- **The plan**: 130 ships set out from Spain in July 1588. The plan was to sail to Calais, pick up soldiers from the Spanish Netherlands, take them to land in Kent, then to attack London.

- **Warning beacons**: Elizabeth knew about the Armada but didn't know where it would land so set up warning beacons along the coast of England.

- **Tight formation**: English ships sighted the Armada off Cornwall and chased them up the English Channel. The Spanish kept their tight crescent formation which made it hard to attack.

- **Waiting in Calais**: the Armada moored off Calais and waited for the Duke of Parma's soldiers who were delayed.

- **Fireships**: the English sent eight **fireships** (unmanned ships filled with burning materials) towards the Spanish fleet. The Spanish boats scattered.

- **Battle of Gravelines**: the English attacked the Spanish boats at the Battle of Gravelines on 8 August 1588. The English destroyed five Spanish ships. Two more ran aground. No English ships were damaged; 1000 Spaniards were killed and 800 wounded; 50 English had been killed.

- **Wind**: strong winds blew the Spanish ships northwards and it was clear they could not get back to meet the Duke of Parma.

- **Shipwreck**: the English chased them northwards. The Spanish tried to sail home round the north of Scotland. In the stormy weather many boats sank on the Scottish and Irish coasts. Only 60 ships made it back to Spain.

The Armada failed for **five main reasons**

- **Flawed plan**: communication between the Armada and the Spanish soldiers was impossible so the rendezvous never happened.
- **Leadership**: Medina Sidonia, the Armada commander, was cautious and inexperienced whereas Lord Howard was decisive and made good use of 'hit and run' specialist Francis Drake.
- **Ships**: Spanish ships called **galleons** were heavier and slower than the swifter, manoeuvrable English vessels that Hawkins had designed.
- **Guns**: the Spanish used short-range guns and relied on getting close to the enemy. The English used accurate long-range guns, **culverins**. English guns could be quickly reloaded and they fired **broadsides**, where all the guns on one side of a ship are fired simultaneously.
- **Weather**: strong winds blew the Spanish north and storms wrecked many ships.

The defeat of the **supposedly 'invincible'** Armada was a **propaganda victory** for Elizabeth

- Elizabeth believed the victory showed that God was on her side. The storm which blew the Spanish north became known as the 'Protestant wind'.
- Victory was celebrated with a special medal and the 'Armada Portrait'.
- Elizabeth made a famous speech to troops at Tilbury: *'I have the body of a weak and feeble woman but I have the heart and stomach of a king.'*
- England's Protestantism and independence had been safeguarded. But it did not end the war with Spain which dragged on until 1604 when both Elizabeth and Philip were dead.

 Test yourself

1 List five reasons why Philip sent the Armada.
2 List five reasons why the Armada failed.
3 When was the war finally over?

 Develop the explanation

The statements below identify some of the reasons why the Armada was important. For each one, add one or two more sentences to turn it from a description into an explanation. One has been done for you.

Description	Explanation
Mary, Queen of Scots' execution angered Philip	Philip felt that Elizabeth had murdered a legitimate Catholic and so a Catholic crusade may be needed to stop the spread of Protestantism. This meant that the 'enterprise of England' was more likely.
The Pope excommunicated Elizabeth	
Philip was angry about English privateers	
The Armada was going to pick up troops	
The Armada was large	

 Practice question

Write an account of the events in the 1580s to show why Philip sent an Armada to England. (8 marks)

Question 1: Evaluate the content of an interpretation

How convincing is Interpretation C about the reasons for the defeat of the Spanish Armada?

(8 marks)

INTERPRETATION C *From* The Spanish Armanda *by F. Fernandez-Armesto (1989)*

Good weather ... was essential for Spanish success ... They needed good weather to preserve their fragile Mediterranean shipping, calm seas to maximise the effectiveness of their galleasses [ships] ... a moderate swell to compensate for the inexperience of their gunners and ...

The interpretation is partially convincing. The weather was certainly a factor which harmed the Spanish Armada. The interpretation suggests that the Spanish were relying on calm conditions because their ships weren't robust and their gunners lacked experience at sea. This is a convincing view because we know the weather played a part during the fighting and after the Battle of Gravelines many of the ships didn't make it back to Spain. Elizabeth had victory medals struck afterwards with the words 'God blew and they were scattered'.

However, there was more to the defeat than just the weather. The Spanish were also unprepared. Sidonia was an inexperienced commander and the whole mission was poorly planned. Philip was relying on communication between Parma in the Netherlands and Sidonia at sea. This was almost impossible. If Parma had met up with the fleet, Philip's original scheme might have worked then the weather would have been less important. The interpretation makes no mention of this.

- Clearly states an answer to the question and accurately sums up the view in the interpretation. At the end of each paragraph it links back to the interpretation

- Uses specific contextual knowledge to challenge or support the interpretation

- Uses clear paragraph starters to show the structure of the answer

Question 2: Explain importance

What was important about the problem of recusancy in Elizabethan England?

(8 marks)

The problem of recusancy was important because it meant that Elizabeth potentially had disloyal subjects In England. She had already seen people refuse to accept her religious settlement and directly challenge her authority during the Northern Rebellion in 1569. The rebels illegally heard mass in Durham Cathedral. This early threat was swiftly and decisively dealt with.

The Papal Bull excommunicating Elizabeth in 1570 made the situation more serious because it encouraged recusancy. Catholics now were ordered to disobey the Queen and refuse to attend church. Recusants were now potential plotters and Mary, Queen of Scots became the focus of Catholic schemes to depose Elizabeth. As a result, Elizabeth was increasingly threatened by Catholic plots and assassination attempts. The authorities were so alarmed that a new Treason Act soon followed in 1571 which meant anyone denying Elizabeth's supremacy could be put to death. Some wealthy recusants harboured missionary priests who influenced wealthy families to stay loyal to the Pope.

The authorities were so concerned that in 1581 recusancy fines were raised to a crippling £20 from 12 pence. This meant that most English Catholics could not afford to continue to miss church and were forced to conform. Those who remained 'obstinate' were associated with England's enemies and so the idea was reinforced that recusants were dangerous, unpatriotic and disloyal. The government campaign against them had worked.

- Directly addresses the question. This helps you to focus your answer

- Uses relevant, precise and detailed knowledge to support the point

- Clearly links each paragraph back to the question

- Links the evidence back to the question by explaining why this was significant

Question 3: Write an account

Write an account of the ways in which the Puritans posed a challenge to Elizabeth and her regime.   (8 marks)

Puritans campaigned in the 1560s, 1570s and 1580s to persuade Elizabeth to further 'purify' the Elizabethan Church of all traces of the Catholic religion.

> Opens with a statement directly linked to the question

Their ideas were spreading, especially in London and the south-east. Influential Privy Councillors such as the Earl of Leicester and Sir Francis Walsingham were Puritans, as were many MPs who put pressure on the Queen to make changes to the Church of England.

> Relevant detailed knowledge shows grasp of the question

Puritans challenged Elizabeth in various ways, for instance, in Parliament in 1566 they argued priests should only wear plain black gowns. In 1571 Walter Strickland aimed to ban vestments and introduce a new prayer book. Elizabeth closed Parliament down before Strickland's ideas could be discussed. Anthony Cope tried in 1584 to establish a new prayer book and ban bishops. This threatened Elizabeth's Church structure, and she had Cope imprisoned.

> Clear paragraph starters give the answer structure

> Analyses developments to assess the nature of the challenge and Elizabeth's rebuttal or the consequences

Further challenges came outside Parliament when Puritans condemned the theatre. William Stubbs wrote in 1583 of the immoral behaviour encouraged by plays and criticised Elizabeth's marriage talks. This encroached on the Queen's prerogative. Elizabeth used theatre as a method of maintaining social control, so this was seen as an attack on her regime. She ordered Stubbs to have his right hand cut off.

Question 4: Historic environment essay

This question will mention one development or cause and you have to argue that this was (or was not) the main change or cause. For example:

> Here is an example paragraph combining general knowledge about Elizabeth theatre with specific site knowledge about The Globe.

'The main reason for the growing popularity of the theatre in Elizabethan England was the development of new purpose-built structures.'
How far does a study of Shakespeare's Globe support this statement?   (16 marks)

This requires a balanced essay combining your general knowledge of Elizabethan England with specific knowledge from the site you have studied. A good answer will weigh up the point mentioned in the question against at least two others.

Going to the theatre was very popular in late Elizabethan England and this was partly the result of purpose-built theatres. Attending plays in the courtyards of inns had always been popular but in 1576 a purpose-built structure called 'The Theatre' was built by James Burbage in Shoreditch near London. It was probably the first ever purpose-built theatre. It allowed Burbage to put on more ambitious productions. Audiences grew as a result and more purpose-built theatres were built. In 1598 there was a dispute over the lease on The Theatre so Burbage's son dismantled it overnight and a team of carpenters led by Peter Street used the timber to build a new, bigger theatre on the south bank of the River Thames called The Globe. It was probably larger than any other London theatre with capacity for 2,000. People flocked there on wherries across the River Thames. The poor could pay 1p to stand in the area around the stage as groundlings or the rich could pay more to sit in the tiered seats. Because it was purpose-built, a stock of props could be stored in the tiring house, and the frons scenae could be elaborately painted or hung with tapestries to suit the play. These features made productions more exciting which boosted the popularity of the theatre. So there is plenty of evidence that the purpose-built theatres boosted the popularity of plays.

> The answer opens by directly addressing the factor which is given in the question. Later paragraphs would deal with other important reasons such as:
> - patronage from the queen and rich courtiers
> - propaganda – telling the Tudor version of English history
> - profit – entrepreneurs such as Burbage
> - playwrights and actors such as Shakespeare

> **General knowledge** of the topic supports the argument of the paragraph

> Detailed, **site-specific knowledge** supports the argument of the paragraph

> Connects the evidence back to the point of the paragraph

Glossary: Elizabethan England, c1568–1603

Abdicate Give up the throne

Alliance An agreement between countries to work together against a shared enemy

Alms Charity given to the poor. Almshouses are houses provided for poor people to live in

Bond of Association Anyone associated with a plot against Elizabeth could not benefit from her death in any way

Broadside Where all the guns on one side of a ship are fired simultaneously

Circumnavigate Sail around the world

Colony An area under the control of another county

Concession Something granted following demands for it

Courtier Member of the royal Court

Culverin Accurate long-range ship's cannon

Enclosure The division of land, including the village common land, into separate fields with hedges, allowing a change from arable to sheep farming

Excommunicated To be expelled from the Church

Fireship Unmanned ship filled with burning material

Flax A plant used to make linen

Galleon A large ship, especially used by Spain, either as a warship or for trading

Humanism Intellectual branch of the Renaissance, drawing on classical texts and stressing the dignity of mankind

Jesuit Roman Catholic missionary priest

Labouring poor Those who work with their hands

Legitimacy Right to rule

Martyr Someone who dies for his or her religious beliefs

Missionary Someone sent on a mission to spread his or her faith

Monopoly The exclusive right to sell a product. Elizabeth sold these monopolies to favourite courtiers as a way of keeping support

Nobility Large landowners

Ordained Made into a priest

Parliament The supreme legislative body. Responsible in the sixteenth century with the Queen for making laws and deciding about taxes

Papal Bull An official document issued by the Pope

Patent A licence

Patronage Duties at Court

Prerogative An exclusive right or privilege

Privateering The actions of pirates licensed by the government to attack and take enemy ships

Privy Council A group of trusted ministers who advise a monarch

Progress When the monarch and courtiers went to stay with powerful nobles

Prorogue Postpone

Propaganda Something that spreads a message in order to encourage people to think or behave in a particular way

Propheysings Prayer meetings where the Bible was discussed and sermons said

Puritan An extreme Protestant, strongly opposed to Catholic ideas and styles of worship

Radical Extreme. Usually used to describe views or someone holding views that are very different from what is commonly accepted

Recusant Someone, usually a Roman Catholic, who refused to go to Church services

Regicide Killing of a monarch

Renaissance An intellectual and cultural movement originating in Italy in the Middle Ages, heavily influenced by the Ancient Greeks and Romans

Seminary A place where priests are trained

Subsidy Grant of money to the Queen

Suitors Possible husbands

Transubstantiation Belief that at mass the bread and wine miraculously turn into Christ's body and blood

Treason Disloyalty to your country, monarch or government

Vagrant A homeless, unemployed person who wanders from place to place and begs

Vestments Clerical robes

Workhouse An umbrella term for the institutions set up by the Poor Law. Separate institutions were envisaged by the laws, but the distinctions between them became blurred over time. In theory, poorhouses were to provide shelter for the 'impotent poor', workhouses to provide work for the 'able-bodied poor', and 'Houses of Correction' were to detain the 'idle poor'

Spelling, Punctuation and Grammar (SPaG)

In each of your exams one question will have 4 marks available for SPaG.

- In Paper 1 your 'How far do you agree?' essay in the World Depth study
- In Paper 2 your 'Factor-based essay' in the Thematic Study.

Together these SPaG marks are nearly 5 per cent of your marks. That's one reason why it is so important to check your work. However, we know you probably won't have time to do this in the exam itself, which is why it is even more important to *do it when you are practising*. Those 8 marks are yours for the taking if you learn to be disciplined about your spelling, punctuation and grammar. Get yourself into the mindset that SPaG matters.

Remember too that it is not just your SPaG marks that are at stake. Accurate spelling, punctuation and grammar also improve the rest of your answers. Examiners have to read hundreds of answers. Good SPaG makes their job easier and more enjoyable. It makes your writing more polished and easier to read.

We can't teach you good SPaG in one page but here are the top eight habits to learn.

Habits to learn
1 **Check and correct your spellings.** Check you can spell the glossary words at the end of each chapter.
2 **Start each sentence** with a capital letter and finish it with a full stop (or a question mark if it is a question).
3 **Avoid exclamation marks**. And never use two explanation marks like this!!
4 **Use commas** to separate the two parts of a sentence, or two or more words in a list. (There are other rules about commas, but we'll keep it simple)
5 **Capitalise proper nouns.** People or places or specific things start with a capital letter.
6 **Use an 's (apostrophe)** only when something belongs to someone, not when it is a plural.
7 **Check your tenses.** Don't change tenses in the middle of an answer. NB You will usually write in the past tense because history is about things that happened in the past.
8 **Use paragraphs.** Each paragraph of an essay should make one supported point and be clearly connected to the answer.

 ## SPaG check

Highlight and correct all the errors in these answers. (Answers over the page.)

1) One way where workers' were effected by Nazi economic policy was that they lost some of there rights, for example the german labour front was set up, which replaced trade unions. Trade union's represent workers interests, but now workers risk losing their jobs if they go on strike or refuse conditions.

2) In 1568 Mary queen of scot's came to England. Mary was arrested and was kept inprisoned but she became the focus of Catholic plots against Elizabeth's rule. the following year there was a major rebelion in the North led by the Earl's of northumberland and westmoreland. An illegal Catholic mass was held at Durham Cathedral and attended by 5000 rebells. The rebellion never recieved the support from Catholic countries in Europe which it had hoped for and were easily defeated over 500 rebels were executed! However, the rebellion led to an increased fear of further plots and as a result the persecution of Catholic's increased.

3) One reason why Harveys work was so significant was that it challenged galen. Harvey discovered that blood is pumped around the body by the constant pumping of the heart and He also discovered that blood is not used up and reprodused in the liver. this was an idea which had been taught by galen and therefore is a dominant idea in medicine since Ancient Times. Although it took many years for Harvey's work to be fully accepted he paved the way for many future discoveries in phsyiology.

4) In 1936 Hitler sends german troops into the Rhineland. he gambled that the french would not respond with militray force as he knew that the German Army was no match for them and he also claimed that placing troops in the Rhineland was justified as it was a part of Germany! France and Britain did nothing to stop Hitler as there attention was focused on the growing crisis in Abysinia and there was some sympathy for Hitlers claim that this was a legitimate defensive action.

1) One way in which workers were affected by Nazi economic policy was that they lost some of their rights. For example, the German Labour Front was set up, which replaced trade unions. Trade unions represented workers' interests, but now workers risked losing their jobs if they went on strike or refused conditions.

2) In 1568, Mary Queen of Scots came to England. Mary was arrested and was kept imprisoned, but she became the focus of Catholic plots against Elizabeth's rule. The following year there was a major rebellion in the North led by the Earls of Northumberland and Westmoreland. An illegal Catholic mass was held at Durham Cathedral and attended by 5000 rebels. The rebellion never received the support from Catholic countries in Europe which it had hoped for and was easily defeated. Over 500 rebels were executed. However, the rebellion led to an increased fear of further plots, and as a result the persecution of Catholics increased.

3) One reason why Harvey's work was so significant was that it challenged Galen. Harvey discovered that blood is pumped around the body by the constant pumping of the heart. He also discovered that blood is not used up and reproduced in the liver. This was an idea which had been taught by Galen, and therefore had been dominant in medicine since ancient times. Although it took many years for Harvey's work to be fully accepted, he paved the way for many future discoveries in physiology.

4) In 1936, Hitler sent German troops into the Rhineland. Hitler gambled that the French would not respond with military force, as he knew that the German Army was no match for them. Hitler also claimed that placing troops in the Rhineland was justified as it was a part of Germany. France and Britain did nothing to stop Hitler as their attention was focused on the growing crisis in Abyssinia, and there was some sympathy for Hitler's claim that this was a legitimate defensive action.